T0238372

Lecture Notes in Computer Science

Commenced Publication in 1973
Founding and Former Series Editors:
Gerhard Goos, Juris Hartmanis, and Jan van Leeuwen

María Alpuente   Byron Cook
Christophe Joubert (Eds.)

Formal Methods for Industrial Critical Systems

14th International Workshop, FMICS 2009
Eindhoven, The Netherlands, November 2-3, 2009
Proceedings

 Springer

Volume Editors

María Alpuente
Christophe Joubert
Universidad Politécnica de Valencia
DSIC/ELP
Camino de Vera s/n, 46022 Valencia, Spain
E-mail: {alpuente,joubert}@dsic.upv.es

Byron Cook
Microsoft Research
Roger Needham Building
J J Thomson Avenue, Cambridge, CB3 0FB, UK
E-mail: bycook@microsoft.com

Library of Congress Control Number: 2009935171

CR Subject Classification (1998): D.2.4, D.2, D.3, C.3, F.3, I.6

LNCS Sublibrary: SL 2 – Programming and Software Engineering

ISSN   0302-9743

ISBN   978-3-642-04569-1 Springer Berlin Heidelberg New York

springer.com

© Springer-Verlag Berlin Heidelberg 2009

Typesetting: Camera-ready by author, data conversion by Scientific Publishing Services, Chennai, India
Printed on acid-free paper   SPIN: 12761746   06/3180   5 4 3 2 1 0

Preface

This volume contains the papers presented at FMICS 2009, the *14th International Workshop on Formal Methods for Industrial Critical Systems*, which was held on November 2–3, 2009, in Eindhoven, The Netherlands. Previous workshops of the ERCIM working group on Formal Methods for Industrial Critical Systems were held in Oxford (March 1996), Cesena (July 1997), Amsterdam (May 1998), Trento (July 1999), Berlin (April 2000), Paris (July 2001), Malaga (July 2002), Trondheim (June 2003), Linz (September 2004), Lisbon (September 2005), Bonn (August 2006), Berlin (July 2007), and L'Aquila (September 2008).

The aim of the FMICS workshop series is to provide a forum for researchers who are interested in the development and application of formal methods in industry. In particular, these workshops bring together scientists and engineers who are active in the area of formal methods and are interested in exchanging their experiences in the industrial usage of these methods. These workshops also strive to promote research and development for the improvement of formal methods and tools for industrial applications.

The FMICS 2009 workshop was part of FMweek, the first Formal Methods Week, which offered a choice of events in the area, including TESTCOM/FATES, *Conference on Testing of Communicating Systems and Workshop on Formal Approaches to Testing of Software*; FACS, *Formal Aspects of Component Software*; PDMC, *Parallel and Distributed Methods of verifiCation*; FM2009, *Symposium of Formal Methods Europe*; CPA, *Communicating Process Architectures*; FAST, *Formal Aspects of Security and Trust*; FMCO, *Formal Methods for Components and Objects*; and the REFINE Workshop. All the information on FMweek can be found at http://www.win.tue.nl/fmweek.

The topics chosen for FMICS 2009 included, but were not restricted to:

- design, specification, code generation and testing based on formal methods;
- methods, techniques and tools to support automated analysis, certification, debugging, learning, optimization and transformation of complex, distributed, real-time and embedded systems;
- verification and validation methods that address shortcomings of existing methods with respect to their industrial applicability (e.g., scalability and usability issues);
- tools for the development of formal design descriptions;
- case studies and experience reports on industrial applications of formal methods, focusing on lessons learned or new research directions;
- impact and costs of the adoption of formal methods;
- application of formal methods in standardization and industrial forums;

In response to the call for papers, 24 contributions were submitted from 16 different countries. The Program Committee selected ten papers, basing this choice on their scientific quality, originality, and relevance to the workshop. Each paper was reviewed by at least three Program Committee members or external referees. This volume also includes four invited contributions by Dino Distefano (Queen Mary, University of London, UK), Diego Latella (CNR/ISTI, Italy), Thierry Lecomte (ClearSy, France), and Ken McMillan (Cadence Berkeley Labs, USA), as well as six poster descriptions. The resulting volume offers the reader a complete landscape of the recent advances in this area.

Following a tradition established over the past few years, the *European Association of Software Science and Technology* (EASST) offered an award to the best FMICS paper. Further information about the FMICS working group and the next FMICS workshop can be found at: http://www.inrialpes.fr/vasy/fmics.

On behalf of the Program Committee, we would like to express our gratitude to all the authors who submitted papers and all external referees for their careful work in the reviewing process. We are very grateful to the members of the ELP group and the local organizers of FMweek who worked with enthusiasm in order to make this event possible. We are also grateful to Andrei Voronkov for making EasyChair available to us. Finally, we gratefully acknowledge the institutions that sponsored this event: the Universidad Politécnica de Valencia, ERCIM, FME, Microsoft Research, the Departamento de Sistemas Informáticos y Computación (UPV), MEC (Feder) TIN2007-30509-E, EASST, and the Technical University of Eindhoven.

November 2009   María Alpuente
                                                           Byron Cook
                                                       Christophe Joubert

Organization

Program Chairs

María Alpuente   Universidad Politécnica de Valencia, Spain
Byron Cook   Microsoft Research, UK

Workshop Chair

Christophe Joubert   Universidad Politécnica de Valencia, Spain

ERCIM FMICS Working Group Coordinator

Alessandro Fantechi   Università degli Studi di Firenze and ISTI-CNR, Italy

Program Committee

Hassan Ait-Kaci	Ilog, Canada
Thomas Arts	IT-Universitetet i Göteborg, Sweden
Demis Ballis	Università degli Studi di Udine, Italy
Josh Berdine	Microsoft Research, UK
Lubos Brim	Masarykova Univerzita, Czech Republic
Darren Cofer	Rockwell Collins, USA
Patrick Cousot	Ecole Normale Supérieure, France
Santiago Escobar	Universidad Politécnica de Valencia, Spain
Azadeh Farzan	University of Toronto, Canada
Hubert Garavel	INRIA Rhône-Alpes, France
Stefania Gnesi	ISTI-CNR, Italy
Alexey Gotsman	University of Cambridge, UK
Holger Hermanns	Universität des Saarlandes, Germany
Daniel Kroening	ETH Zürich, Switzerland
Michael Leuschel	Heinrich-Heine-Universität Düsseldorf, Germany
Pedro Merino	Universidad de Málaga, Spain
Juan José Moreno-Navarro	Universidad Politécnica de Madrid, Spain
Corina Pasareanu	NASA Ames Research Center, USA
Murali Rangarajan	Honeywell, USA
Jakob Rehof	Technische Universität Dortmund, Germany
Andrey Rybalchenko	Max-Planck-Gesellschaft, Germany
Marcel Verhoef	Chess, The Netherlands
Martin Wirsing	Ludwig-Maximilians-Universität München, Germany

Hongseok Yang	Queen Mary, University of London, UK
Greta Yorsh	IBM T.J. Watson Research Center, USA
Jaco van de Pol	Universiteit Twente, The Netherlands

Local Organization

Erik de Vink	Technische Universiteit Eindhoven, The Netherlands
Tijn Borghuis	Technische Universiteit Eindhoven, The Netherlands

External Reviewers

Michele Baggi	Università degli Studi di Siena, Italy
Jiri Barnat	Masarykova Univerzita, Czech Republic
Axel Belinfante	Universiteit Twente, The Netherlands
Jens Bendisposto	Heinrich-Heine-Universität Düsseldorf, Germany
Nicolas Blanc	ETH Zürich, Switzerland
Ivana Cerna	Masarykova Univerzita, Czech Republic
Jerome Feret	Ecole Normale Supérieure, France
Raúl Gutiérrez	Universidad Politécnica de Valencia, Spain
Joe Hendrix	Microsoft Corporation, USA
Ángel Herranz	Universidad Politécnica de Madrid, Spain
José Iborra	Universidad Politécnica de Valencia, Spain
Sumit Kumar Jha	Carnegie Mellon University, USA
Zachary Kincaid	University of Western Ontario, Canada
Franco Mazzanti	ISTI-CNR, Italy
Antoine Miné	Ecole Normale Supérieure, France
John Regehr	University of Utah, USA
Daniel Romero	Universidad Politécnica de Valencia, Spain
Philipp Ruemmer	Oxford University, UK
Theo Ruys	Universiteit Twente, The Netherlands
Wendelin Serwe	INRIA Rhône-Alpes, France
Pavel Simecek	Masarykova Univerzita, Czech Republic
Ofer Strichman	Technion, Israel
Salvador Tamarit	Universidad Politécnica de Valencia, Spain
Damien Thivolle	INRIA Rhône-Alpes, France
Enrico Vicario	Università degli Studi di Firenze, Italy
Georg Weissenbacher	ETH Zürich, Switzerland
Michael Katelman	University of Illinois at Urbana-Champaign, USA

Table of Contents

Invited Papers

Contributed Papers

Selected Posters

Attacking Large Industrial Code with Bi-abductive Inference

Dino Distefano

Queen Mary, University of London

Abstract. In joint work with Cristiano Calcagno, Peter O'Hearn, and Hongseok Yang, we have introduced *bi-abductive inference* and its use in reasoning about heap manipulating programs [5]. This extended abstract briefly surveys the key concepts and describes our experience in the application of bi-abduction to real-world applications and systems programs of over one million lines of code.

1 Introduction

Automatic software verification has seen an upsurge of interest in recent years. This is exemplified by tools such as SLAM [1] and ASTRÉE [4], which have been used to verify properties of special classes of real-world software, e.g., device drivers and avionics code. Crucial in this reinvigoration of software verification has been the employment of methods from static program analysis which have the advantage to lessen annotation burden (e.g., by automatically inferring loop invariants and procedure summaries).

While these advances are impressive, a persistent trouble area stands in the way of verification-oriented program analysis for a wider range of real software: *the heap.* The heap is one of the hardest open problems in automatic verification and prominent tools such as ASTRÉE and SLAM either eschew dynamic allocation altogether or use coarse models that assume pointer safety.

Shallow pointer analyses, which infer dereferencing information of bounded length, often do not give enough information for verification purposes. For example, for automatically proving that a device driver manipulating a collection of nested cyclic linked lists, does not dereference `null` or a dangling pointer, the analysis technique needs to be able to look unboundedly deep into the heap. This is done by shape analyses [13]. Shape analyses are program analyses which aim to be accurate in the presence of deep-heap update—They go beyond aliasing or points-to relationships to infer properties such as whether a variable points to a cyclic or acyclic linked list.

Until very recently shape analyses could only be applied to tiny toy programs written to test an analysis. SpaceInvader [8,2,10] is an automatic tool aiming at bringing such analyses into the real world. The driving force behind Space Invader is the idea of local reasoning, which is enabled by the Frame Rule of separation logic [11]:

$$\frac{\{P\}\,C\,\{Q\}}{\{P * R\}\,C\,\{Q * R\}}$$

M. Alpuente, B. Cook, and C. Joubert (Eds.): FMICS 2009, LNCS 5825, pp. 1–8, 2009.

In this rule R is the *frame*, i.e., the part of the heap which is not touched by the execution of the command C. The connective $*$ is called *separating conjunction* and it states that its operands hold for disjoint parts of memory. The Frame Rule allows pre and postconditions to concentrate on the *footprint*: the cells touched by command C. In by-hand proofs this enables specifications to be much more succinct than they might otherwise be. SpaceInvader takes as its aim to port the concept of footprint into automatic verification in order to enjoy similar benefits and keep the proof process manageable.

2   Bi-Abduction

In moving from by-hand to automatic verification the ability to deduce the frame becomes a central task. Computation of the frame is done by *frame inference*, which can be formally defined as:

Definition 1 (Frame inference). *Given (separation logic) formulae H and H' compute a formula $\mathcal{F}$ such that $H \vdash H' * \mathcal{F}$ holds.*

An algorithm for inferring frames was introduced in [3]. Interestingly, crucial tasks necessary to perform automatic heap analysis — such as rearrangement (materialization) and abstraction — can be reduced to solving frame inference questions [9].

In our attempts to deal with incomplete code and increase automation in Space Invader, we discovered that the idea of *abductive inference* (or abduction) — introduced by Charles Peirce in the early 1900s in his writings on the scientific process [12] — is highly valuable. When reasoning about the heap, abductive inference, often known as inference of explanatory hypotheses, is a natural dual to the notion of frame inference, and can be defined as follows:

Definition 2 (Abductive Inference). *Given (separation logic) formulae H and H' compute a formula $\mathcal{A}$ such that $H * \mathcal{A} \vdash H'$ holds.*

In this definition we call $\mathcal{A}$ the "anti-frame".

Bi-abductive inference (or bi-abduction) is the combination of frame inference and abduction. It consists of deriving at the same time frames and anti-frames.

Definition 3 (Bi-Abductive inference). *Given (separation logic) formulae H and H' compute a frame $\mathcal{F}$ and an anti-frame $\mathcal{A}$ such that $H * \mathcal{A} \vdash H' * \mathcal{F}$ holds.*

Many solutions are possible for $\mathcal{A}$ and $\mathcal{F}$. A criterion to judge the quality of solutions as well as a bi-abductive prover were defined in [5].

Example 1. Let $H \triangleq z \mapsto \mathsf{nil} * x \mapsto \mathsf{nil}$ and $H' \triangleq \mathsf{list}(x) * \mathsf{list}(y)$. Informally H represents a heap with two disjoint cells allocated at addresses x and z which contain the value nil[1]. H' stands for a heap with two disjoint allocated lists starting at x and y, respectively. Consider now the bi-abduction question:

---

[1] The semantics of the predicate $a \mapsto b$ is a heap with precisely one allocated cell at address a with content b.

$$z \mapsto \text{nil} * x \mapsto \text{nil} * \mathcal{A} \vdash \text{list}(x) * \text{list}(y) * \mathcal{F}$$

There are many solutions for the pair $\mathcal{A}$ and $\mathcal{F}$, some of which are

$$
\begin{array}{ll}
\mathcal{A} \triangleq \text{list}(y) & \mathcal{F} \triangleq z \mapsto \text{nil} \\
\mathcal{A} \triangleq y \mapsto \text{nil} & \mathcal{F} \triangleq \exists v.z \mapsto v \\
\mathcal{A} \triangleq y \mapsto \text{nil} & \mathcal{F} \triangleq \text{list}(z) \\
\mathcal{A} \triangleq y \mapsto \text{nil} * w \mapsto 0 & \mathcal{F} \triangleq \text{list}(z) * \exists v.w \mapsto v
\end{array}
$$

Notice how in synthesizing $\mathcal{A}$ we are discovering the part of the heap which is missing in H w.r.t. H'. Dually, $\mathcal{F}$ represents the part of the heap H which is superfluous w.r.t. H'. Given that there are many solutions, an automatic prover will essentially make pragmatic choices in order to synthesize only one. In our experience aiming for the "best" solution is hard.

3 Compositional Shape Analysis

Bi-abduction allows us to automatically compute (approximations of) *footprints* of commands and preconditions of procedures. In particular, bi-abduction is the main ingredient which allows for an analysis method where pre/post specs of procedures are inferred independently of their context. This has opened up a way to design compositional shape analyses for sequential [5], and recently concurrent programs [6]. Such analyses can be seen as the attempt to build proofs for Hoare triples of a program. More precisely, given a program composed by procedures $p_1(\boldsymbol{x_1}), \ldots, p_n(\boldsymbol{x_n})$ a compositional analysis automatically synthesizes preconditions $P_1, \ldots, P_n$ and postconditions $Q_1, \ldots, Q_n$ such that the following are valid Hoare triples:

$$\{P_1\}\, p_1(\boldsymbol{x_1})\, \{Q_1\}, \ldots, \{P_n\}\, p_n(\boldsymbol{x_n})\, \{Q_n\}$$

The triples are constructed by symbolically executing the program and by *composing* existing triples. The composition (and therefore the construction of the proof) is done in a bottom-up fashion starting from the leaves of the call-graph and then using their triples to build other proofs for procedures which are on a higher-level in the call-graph. To achieve that we use a special rule for sequential composition which embeds directly the concept of bi-abduction:

$$\frac{\{P_1\}\, C_1\, \{Q_1\} \qquad \{P_2\}\, C_2\, \{Q_2\}}{\{P_1 * \mathcal{A}\}\, C_1; C_2\, \{Q_2 * \mathcal{F}\}} \qquad Q_1 * \mathcal{A} \vdash P_2 * \mathcal{F}$$

A compositional analysis has a great ability to scale since procedures are analyzed in isolation and, moreover, the analysis results of procedures can be easily reused. When dealing with large programs, the ability to analyze parts of the program independently of others, allows us to load only small parts of the source program into memory avoiding to overspill the RAM and cause the analysis to thrash. Finally, compositional analysis is *incremental*: that is, if the program changes after being analyzed, only the modified part need to be re-analyzed.

The results of the previous analysis are still valid for those parts of the program which did not change. All these features provide a strong boost to accurate heap analysis and make it scale up to millions of lines of code. Previous shape analyses were whole-program, non-compositional and therefore did not scale.[2]

We have implemented a compositional shape analysis which uses abduction in a new version of SpaceInvader called SpaceInvader/Abductor (or Abductor for short).

4   Application to Real Code

In this section we discuss our experience of running SpaceInvader/Abductor on large open source codebases (e.g. a complete Linux Kernel distribution with over 2.5 million lines of code). Figure 1 reports the results we obtained from these experiments. The case studies were run on a machine with two 2.66GHz Quad-Core Intel Xeon processors with 4GB memory. The number of lines of C code was measured by instrumenting gcc so that only code actually compiled was counted. The analysis was run using only one core in all examples except Linux for which, instead, we used 8 cores. The experiments were run using a timeout of one second.

The green bars indicate the percentage of procedures with at least one consistent non-trivial specification found from the analyzer. The precondition of a discovered specification denotes a set of states on which it is safe to run the procedure: that is, states for which one will not get pointer errors such as a double-free, dereference of null/dangling pointers, or memory leaks. Thus, for example, if a procedure disposes an acyclic list the precondition will not describe cyclic lists, because otherwise the procedure would commit a null-pointer violation.

The red bars instead show the percentage of procedures for which the analyzer was not able to synthesize any specification. The best results were obtained for the IMAP experiment for which SpaceInvader/Abductor synthesized specifications for 68.3% of the total number of procedures. The worst was OpenSSH for which 45.3% of consistent specs were found. For Linux, specs for 58.4% of procedures were discovered.

Focussing on the IMap example. Currently, Space Invader/Abductor provides little support for interpreting the data resulting from the analysis. Given this current user support and the huge quantity of results we decided to look closely only at the data related to IMAP.[3] Here we briefly summarize the outcomes. As indicated above consistent specifications were found for 68.3% of the procedures. Among the discovered specifications, we observed that 18 procedures (i.e., 1% of the total and 1.5% of the successfully analyzed procedures) reported preconditions involving complex data structures (e.g., different kinds of nested and

---

[2] The largest example of whole-program shape analysis in the literature is around 10K lines of code [10].

[3] We used cyrus-impad-2.3.13 downloaded from http://cyrusimap.web.cmu.edu

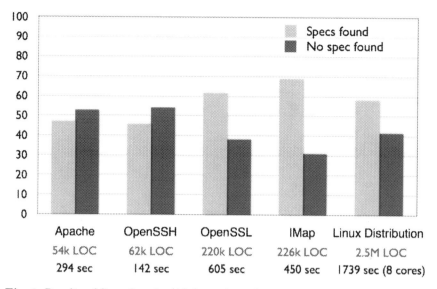

Fig. 1. Results of SpaceInvader/Abductor's analysis on large open source projects

non-nested lists). This indicates that a minority of procedures actually traverse data structures.

Figure 2 reports (in a pictorial form) one of the three (heap) specifications discovered for the procedure freeentryatts. The precondition is given by the box on the top labelled by "PRE1". On the bottom there are two post-conditions labelled by "POST1" and "POST2", respectively. The intuitive meaning is that when running the procedure freeentryatts starting from a state satisfying PRE1, the procedure does not commit any pointer errors, and if it terminates it will reach a state satisfying either POST1 or POST2. A pre (or a post) displays a heap structure. A small white rectangle with a label denotes an allocated cell, a red rectangle stands for a possibly dangling pointer and a green rectangle denotes nil. A long grey rectangle represents a list. A dashed blue box shows the internal structure of the elements of a list. Hence we can observe that the footprint of freeentryatts consists of a nested non-circular singly linked-list.

Figure 3 shows one specification of the function freeattvalues. It deallocates the fields in the list pointed to by its formal parameter l. The procedure freeentryatts calls freeattvalues(l->attvalues) asking to free the elements of the inner list. Notice how the bottom-up analysis composes these specifications. In freeentryatts the elements of the inner list pointed to by attvalues are deallocated by using (composing) the specification found for freeattvalues which acts on a smaller footprint. The field entry is instead deallocated directly inside freeentryatts.

This relation between freeentryatts and freeentryattvalues illustrates, in microcosm, the modularizing effect of bi-abductive inference. The specification of freeentryattvalues does not need to mention the enclosing list from freeentryatts, because of the principle of local reasoning. In a similar way, if

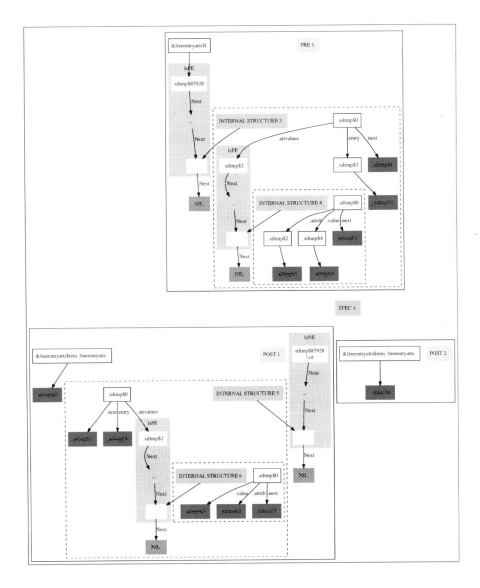

Fig. 2. A specification automatically synthesized by SpaceInvader/Abductor for the procedure `freeentryatts` of the IMap example

a procedure touches only two or three cells, there will be no need to add any predicates describing entire linked structures through its verification. In general, analysis of a procedure does not need to be concerned with tracking an explicit description of the entire global state of a system, which would be prohibitively expensive.

Only 4 procedures timed out (that is 0.4% of the total). Among the procedures for which the analysis was unable to synthesize specifications, 84 potential

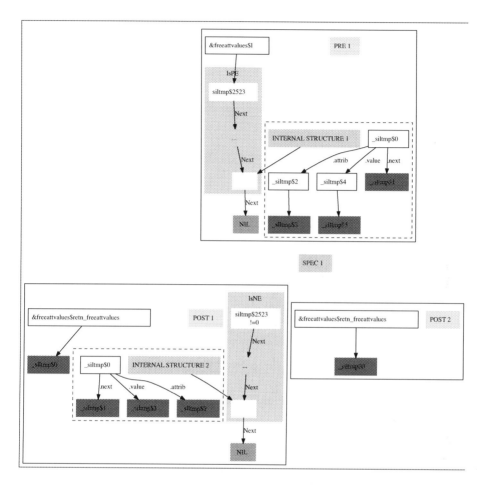

Fig. 3. A specification for the procedure `freeattvalues` called by `freeentryatts`

memory leaks were reported by SpaceInvader/Abductor. A quick inspection of these possible errors revealed that 19 cases (22.6%) were clearly real leaks, whereas 26 cases (30.9%) were false bugs. For the remaining 39 cases (46.4%), it was not easy to establish whether or not they were genuine bugs. This would require a good knowledge of the source code and/or better user support in reporting possible errors, a feature that is currently lacking in Abductor.[4] Nevertheless, given that SpaceInvader/Abductor was not designed as a bug catcher, but rather as a proof tool, we found the unveiling of several real bugs a pleasant surprising feature of our technology. In this context, we add a final consideration. We emphasize that SpaceInvader/Abductor computes a genuine over-approximation (with respect to an idealized model) in the sense of abstract interpretation [7]. Thus, in contrast to several unsound bug-catching tools that can detect some

---

[4] This feature has high priority in our to-do list of future work.

heap errors, when Abductor finds a specification it has constructed a proof which shows that no pointer errors can occur. For instance, from Figure 2 we can infer that `freeentryatts` *does not* leak memory, *does not* dereference a null/dangling pointer, and *does not* double-free memory.

Acknowledgments. I would like to thank Peter O'Hearn for many invaluable suggestions and helpful ideas on preliminary versions of this paper. This work was supported by a Royal Academy of Engineering research fellowship.

References

1. Ball, T., Majumdar, R., Millstein, T., Rajamani, S.: Automatic predicate abstraction of C programs. In: PLDI, pp. 203–213. ACM, New York (2001)
2. Berdine, J., Calcagno, C., Cook, B., Distefano, D., O'Hearn, P., Wies, T., Yang, H.: Shape analysis of composite data structures. In: Damm, W., Hermanns, H. (eds.) CAV 2007. LNCS, vol. 4590, pp. 178–192. Springer, Heidelberg (2007)
3. Berdine, J., Calcagno, C., O'Hearn, P.: Symbolic execution with separation logic. In: Yi, K. (ed.) APLAS 2005. LNCS, vol. 3780, pp. 52–68. Springer, Heidelberg (2005)
4. Blanchet, B., Cousot, P., Cousot, R., Feret, J., Mauborgne, L., Miné, A., Monniaux, D., Rival, X.: A static analyzer for large safety-critical software. In: PLDI 2003, pp. 196–207. ACM, New York (2003)
5. Calcagno, C., Distefano, D., O'Hearn, P.W., Yang, H.: Compositional shape analysis by means of bi-abduction. In: POPL, pp. 289–300. ACM, New York (2009)
6. Calcagno, C., Distefano, D., Vafeiadis, V.: Compositional resource invariant synthesis (submitted, 2009)
7. Cousot, P., Cousot, R.: Abstract interpretation: A unified lattice model for static analysis of programs by construction or approximation of fixpoints. In: POPL, pp. 238–252. ACM, New York (1977)
8. Distefano, D., O'Hearn, P., Yang, H.: A local shape analysis based on separation logic. In: Hermanns, H., Palsberg, J. (eds.) TACAS 2006. LNCS, vol. 3920, pp. 287–302. Springer, Heidelberg (2006)
9. Distefano, D., Parkinson, M.: jStar: Towards Practical Verification for Java. In: OOPSLA, pp. 213–226. ACM, New York (2008)
10. Yang, H., Lee, O., Berdine, J., Calcagno, C., Cook, B., Distefano, D., O'Hearn, P.: Scalable shape analysis for systems code. In: Gupta, A., Malik, S. (eds.) CAV 2008. LNCS, vol. 5123, pp. 385–398. Springer, Heidelberg (2008)
11. O'Hearn, P., Reynolds, J., Yang, H.: Local reasoning about programs that alter data structures. In: Fribourg, L. (ed.) CSL 2001 and EACSL 2001. LNCS, vol. 2142, pp. 1–19. Springer, Heidelberg (2001)
12. Peirce, C.: Collected papers of Charles Sanders Peirce. Harvard University Press, Cambridge (1958)
13. Sagiv, M., Reps, T., Wilhelm, R.: Solving shape-analysis problems in languages with destructive updating. ACM TOPLAS 20(1), 1–50 (1998)

On a Uniform Framework for
the Definition of Stochastic Process Languages*

Rocco De Nicola[1], Diego Latella[2], Michele Loreti[1], and Mieke Massink[2]

[1] Dipartimento di Sistemi e Informatica - Università di Firenze
[2] Istituto di Scienza e Tecnologie dell'Informazione "A. Faedo"- CNR

Abstract. In this paper we show how *Rate Transition Systems* (*RTS*s) can be used as a unifying framework for the definition of the semantics of stochastic process algebras. *RTS*s facilitate the *compositional* definition of such semantics exploiting operators on the next state functions which are the functional counterpart of classical process algebra operators. We apply this framework to representative fragments of major stochastic process calculi namely *TIPP*, *PEPA* and *IML* and show how they solve the issue of transition multiplicity in a simple and elegant way. We, moreover, show how *RTS*s help describing different languages, their differences and their similarities. For each calculus, we also show the formal correspondence between the *RTS*s semantics and the standard SOS one.

1 Introduction

Several stochastic, and in particular Markovian, process algebras have been proposed in the recent past. An overview can be found in [16]. Examples include *TIPP* [13,17], *PEPA* [19], *EMPA* [3], stochastic π-calculus [24] and, more recently, calculi for Mobile and Service Oriented Computing [10,6,7,23,4,8]. The main aim has been the integration of qualitative behavioural descriptions with non-functional ones, e.g. performance, in a single mathematical framework, namely that of process algebras. This has lead to the combination of two very successful approaches to concurrent systems modelling and analysis, namely Labeled Transition Systems (LTSs), widely used in the framework of process algebra, and Continuous Time Markov Chains (CTMCs), one of the most successful approaches to modelling and analysing system performance. The common feature of the most prominent stochastic process algebra proposals, including all the above mentioned ones, is that the actions used to label transitions are enriched with rates of exponentially distributed random variables (r.v.) characterising their duration[1]. Although all these languages relay on the same class of r.v., the underlying models and notions are significantly different, in particular with regards to the issue of the correct representation of the *race condition* principle for

---

* Research partially funded by EU IP SENSORIA (contract n. 016004), CNR-RSTL project XXL, FIRB-MUR project TOCAI.IT and by PRIN-MIUR PACO.

[1] Sometimes actions are assumed to have zero duration; then the associated r.v. is interpreted as a *delay*, before the action takes place.

M. Alpuente, B. Cook, and C. Joubert (Eds.): FMICS 2009, LNCS 5825, pp. 9–25, 2009.
© Springer-Verlag Berlin Heidelberg 2009

the choice operator, inherited from the theory of CTMCs. This principle implies that an expression like $(\alpha, \lambda).P + (\alpha, \lambda).P$, where there are two different ways of executing α, both with (exponentially distributed duration with) rate λ should model the same behavior as $(\alpha, 2 \cdot \lambda).P$, and not as $(\alpha, \lambda).P$, as it would be the case if one would look at the term as a standard process algebra one. Several, significantly different, approaches have been proposed for addressing the issue of *transition multiplicity* raised by the race condition principle ranging, e.g. from *multi relations* [19], to *proved transition systems* [24,13], to LTS with *numbered transitions* [16], to *unique rate names* [10,6]. A different approach has been taken in [15] for IML, a language for Interactive Markov Chains, $IMCs$, where actions are de-coupled from rates and interaction transitions, labelled with actions, are kept separated from Markovian ones, labelled by rates. Multi-relations are used for Markovian transitions. It should also be noted that some of the most successful approaches, e.g. [19,15] suffer from technical imprecision in that they define the relevant transition multi-relation as the *least* multi-relation satisfying a set of Structured Operational Semantics (SOS) axioms and rules. Unfortunately, such a least multi-relation turns out to be a relation, thus failing to formally representing transition multiplicity. In [20] a variant of LTSs, namely *Rated Transition Systems* ($RdTS$) has been proposed as a model for the definition of the semantics of Markovian process calculi by relying on the general framework of SGSOS. Moreover, in [20] conditions are put forward for guaranteeing associativity of the parallel composition operator in the SGSOS framework. It is then proved that one cannot guarantee associativity of the parallel composition operator up to stochastic bisimilarity when the synchronisation paradigm of CCS is used in combination with the synchronisation rate computation based on *apparent rates* [19]. This implies for instance that parallel composition of the Stochastic π-calculus is not associative.

In the present paper, we use *Rate Transition Systems* (RTS) a variant of $RdTS$ where the transition relation $\rightarrowtail$ associates to a given process P and a given transition label α a *next state* function, say $\mathscr{P}$, mapping each term into a non-negative real number. The transition $P \stackrel{\alpha}{\rightarrowtail} \mathscr{P}$ has the following meaning: if $\mathscr{P}(Q) = v$, (with $v \neq 0$), then Q is reachable from P by executing α, the duration of such execution being exponentially distributed with rate v; if $\mathscr{P}(Q) = 0$, then Q is not reachable from P via α. The approach is somewhat reminiscent of that of Deng et al. [12] where probabilistic process algebra terms are associated to a discrete probability distribution over such terms. $RTSs$ are similar to Continuous Time Markov Decision Processes (CTMDPs) as defined, e.g., in [18,2] or Continuous Time Probabilistic Automata (CPA) (see [21,22,5]), as we shall discuss in more detail in Sect. 2. A distinguishing feature of our approach is compositionality, which, as in [20], is a direct consequence of a structured approach to semantics; furthermore, in our approach, next state functions are composed and manipulated using operators which are in one to one correspondence with those of process calculi. A pleasant side-effect of the resulting framework is a simple and elegant solution to the transition multiplicity problem. Furthermore, $RTSs$ make it relatively easy to define *associative* parallel composition operators for calculi based on the CCS interaction paradigm. Finally, the possibility of defining different stochastic process languages within a single, uniform framework facilitates reasoning about them; their similarities and their major differences. In this paper we will consider only a small number of stochastic process calculi, due to space limitations. Moreover, we will focus only on the fragment of each calculus which is relevant for the stochastic extension. For the sake of conciseness, we will introduce the operators in an incremental fashion, pointing out the relative differences, avoiding repeating the relevant definitions for each language. We will not deal with behavioural relations and we will focus only on language definition: that is why in the title we mention process *languages* and not *calculi*. The reader interested in process equivalencies is referred to [8,9] for some initial results. The rest of the paper is organised as follows: in Sect. 2 some preliminary notions and definitions are recalled. Sect. 3 introduces the RTS semantics for a simple language for CTMCs. Sect. 4 shows the RTS semantics of significant fragments of major Markovian Process Calculi. Emphasis is put on calculi based on the multi-party CSP interaction paradigm, like $TIPP$ and $PEPA$. A brief discussion of other calculi, based on the binary, CCS, interaction paradigm is also provided. The RTS semantics of a language based on the Interactive Markov Chain principle of separating actions from rates is presented in Sect.5. Irrelevance of self-loops for transient analysis of CTMCs is proved in the appendix; for all other proofs concerning results presented in this paper the interested reader is referred to [11], where the $EMPA$ calculus is dealt with as well; results are proved by induction either on the structure of terms or on the length of the derivation in the relevant semantics deduction system. Basic knowledge of prominent stochastic process calculi is assumed in the rest of the paper.

2   Preliminaries

We let $\mathbb{N}_{\geq 0}$ ($\mathbb{R}_{\geq 0}$, respectively) denote the set $\{n \in \mathbb{N} \mid n \geq 0\}$ ($\{x \in \mathbb{R} \mid x \geq 0\}$, respectively) and, similarly, $\mathbb{N}_{>0}$ ($\mathbb{R}_{>0}$, respectively) denote the set $\{n \in \mathbb{N} \mid n > 0\}$ ($\{x \in \mathbb{R} \mid x > 0\}$, respectively). For set S we let 2^S denote the power-set of S and 2^S_{fin} the set of *finite* subsets of S. In function definitions as well as application *Currying* will be used whenever convenient.

Definition 1 (Negative Exponential Distributions). *A random variable X has a negative exponential distribution with rate λ if and only if $\mathbb{P}\{X \leq t\} = 1 - e^{\lambda \cdot t}$ for $t > 0$ and 0 otherwise.*   •

The expected value of an exponentially distributed r.v. with rate λ is λ^{-1} while its variance is λ^{-2}. The *min* of exponentially distributed independent r.v. $X_1, \ldots, X_n$ with rates $\lambda_1, \ldots, \lambda_n$ respectively is an exponentially distributed r.v. with rate $\lambda_1 + \ldots + \lambda_n$ while the probability that X_j is the *min* is $\frac{\lambda_j}{\lambda_1 + \ldots + \lambda_n}$. The *max* of exponentially distributed r.v. is not exponentially distributed. For the purpose of the present paper, CTMCs are defined as follows:

Definition 2 (Continuous Time Markov Chains). *A* Continuous Time Markov Chain (CTMC) *is a tuple* $(S, \mathbf{R})$ *where* S *is a countable non-empty set of states, and* $\mathbf{R} : S \to S \to \mathbb{R}_{\geq 0}$ *is the* rate matrix, *where for all* $s \in S$ *there exists* $K_s < \infty$ *such that* $\sum_{s' \in S} \mathbf{R} \, s \, s' = K_s$.   •

We will often use the matrix notation $\mathbf{R}[s, s']$ for $\mathbf{R} \, s \, s'$. $\mathbf{R}[s, s'] > 0$ means that a transition from s to s' can be taken. The sojourn time at state s before taking a transition is an exponentially distributed r.v. with rate $\sum_{s' \in S} \mathbf{R}[s, s']$ and the probability that the transition from s to s' is taken is $\mathbf{R}[s, s'] / \sum_{s'' \in S} \mathbf{R}[s, s'']$.

Notice that the above definition allows $\mathbf{R}[s, s] > 0$, i.e. self-loops are allowed, which is not the case in traditional definitions of CTMCs. The following proposition, proved in Appendix A, shows that, as long as traditional measures of CTMCs like transient (and consequently steady state) probabilities are concerned, this more liberal definition does not affect the meaning of the CTMC and, in fact, self-loops can be removed (i.e. $\mathbf{R}[s, s]$ set to zero) or added without affecting transient and steady state probability analysis results.

Proposition 1. *The transient behaviour of CTMC* $C = (S, \mathbf{R})$ *with* $\mathbf{R}[\bar{s}, \bar{s}] > 0$ *for some* $\bar{s} \in S$ *coincides with that of CTMC* $\tilde{C} = (S, \tilde{\mathbf{R}})$, *such that* $\tilde{\mathbf{R}}[s, s']$ $=_{\text{def}}$ 0, *if* $s = s'$, *and* $\tilde{\mathbf{R}}[s, s']$ $=_{\text{def}}$ $\mathbf{R}[s, s']$ *otherwise.*   □

As a consequence of the above result, the infinitesimal generator matrix representation of CTMCs, traditionally used for CTMCs without self-loops, can be safely used also for those with such loops.

For countable non-empty set S, we consider the set $S \to \mathbb{R}_{\geq 0}$ of total functions from S to $\mathbb{R}_{\geq 0}$. We let $\mathscr{P}, \mathscr{Q}, \mathscr{R}, \ldots$ range over $S \to \mathbb{R}_{\geq 0}$. We let $[]$ denote the 0 constant function in $S \to \mathbb{R}_{\geq 0}$, i.e. $[] \, s$ $=_{\text{def}}$ 0 for all $s \in S$; moreover given $s_1, \ldots, s_n \in S$ and, $\lambda_1, \ldots, \lambda_n \in \mathbb{R}_{>0}$ we let $[s_1 \mapsto \lambda_1, \ldots, s_n \mapsto \lambda_n]$ denote the function in $S \to \mathbb{R}_{\geq 0}$ which maps s_1 to $\lambda_1, \ldots, s_n$ to λ_n and any $s \in S \setminus \{s_1, \ldots, s_n\}$ to 0. The following definition characterises *Rate Transition Systems* [8,9].

Definition 3 (Rate Transition Systems). *A* Rate Transition System (RTS) *is a tuple* $(S, A, \rightarrowtail)$ *where* S *is a countable non-empty set of states,* A *is a countable non-empty set of labels and* $\rightarrowtail \subseteq S \times A \times (S \to \mathbb{R}_{\geq 0})$ *is the transition relation.*

In the sequel *RTSs* will be denoted by $\mathcal{R}, \mathcal{R}_1, \mathcal{R}', \ldots$ As usual, we let $s \xrightarrow{\alpha} \mathscr{P}$ denote $(s, \alpha, \mathscr{P}) \in \rightarrowtail$. Intuitively, $s_1 \xrightarrow{\alpha} \mathscr{P}$ and $(\mathscr{P} \, s_2) = \lambda \neq 0$ means that s_2 is reachable from s_1 via the execution of α and that the duration of such an execution is characterised by a random variable whose distribution function is negative exponential with rate λ. On the other hand, $(\mathscr{P} \, s_2) = 0$ means that s_2 is not reachable from s_1 via α.

Definition 4 (Σ_S). Σ_S *denotes the subset of* $S \to \mathbb{R}_{\geq 0}$ *including only all functions expressed using the* $[\ldots]$ *notation, i.e.* $\mathscr{P} \in \Sigma_S$ *if and only if* $\mathscr{P} = []$ *or there exist* $n > 0$, $s_1, \ldots, s_n \in S$ *and* $\lambda_1, \ldots, \lambda_n \in \mathbb{R}_{>0}$ *such that* $\mathscr{P} = [s_1 \mapsto \lambda_1, \ldots, s_n \mapsto \lambda_n]$ •

We equip Σ_S with a few useful operations, i.e. $+ : \Sigma_S \times \Sigma_S \rightarrow (S \rightarrow \mathbb{R}_{\geq 0})$ with $(\mathscr{P} + \mathscr{Q}) s =_{\text{def}} (\mathscr{P} s) + (\mathscr{Q} s)$ and $\bigoplus : \Sigma_S \rightarrow 2^S \rightarrow \mathbb{R}_{\geq 0}$ with $\bigoplus \mathscr{P} C =_{\text{def}} \sum_{s \in C} (\mathscr{P} s)$, for $C \subseteq S$, and we use the shorthand $\bigoplus \mathscr{P}$ for $\bigoplus \mathscr{P} S$. The proposition below trivially follows from the relevant definitions:

Proposition 2. *(i) All functions in Σ_S yield zero almost everywhere, i.e. for all $\mathscr{P} \in \Sigma_S$ the set $\{s \in S \mid (\mathscr{P} s) \neq 0\}$ is finite; (ii) Σ_S is closed under $+$, i.e. $+ : \Sigma_S \rightarrow \Sigma_S \rightarrow \Sigma_S$.* □

Proposition 2(i) above guarantees that $\bigoplus$ is well defined.

Definition 5. *Let $\mathcal{R} = (S, A, \rightarrowtail)$ be an RTS, then: (i) $\mathcal{R}$ is* total *if for all $s \in S$ and $\alpha \in A$ there exists $\mathscr{P} \in (S \rightarrow \mathbb{R}_{\geq 0})$ such that $s \overset{\alpha}{\rightarrowtail} \mathscr{P}$; (ii) $\mathcal{R}$ is* functional[2] *if for all $s \in S$, $\alpha \in A$, and $\mathscr{P}, \mathscr{Q} \in (S \rightarrow \mathbb{R}_{\geq 0})$ we have: $s \overset{\alpha}{\rightarrowtail} \mathscr{P}, s \overset{\alpha}{\rightarrowtail} \mathscr{Q} \Longrightarrow \mathscr{P} = \mathscr{Q}$; (iii) $\mathcal{R}$ is* well formed *if $\rightarrowtail \subseteq S \times A \times \Sigma_S$.* ●

Discussion

It is worth noting that RTSs are a slight generalization of Continuous Time Markov Decision Processes (CTMDPs) as defined by Hermanns and Johr [18] and Continuous Time Probabilistic Automata, as defined in [22]. In [18,22], in fact, the transition relation is a subset of $S \times A \times (S \rightarrow \mathbb{R}_{\geq 0})$, i.e. it is *not* required to be a *function* in $S \times A \rightarrow (S \rightarrow \mathbb{R}_{\geq 0})$, but sets S and A are required to be *finite* and in [18] an *initial state* is assumed as well. There is also a direct relationship between RTSs and Continuous Time Probabilistic Automata proposed by Knast in [21], although the latter are studied in a language theoretic framework: the element $a_{i,j}(x)$ of the infinitesimal matrix used in [21] coincides with $(\mathscr{P} j)$ for $i \overset{x}{\rightarrowtail} \mathscr{P}$. Finally, the Continuous Time Probabilistic Automata used by Dang Van Hung and Zhou Chaochen in [5] are based on standard automata, where transitions are elements of $S \times S$ and have a rate and no label associated. In [20] *Rated Transition Systems* (RdTSs) are proposed by Klin and Sassone. RdTSs coincide with the class of *functional RTS*: the transition relation is required to be a *function* in $S \times A \times S \rightarrow \mathbb{R}_{\geq 0} = S \times A \rightarrow (S \rightarrow \mathbb{R}_{\geq 0})$. In [2], Baier et al. define CTMDPs as tuples $(S, A, \rightarrowtail)$ where S and A are *finite* sets and $\rightarrowtail$ is a function in $S \times A \times S \rightarrow \mathbb{R}_{\geq 0}$, while we allow also infinite sets and relations over $S \times A \times (S \rightarrow \mathbb{R}_{\geq 0})$. Finally, we point out that RTSs can be used also to model (passive) action *weights*, e.g. in $EMPA$ or $PEPA$ as well as *interactive* transitions of Interactive Markov Chains in a natural way.

In the rest of the present paper we will consider only *well-formed RTSs*, since they are powerful enough to provide a semantic model for the stochastic process calculi we are interested in.

Definition 6 (Derivatives). *Let $\mathcal{R} = (S, A, \rightarrowtail)$ be an RTS; for sets $S' \subseteq S$ and $A' \subseteq A$, the set of* derivatives *of S' through A', denoted $Der(S', A')$, is the smallest set such that: (i) $S' \subseteq Der(S', A')$, and (ii) if $s \in Der(S', A')$ and there exists $\alpha \in A'$ and $\mathscr{Q} \in \Sigma_S$ such that $s \overset{\alpha}{\rightarrowtail} \mathscr{Q}$ then $\{s' \in S \mid \mathscr{Q}(s') \neq 0\} \subseteq Der(S', A')$.* ●

---

[2] *Fully-stochastic according to the terminology used in [9].*

Definition 7 (Derived CTMC). *Let* $\mathcal{R} = (S, A, \rightarrowtail)$ *be a functional RTS; for* $S' \subseteq S$, *the CTMC of* S', *when one considers only labels in* finite *set* $A' \subseteq A$ *is defined as* $CTMC[S', A']$ $=_{\text{def}}$ $(Der(S', A'), \mathbf{R})$ *where, for all* $s_1, s_2 \in Der(S', A')$, $\mathbf{R}[s_1, s_2]$ $=_{\text{def}}$ $\sum_{\alpha \in A', s_1 \overset{\alpha}{\rightarrowtail} \mathscr{P}} \mathscr{P}(s_2)$. •

We write $Der(s, A')$ and $CTMC[s, A']$ when $S' = \{s\}$.

The semantics of stochastic process calculi are often defined in the literature by means of Structured Operational Semantics (SOS) which characterize transition systems or *multi*-transition systems, i.e. transition systems where the transition relation is instead a *multi*-relation. Such (multi-)transitions are usually labelled by *rates* $\lambda \in \mathbb{R}_{>0}$, but sometimes they are also labelled with *actions* drawn from some set A. In such LTSs there may be two or more transitions with (the same action label and) different rates from a state to another one; in case of multi-transition systems such distinct transitions may even have the same rate. Henceforth we let $\mathbf{rt}(s_1, s_2)$ and $\mathbf{rt}_a(s_1, s_2)$ denote the *cumulative* rate over *all* transitions from s_1 to s_2 and the *cumulative* rate over *all* a-*labelled* transitions from s_1 to s_2 as defined below, where we use $\{\!| \_ |\!\}$ as a notation for multi-sets, and $\overset{\lambda}{\longrightarrow}$ ($\overset{a,\lambda}{\longrightarrow}$, respectively) for a generic transition (a-labelled transition, respectively):

Definition 8. *The* cumulative rates $\mathbf{rt}(s_1, s_2)$ *and* $\mathbf{rt}_a(s_1, s_2)$ *are defined as follows:* $\mathbf{rt}(s_1, s_2)$ $=_{\text{def}}$ $\sum\{\!| \lambda | s_1 \overset{\lambda}{\longrightarrow} s_2 |\!\}$ *and* $\mathbf{rt}_a(s_1, s_2)$ $=_{\text{def}}$ $\sum\{\!| \lambda | s_1 \overset{a,\lambda}{\longrightarrow} s_2 |\!\}$, *with* $\sum\{\!| |\!\} =_{\text{def}} 0$. •

3   A Language for CTMCs

In this section we define a simple language for CTMCs, in a similar way as in [16]. The set $\mathcal{P}_{CTMC}$ of CTMC terms includes *inaction*, *rate-prefix-*, *choice-*, and *constant-*terms as defined by the following grammar:

$$P ::= \mathbf{nil} \quad \Big| \quad \lambda.P \quad \Big| \quad P + P \quad \Big| \quad X$$

where $\lambda \in \mathbb{R}_{>0}$ and X is a constant defined by means of an equation of the form $X \overset{\Delta}{=} P$ where constants $X, X_1, X', \ldots$ may occur only guarded, i.e. under the scope of a prefix $\lambda.\_$, in *defining body* P.

In order to give an *RTS* semantics to the calculus we first of all choose the set $\mathcal{A}_{CTMC}$ $=_{\text{def}}$ $\{\sqrt{}\}$ as labels set; transitions have no action labels in standard CTMCs. The transition relation $\rightarrowtail$, is defined in Fig. 1, where $\alpha = \sqrt{}$ is assumed.

Intuitively, from Fig. 1 it is clear that there is no transition from **nil** to any other state, while there is a single transition from $\lambda.P$ to P and λ is the rate associated to such a transition. The rule for choice postulates that if there is a transition from P to a state, say R, with rate $(\mathscr{P}R)$ and a transition from Q to the same state R, with rate $(\mathscr{Q}R)$, then there is a transition from $P + Q$ to R with rate $(\mathscr{P}R) + (\mathscr{Q}R)$. Notice that, for term $P + Q$, if there is a transition *only* from P to R (i.e. not from Q to R) then $(\mathscr{Q}R) = 0$. Similarly, $(\mathscr{P}R) = 0$ if

$$(\text{NIL}) \; \overline{\text{nil} \overset{\alpha}{\rightarrowtail} []} \quad (\text{PRF}) \; \overline{\lambda.P \overset{\alpha}{\rightarrowtail} [P \mapsto \lambda]} \quad (\text{CHO}) \; \frac{P \overset{\alpha}{\rightarrowtail} \mathscr{P}, Q \overset{\alpha}{\rightarrowtail} \mathscr{Q}}{P+Q \overset{\alpha}{\rightarrowtail} \mathscr{P}+\mathscr{Q}} \quad (\text{CNT}) \; \frac{P \overset{\alpha}{\rightarrowtail} \mathscr{P}, X \overset{\Delta}{=} P}{X \overset{\alpha}{\rightarrowtail} \mathscr{P}}$$

Fig. 1. Semantics Rules for the CTMC Language

there is only a transition from Q to R. If, instead, there is *both* a transition from P to R (i.e. $(\mathscr{P}R) > 0$) *and* a transition from Q to R (i.e. $(\mathscr{Q}R) > 0$), then the cumulative rate $(\mathscr{P}R) + (\mathscr{Q}R)$ will be associated directly to the transition from $P + Q$ to R. The use of $RTSs$, in particular in the rule for choice, incorporates the *race condition* principle and solves the related *transition multiplicity* issue in a simple and elegant way. In fact, from Fig. 1, for $R_1 \neq R_2$ we get $\lambda.R_1 + \mu.R_2 \overset{\checkmark}{\rightarrowtail} [R_1 \mapsto \lambda, R_2 \mapsto \mu]$ where $\oplus[R_1 \mapsto \lambda, R_2 \mapsto \mu] = \lambda + \mu$ is the exit rate of state $\lambda.R_1 + \mu.R_2$ while $\lambda/(\lambda+\mu)$ and $\mu/(\lambda+\mu)$ are the probabilities of moving to R_1 and R_2, respectively. If $R_1 = R_2 = R$ then we get $\lambda.R + \mu.R \overset{\checkmark}{\rightarrowtail} [R \mapsto \lambda+\mu]$ and if, moreover, $\lambda = \mu$, we get $\lambda.R + \lambda.R \overset{\checkmark}{\rightarrowtail} [R \mapsto 2\lambda]$. The following proposition ensures that the semantics are closed w.r.t. $\Sigma_{\mathcal{P}_{CTMC}}$.

Proposition 3. *For all $P \in \mathcal{P}_{CTMC}$ and $\mathscr{P} \in \mathcal{P}_{CTMC} \rightarrow \mathbb{R}_{\geq 0}$, if $P \rightarrowtail \mathscr{P}$ can be derived from the rules of Fig. 1, then $\mathscr{P} \in \Sigma_{\mathcal{P}_{CTMC}}$.* □

Definition 9 (Formal semantics of the Language for CTMCs). *The formal semantics of the calculus for CTMCs is the RTS $\mathcal{R}_{CTMC}$ $=_{\text{def}}$ $(\mathcal{P}_{CTMC}, \mathcal{A}_{CTMC}, \rightarrowtail)$ where $\rightarrowtail \subseteq \mathcal{P}_{CTMC} \times \mathcal{A}_{CTMC} \times \Sigma_{\mathcal{P}_{CTMC}}$ is the least relation satisfying the rules of Fig. 1.* ●

The following theorem characterises the structure of $\mathcal{R}_{CTMC}$.

Theorem 1. *$\mathcal{R}_{CTMC}$ is total and functional.* □

The CTMC associated to a given term $P \in \mathcal{P}_{CTMC}$, $CTMC[P, \{\sqrt{}\}]$ is generated according to Def. 7. As a corollary of Theorem 1 we get that whenever $P \overset{\checkmark}{\rightarrowtail} \mathscr{P}$, the exit rate of P is given by $\oplus\mathscr{P}$ and $\mathscr{P}$ is the row of the rate matrix corresponding to P.

4 Fully Markovian Stochastic Process Calculi

We first introduce some additional notation. Let S and A be countable nonempty sets. We define function $\chi : S \rightarrow S \rightarrow \mathbb{R}_{\geq 0}$ as $\chi s =_{\text{def}} [s \mapsto 1]$. Let, moreover, $\_ \otimes \_ \_ : 2^A_{fin} \rightarrow S \rightarrow S \rightarrow S$ be a total function and let us define, with a little bit of overloading, function $\_ \otimes \_ \_ : 2^A_{fin} \rightarrow (S \rightarrow \mathbb{R}_{\geq 0}) \rightarrow (S \rightarrow \mathbb{R}_{\geq 0}) \rightarrow (S \rightarrow \mathbb{R}_{\geq 0})$ as follows:

$$(\mathscr{P} \otimes_L \mathscr{Q}) s =_{\text{def}} \begin{cases} (\mathscr{P} s_1) \cdot (\mathscr{Q} s_2), & \text{if } \exists s_1, s_2 \in S.\, s = s_1 \otimes_L s_2 \\ 0 & , \text{ otherwise} \end{cases}$$

$$(\text{PRF1}) \frac{}{(\alpha,\lambda).P \overset{\alpha}{\rightarrowtail} [P \mapsto \lambda]} \qquad (\text{PRF2}) \frac{\alpha \neq \beta}{(\alpha,\lambda).P \overset{\beta}{\rightarrowtail} []}$$

$$(\text{PAR1}) \frac{\alpha \notin L, P \overset{\alpha}{\rightarrowtail} \mathscr{P}, Q \overset{\alpha}{\rightarrowtail} \mathscr{Q}}{P||_L Q \overset{\alpha}{\rightarrowtail} (\mathscr{P}||_L(\chi Q)) + ((\chi P)||_L \mathscr{Q})} \qquad (\text{PAR2}) \frac{\alpha \in L, P \overset{\alpha}{\rightarrowtail} \mathscr{P}, Q \overset{\alpha}{\rightarrowtail} \mathscr{Q}}{P||_L Q \overset{\alpha}{\rightarrowtail} \mathscr{P}||_L \mathscr{Q}}$$

Fig. 2. Additional Semantics Rules for $TIPP_k$

We also define function $\_ \cdot \_/\_ : (S \to \mathbb{R}_{\geq 0}) \to \mathbb{R}_{\geq 0} \to \mathbb{R}_{\geq 0} \to S \to \mathbb{R}_{\geq 0}$ as follows:

$$\left(\mathscr{P} \cdot \frac{x}{y}\right) s =_{\text{def}} \begin{cases} (\mathscr{P}\,s) \cdot \frac{x}{y} \text{ , if } y \neq 0 \\ 0 \qquad\qquad \text{, otherwise} \end{cases}$$

The proposition below trivially follows from the relevant definitions:

Proposition 4. Σ_S *is* closed *under the operations* $\chi, (\_ \otimes \_)$, *and* $\_ \cdot \_/\_$, *i.e.* $\chi : S \to \Sigma_S$, $(\_ \otimes \_) : 2^A_{fin} \to \Sigma_S \to \Sigma_S \to \Sigma_S$, *and* $\_ \cdot \_/\_ : \Sigma_S \to \mathbb{R}_{\geq 0} \to \mathbb{R}_{\geq 0} \to \Sigma_S$. $\qquad\square$

4.1 $TIPP_k$

Here we consider a kernel language $TIPP_k$ of the version[3] of $TIPP$ presented in [17]. Let $\mathcal{A}_{TIPP_k}$ be a countable set of *actions*, $\tau \notin \mathcal{A}_{TIPP_k}$, and $\mathcal{A}^\tau_{TIPP_k} =_{\text{def}} \mathcal{A}_{TIPP_k} \cup \{\tau\}$, with τ representing the internal action. The set $\mathcal{P}_{TIPP_k}$ of $TIPP$ terms we consider includes *inaction, choice-,* and *constant*-terms, defined as in Sect. 3; moreover, $\mathcal{P}_{TIPP_k}$ includes *action-prefix* (which replaces rate-prefix) and *parallel composition*, as defined by the following grammar[4]:

$$P ::= (\alpha, \lambda).P \quad \Big| \quad P||_L P$$

where $\alpha \in \mathcal{A}^\tau_{TIPP_k}$, $\lambda \in \mathbb{R}_{>0}$, and finite *synchronisation* set $L \in 2^{\mathcal{A}_{TIPP_k}}_{fin}$. Constants $X, X_1, X', \ldots$ may only occur guarded, i.e. under the scope of a prefix $(\alpha, \lambda).\_$, in defining bodies.

The transition relation $\rightarrowtail$ for $TIPP_k$ is characterised by the set of rules RLS_{TIPP_k} defined below:

Definition 10 (RLS_{TIPP_k}). *Set* RLS_{TIPP_k} *is the least set of semantics rules including the rules in Fig. 2 plus rules (NIL), (CHO), (CNT) of Fig. 1, where terms P, Q, X are assumed to range over $\mathcal{P}_{TIPP_k}$ and $\alpha, \beta \in \mathcal{A}^\tau_{TIPP_k}$.* $\qquad\bullet$

---

[3] In [17] the synchronisation rate is defined as the product of those of the synchronising actions, as opposed to the original definition of $TIPP$, given in [13], where, instead, such rate is the *max* of the component rates.

[4] In $TIPP$ the notation **stop**, **i**, [] and $P|[L]|P$ is used instead of **nil**, τ, +, and $P||_L P$. Here we prefer to use a standard notation for the sake of uniformity.

In the rules, the generic functions χ and $\otimes$ on S are instantiated with specific functions for $\mathcal{P}_{TIPP_k}$. In particular the specific function $\|$ is used in place of the generic function $\otimes$; the specific function $\_\|\_\_ : 2_{fin}^{\mathcal{A}_{TIPP_k}} \to \mathcal{P}_{TIPP_k} \to \mathcal{P}_{TIPP_k} \to \mathcal{P}_{TIPP_k}$ is just the syntactical constructor for parallel composition on $TIPP$ terms. Rule (PAR1) ensures that all interesting continuations of $P \|_L Q$ are of the form $R \|_L Q$ where $P \overset{\alpha}{\rightarrowtail} \mathcal{P}$ and $(\mathcal{P} R) > 0$, for some $\mathcal{P}$ and $\alpha \notin L$, or of the form $P \|_L R$ where $Q \overset{\alpha}{\rightarrowtail} \mathcal{Q}$ and $(\mathcal{Q} R) > 0$, for some $\mathcal{Q}$ and $\alpha \notin L$. Rule (PAR2), instead, formalizes the *rate multiplication* principle of $TIPP$: if $\alpha \in L$, $P \overset{\alpha}{\rightarrowtail} \mathcal{P}, Q \overset{\alpha}{\rightarrowtail} \mathcal{Q}, (\mathcal{P} R_P) = \lambda_P > 0$, and $(\mathcal{Q} R_Q) = \lambda_Q > 0$, then $P \|_L Q$ evolves, via α, to $R_P \|_L R_Q$ with rate $\lambda_P \cdot \lambda_Q$.

The following proposition ensures that the semantics are closed w.r.t. $\Sigma_{\mathcal{P}_{TIPP_k}}$.

Proposition 5. *For all* $P \in \mathcal{P}_{TIPP_k}$, $\alpha \in \mathcal{A}_{TIPP_k}^{\tau}$ *and* $\mathcal{P} \in \mathcal{P}_{TIPP_k} \to \mathbb{R}_{\geq 0}$, *if* $P \overset{\alpha}{\rightarrowtail} \mathcal{P}$ *can be derived using only the rules in set* RLS_{TIPP_k} *of Def. 10, then* $\mathcal{P} \in \Sigma_{\mathcal{P}_{TIPP_k}}$. □

Definition 11 (Formal semantics of $TIPP_k$). *The formal semantics of* $TIPP_k$ *is the RTS* $\mathcal{R}_{TIPP_k} =_{\mathrm{def}} (\mathcal{P}_{TIPP_k}, \mathcal{A}_{TIPP_k}^{\tau}, \rightarrowtail)$ *where* $\rightarrowtail \subseteq \mathcal{P}_{TIPP_k} \times \mathcal{A}_{TIPP_k}^{\tau} \times \Sigma_{\mathcal{P}_{TIPP_k}}$ *is the least relation satisfying the rules of set* RLS_{TIPP_k} *(Def. 10).* ●

The following theorem characterises the structure of $\mathcal{R}_{TIPP_k}$.

Theorem 2. $\mathcal{R}_{TIPP_k}$ *is total and functional.*

Corollary 1. *For all* $P \in \mathcal{P}_{TIPP_k}, \alpha \in \mathcal{A}_{TIPP_k}^{\tau}$ *there exists a unique* $\mathcal{P}$ *such that* $P \overset{\alpha}{\rightarrowtail} \mathcal{P}$.

The following theorem establishes the formal correspondence between the RTS semantics of $TIPP_k$ and the semantics definition given in [17].

Theorem 3. *For all* $P, Q \in \mathcal{P}_{TIPP_k}$, $\alpha \in \mathcal{A}_{TIPP_k}^{\tau}$, *and unique* $\mathcal{P} \in \Sigma_{\mathcal{P}_{TIPP_k}}$ *such that* $P \overset{\alpha}{\rightarrowtail} \mathcal{P}$ *the following holds:* $(\mathcal{P} Q) = \mathbf{rt}_{\alpha}(P, Q)$ □

4.2 $PEPA_k$

The RTS semantics of the full $PEPA$ [19] calculus can be found in [9]. Here we confine our presentation to the kernel language $PEPA_k$. Let $\mathcal{A}_{PEPA_k}$, ranged over by $\alpha, \alpha', \dots$ be a countable set of *actions*. The set $\mathcal{P}_{PEPA_k}$ of $PEPA$ terms we consider includes *choice-* and *constant-*terms, defined as in Sect. 3, and *action-prefix* and *parallel composition*, defined as in Sect. 4.1, but with synchronisation set[5] $L \in 2_{fin}^{\mathcal{A}_{PEPA_k}}$. Constants $X, X_1, X', \dots$ may occur only guarded, i.e. under the scope of a prefix $(\alpha, \lambda).\_$, in defining bodies.

The transition relation $\rightarrowtail$ for $PEPA_k$ is characterised by the set of rules RLS_{PEPA_k} defined below:

---

[5] In $PEPA$ the notation $P \bowtie_L P$ is used instead of $P \|_L P$. Here we prefer to use a standard notation for the sake of uniformity.

$$\left(\begin{array}{c} \text{PAR} \\ \text{PEPA} \end{array}\right) \frac{\alpha \in L, P \xrightarrow{\alpha} \mathscr{P}, Q \xrightarrow{\alpha} \mathscr{Q}}{P\|_L Q \xrightarrow{\alpha} \mathscr{P}\|_L \mathscr{Q} \cdot \frac{min\{\oplus\mathscr{P}, \oplus\mathscr{Q}\}}{\oplus\mathscr{P} \cdot \oplus\mathscr{Q}}}$$

Fig. 3. Additional Semantics Rule for $PEPA_k$

Definition 12 (RLS_{PEPA_k}). *Set* RLS_{PEPA_k} *is the least set of semantics rules including the rule in Fig.3 plus rules (CHO), (CNT) of Fig. 1 and Rules (PRF1), (PRF2), and (PAR1) of Fig. 2. In all the above rules terms* P, Q, X *are assumed to range over* $\mathcal{P}_{PEPA_k}$ *and* $\alpha \in \mathcal{A}_{PEPA_k}$. •

In the rules, the generic functions χ and $\otimes$ on S are instantiated with specific functions on $\mathcal{P}_{PEPA_k}$. In particular the specific function $\|$ is used in place of the generic function $\otimes$; the specific function $\_\|\_\_ : 2^{\mathcal{A}_{PEPA_k}}_{fin} \rightarrow \mathcal{P}_{PEPA_k} \rightarrow \mathcal{P}_{PEPA_k} \rightarrow \mathcal{P}_{PEPA_k}$ is just the syntactical constructor for co-operation on $PEPA$ terms. The rule for interleaving ensures that all continuations of $P\|_L Q$ are of the form $R\|_L Q$ where $P \xrightarrow{\alpha} \mathscr{P}$ and $(\mathscr{P} R) > 0$, for some α and $\mathscr{P}$ or of the form $P\|_L R$ where $Q \xrightarrow{\alpha} \mathscr{Q}$ and $(\mathscr{Q} R) > 0$, for some α and $\mathscr{Q}$. The rule for co-operation, instead, implements the *apparent rate* principle of $PEPA$ (see corollary of Theorem 4): if $\alpha \in L$, $P \xrightarrow{\alpha} \mathscr{P}$, $Q \xrightarrow{\alpha} \mathscr{Q}$, $(\mathscr{P} R_P) = \lambda_P > 0$, and $(\mathscr{Q} R_Q) = \lambda_Q > 0$, then $P\|_L Q$ evolves to $R_P\|_L R_Q$ with rate $\frac{\lambda_P}{\oplus\mathscr{P}} \cdot \frac{\lambda_Q}{\oplus\mathscr{Q}} \cdot min\{\oplus\mathscr{P}, \oplus\mathscr{Q}\}$.

The following proposition ensures that the semantics are closed w.r.t. $\Sigma_{\mathcal{P}_{PEPA_k}}$.

Proposition 6. *For all* $P \in \mathcal{P}_{PEPA_k}$, $\alpha \in \mathcal{A}_{PEPA_k}$ *and* $\mathscr{P} \in \mathcal{P}_{PEPA_k} \rightarrow \mathbb{R}_{\geq 0}$, *if* $P \xrightarrow{\alpha} \mathscr{P}$ *can be derived from the rules of Fig. 3, then* $\mathscr{P} \in \Sigma_{\mathcal{P}_{PEPA_k}}$. □

Definition 13 (Formal semantics of $PEPA_k$). *The formal semantics of* $PEPA_k$ *is the RTS* $\mathcal{R}_{PEPA_k} =_{def} (\mathcal{P}_{PEPA_k}, \mathcal{A}_{PEPA_k}, \rightarrowtail)$ *where* $\rightarrowtail \subseteq \mathcal{P}_{PEPA_k} \times \mathcal{A}_{PEPA_k} \times \Sigma_{\mathcal{P}_{PEPA_k}}$ *is the least relation satisfying the rules of set* RLS_{PEPA_k} *(Def. 12).* •

Theorem 4. $\mathcal{R}_{PEPA_k}$ *is total and functional.*

As a corollary of Theorem 4 we get that whenever $P \xrightarrow{\alpha} \mathscr{P}$ the apparent rate of α in P—namely the exit rate of P relative to α, denoted by $r_\alpha(P)$ in [19]—is given by $\oplus\mathscr{P}$. In [9] it is shown that the RTS semantics of $PEPA$ coincides with the original one.

We close this section by observing that $PEPA$ passive actions [19] can be easily dealt with in the RTS approach. One has to consider total functions in $\mathcal{P}_{PEPA_k} \rightarrow (\mathbb{R}_{\geq 0} \cup \{w \cdot \top \mid w \in \mathbb{N}_{>0}\})$ and define $\Sigma^\top_{\mathcal{P}_{PEPA_k}}$ by restricting only to functions expressed using the $[\ldots]$ notation; all definitions involving $\Sigma_{\mathcal{P}_{PEPA_k}}$ must be extended to $\Sigma^\top_{\mathcal{P}_{PEPA_k}}$ accordingly and taking into account the equations for $\top$ introduced in [19]. The following is an example resulting from the related derivation using the extended definitions:

$$(\alpha, \sqrt{2}).P\|_{\{a\}}((\alpha, 2\top).Q + (\alpha, 4\top).R) \xrightarrow{\alpha} [P\|_{\{a\}}Q \mapsto \frac{\sqrt{2}}{3}, P\|_{\{a\}}R \mapsto \frac{2 \cdot \sqrt{2}}{3}]$$

4.3 CCS-Based Stochastic Process Calculi

Our RTS approach has been successfully applied to several CCS-based calculi including Stochastic CCS [20], Stochastic π-calculus [24] and calculi for modeling Service Oriented Computing [8]. The main issue is the treatment of the CCS one-to-one synchronisation paradigm, as opposed to the CSP multicast one adopted by $TIPP$, $PEPA$ and $EMPA$. RTS semantics allows for an adequate and elegant calculation of normalisation factors which make it possible to preserve nice properties of the original calculi, like associativity of parallel composition, which is not possible using other approaches, as discussed in e.g. [20]. Due to space limitations we do not show the RTS semantics of Stochastic CCS and SOC calculi here and we refer to [8,9].

5   A Language of Interactive Markov Chains

In this section we show an RTS semantics of Hermanns' Language of Interactive Markov Chains (IML). The definition of Interactive Markov Chains (IMC) follows [15]:

Definition 14. *An Interactive Markov Chain is a tuple* $(S, A, \rightarrow, \dashrightarrow, s_0)$ *where* S *is a nonempty, finite set of states,* A *a finite set of actions,* $\rightarrow \subseteq S \times A \times S$ *the set of* interactive transitions, $\dashrightarrow \subseteq S \times \mathbb{R}_{>0} \times S$ *the set of* Markov transitions, *and* $s_0 \in S$ *the initial state.*   •

Also for IMCs we let the cumulative transition rate from s to s' be denoted by $\mathbf{rt}(s, s')$. For the sake of simplicity and due to space limitations, in this section we consider a kernel subset IML_k of the language IML defined in [15], which is anyway sufficient for showing how $RTSs$ can be used as a semantic model for IML. Let $\mathcal{A}_{IML_k}$ be a countable set of *actions*. The set $\mathcal{P}_{IML_k}$ of IML_k terms we consider includes *inaction*, *rate-prefix-*, *choice-*, and *constant-*terms, defined as in Sect. 3, and *action-prefix-* and *parallel composition-*terms, defined as in Sect. 4.1, but with $\alpha \in \mathcal{A}_{IML_k}$ and $L \in 2^{\mathcal{A}_{IML_k}}_{fin}$ as synchronisation set[6]. Constants $X, X_1, X', \ldots$ may occur only guarded, i.e. under the scope of a prefix $\lambda.\_$ or $\alpha.\_$, in defining bodies.

In order to give interactive transitions a "first-class objects" status, we consider a slight extension of RTS. We point out here that, technically, such an extension is not necessary, as we shall briefly discuss later on. We use it only because it makes our framework closer to the original model of IMCs. The extension of interest, namely RTS^ι, differs from RTS only because, instead of using functions in $\mathcal{P}_{IML_k} \rightarrow \mathbb{R}_{\geq 0}$, we consider those in $\mathcal{P}_{IML_k} \rightarrow \mathbb{R}^\iota_{\geq 0}$, where $\mathbb{R}^\iota_{\geq 0}$

---

[6] In IML_k the notation $\mathbf{0}$ and $P\|[L]\|P$ is used instead of $\mathbf{nil}$ and $P\|_L P$. Here we prefer to use a standard notation for the sake of uniformity.

$+^{\iota}$	0	ι	v_2
0	0	ι	v_2
ι	ι	ι	ι
v_1	v_1	ι	$v_1 + v_2$

$\cdot^{\iota}$	0	ι	v_2
0	0	0	0
ι	0	ι	ι
v_1	0	ι	$v_1 \cdot v_2$

Fig. 4. Definition of $+^{\iota}$ and $\cdot^{\iota}$

denotes $\mathbb{R}_{\geq 0} \cup \{\iota\}$, with ι a distinguished value such that $\iota \notin \mathbb{R}_{\geq 0}$. Markov transitions are modeled as in Sect. 3, using the special element $\sqrt{} \notin \mathcal{A}_{IML_k}$ as a label and defining the label set of the relevant RTS^{ι} as $\mathcal{A}^{\sqrt{}}_{IML_k} =_{\text{def}} \mathcal{A}_{IML_k} \cup \{\sqrt{}\}$, ranged over by $\alpha, \alpha_1, \alpha', \ldots$. We define $\Sigma^{\iota}_{\mathcal{P}_{IML_k}}$ as expected:

Definition 15 ($\Sigma^{\iota}_{\mathcal{P}_{IML_k}}$). $\Sigma^{\iota}_{\mathcal{P}_{IML_k}}$ *denotes the subset of* $\mathcal{P}_{IML_k} \to \mathbb{R}^{\iota}_{\geq 0}$ *including only all functions expressed using the* $[\ldots]$ *notation, i.e.* $\mathscr{P} \in \Sigma^{\iota}_{\mathcal{P}_{IML_k}}$ *if and only if* $\mathscr{P} = [\,]$ *or* $\mathscr{P} = [P_1 \mapsto v_1, \ldots, P_n \mapsto v_n]$ *for* $n \in \mathbb{N}_{>0}$, $P_1, \ldots, P_n \in \mathcal{P}_{IML_k}$ *and* $v_1, \ldots, v_n \in \mathbb{R}_{>0} \cup \{\iota\}$, *with* $([\,] P) =_{\text{def}} 0$ *and* $[P_1 \mapsto v_1, \ldots, P_n \mapsto v_n] P$ *yielding* v_j *if* $P = P_j$ *for* $1 \leq j \leq n$ *and* 0 *otherwise.* •

We extend operations $+$ and $\cdot$ to $+^{\iota}, \cdot^{\iota} : \mathbb{R}^{\iota}_{\geq 0} \to \mathbb{R}^{\iota}_{\geq 0} \to \mathbb{R}^{\iota}_{\geq 0}$ as in Fig. 4, where we assume that $v_1, v_2 \notin \{0, \iota\}$. We lift $+^{\iota} : \mathbb{R}^{\iota}_{\geq 0} \to \mathbb{R}^{\iota}_{\geq 0} \to \mathbb{R}^{\iota}_{\geq 0}$ to $+^{\iota} : \Sigma^{\iota}_{\mathcal{P}_{IML_k}} \to \Sigma^{\iota}_{\mathcal{P}_{IML_k}} \to \mathcal{P}_{IML_k} \to \mathbb{R}^{\iota}_{\geq 0}$; we moreover define $_-\|_L{_-} : \Sigma^{\iota}_{\mathcal{P}_{IML_k}} \to \Sigma^{\iota}_{\mathcal{P}_{IML_k}} \to \mathcal{P}_{IML_k} \to \mathbb{R}^{\iota}_{\geq 0}$ by instantiating $\otimes_L$ on the syntactical constructor for parallel composition on IML_k terms and using $\cdot^{\iota}$ instead of $\cdot$. In the sequel we refrain from using the superscript ι in $+^{\iota}$ and $\cdot^{\iota}$ when it is clear from the context that we are using the extended operators. The following proposition trivially follows from the relevant definitions.

Proposition 7. *(i) All functions in* $\Sigma^{\iota}_{\mathcal{P}_{IML_k}}$ *yield zero almost everywhere, i.e. for all* $\mathscr{P} \in \Sigma^{\iota}_{\mathcal{P}_{IML_k}}$ *the set* $\{P \in \mathcal{P}_{IML_k} \mid \mathscr{P} P \neq 0\}$ *is finite; (ii)* $\Sigma^{\iota}_{\mathcal{P}_{IML_k}}$ *is closed under the extended operators, namely* $+, \|_L : \Sigma^{\iota}_{\mathcal{P}_{IML_k}} \to \Sigma^{\iota}_{\mathcal{P}_{IML_k}} \to \Sigma^{\iota}_{\mathcal{P}_{IML_k}}$. □

We finally extend the notion of Derived CTMC (see Def. 7) to IMCs in the obvious way:

Definition 16 (Derived IMC). *Let* $\mathcal{R} = (S, A, \rightarrowtail)$ *be a functional* RTS^{ι}; *for* $s_0 \in S$, *the IMC of* s_0, *when one considers only labels in finite set* $A' \subseteq A$ *is defined as* $IMC[\{s_0\}, A'] =_{\text{def}} (Der(\{s_0\}, A'), A', \to, \dashrightarrow, s_0)$ *where for all* $s_1, s_2 \in Der(\{s_0\}, A')$, $\alpha \in A'$ *such that* $s_1 \overset{\alpha}{\rightarrowtail} \mathscr{P}$: *(i)* $s_1 \overset{\alpha}{\to} s_2$ *iff* $(\mathscr{P} s_2) = \iota$, *and (ii)* $s_1 \overset{\lambda}{\dashrightarrow} s_2$ *iff* $(\mathscr{P} s_2) = \lambda > 0$. •

The transition relation $\rightarrowtail$ for IML_k is characterised by the set of rules RLS_{IML_k} defined below:

$$\frac{}{\lambda.P \overset{\checkmark}{\rightarrowtail} [P \mapsto \lambda]} \qquad \frac{\alpha \neq \checkmark}{\lambda.P \overset{\alpha}{\rightarrowtail} []} \qquad \frac{\alpha \neq \checkmark}{\alpha.P \overset{\alpha}{\rightarrowtail} [P \mapsto \iota]} \qquad \frac{\checkmark \neq \alpha \neq \beta}{\alpha.P \overset{\beta}{\rightarrowtail} []}$$

Fig. 5. Additional Semantics Rules for the IML_k

Definition 17 (RLS_{IML_k}). *Set* RLS_{IML_k} *is the least set of semantics rules including the rules in Fig.5 plus rules (NIL), (CHO), (CNT) of Fig. 1, and rules (PAR1) and (PAR2) of Fig. 2. In all the above rules, terms P, Q, X are assumed to range over $\mathcal{P}_{IML_k}$ and $\alpha, \beta \in \mathcal{A}_{IML_k}^{\checkmark}$.* •

The rule for choice allows for the integration of Markov transitions with interaction ones; as usual, if $P \overset{\checkmark}{\rightarrowtail} \mathcal{P}$ and $(\mathcal{P} Q) = \lambda$ then λ is the cumulative rate for reaching Q from P, i.e. $\lambda = \mathbf{rt}(P, Q)$. For instance, for

$$P \overset{\Delta}{=} (\lambda_1.P_1 + \alpha.P_2) + (\alpha.P_2 + \lambda_2.P_1)$$

we have $P \overset{\checkmark}{\rightarrowtail} [P_1 \mapsto \lambda_1 + \lambda_2]$ and $P \overset{\alpha}{\rightarrowtail} [P_2 \mapsto \iota]$ with, moreover, $P \overset{\alpha'}{\rightarrowtail} []$ for all $\alpha' \notin \{\alpha, \checkmark\}$. The rule for interleaving ensures that all continuations of $P \|_L Q$ are of the form $R \|_L Q$ where $P \overset{\checkmark}{\rightarrowtail} \mathcal{P}$ and $(\mathcal{P} R) > 0$ or $P \overset{\alpha}{\rightarrowtail} \mathcal{P}$ and $(\mathcal{P} R) = \iota$ for some $\mathcal{P}$ and α, or of the form $P \|_L R$ where $Q \overset{\checkmark}{\rightarrowtail} \mathcal{Q}$ and $(\mathcal{Q} R) > 0$ or $Q \overset{\alpha}{\rightarrowtail} \mathcal{Q}$ and $(\mathcal{Q} R) = \iota$, for $\alpha \notin L$. The rule for synchronisation, instead, applies only in the case of interactive transitions and postulates that the only terms which can be reached from $P \|_L Q$, via $\alpha \in L$ are those of the form $P' \|_L Q'$ with $(\mathcal{P} P') = (\mathcal{Q} Q') = \iota$, where $P \overset{\alpha}{\rightarrowtail} \mathcal{P}$ and $Q \overset{\alpha}{\rightarrowtail} \mathcal{Q}$. It is worth noting that we could have chosen to use standard $\Sigma_{\mathcal{P}_{IML_k}}$ instead of its extension $\Sigma_{\mathcal{P}_{IML_k}}^{\iota}$ by replacing axiom $\alpha.P \overset{\alpha}{\rightarrowtail} [P \mapsto \iota]$ with $\alpha.P \overset{\alpha}{\rightarrowtail} [P \mapsto 1]$. In particular, whenever $P \overset{\alpha}{\rightarrowtail} \mathcal{P}$ the number of *different* (interaction) α-transitions from P to Q would be given by $(\mathcal{P} Q)$. We preferred the first alternative because we are not interested in counting such transition and we think that keeping different types for the range of the two kinds of transitions makes the framework more clear and closer to the original model of IMCs. We note also a clean separation between internal non-determinism, represented *within* functions, and external non-determinism, represented by different transitions. For instance, assuming P_1, P_2 and P_3 all different terms, the term

$$P \overset{\Delta}{=} \alpha.P_1 + \beta.P_2 + \alpha.P_3$$

has the following transitions: $P \overset{\alpha}{\rightarrowtail} [P_1 \mapsto \iota, P_3 \mapsto \iota]$, $P \overset{\beta}{\rightarrowtail} [P_2 \mapsto \iota]$, and $P \overset{\alpha'}{\rightarrowtail} []$ for all $\alpha' \notin \{\alpha, \beta\}$

Proposition 8. *For all $P \in \mathcal{P}_{IML_k}$, $\alpha \in \mathcal{A}_{IML_k}^{\checkmark}$ and $\mathcal{P} \in \mathcal{P}_{IML_k} \to \mathbb{R}_{\geq 0}^{\iota}$, if $P \overset{\alpha}{\rightarrowtail} \mathcal{P}$ can be derived from the rules in set RLS_{IML_k} of Def. 17, then $\mathcal{P} \in \Sigma_{\mathcal{P}_{IMC}}^{\iota}$.* □

Proposition 9. *For all* $P \in \mathcal{P}_{IML_k}$, $\alpha \in \mathcal{A}^{\vee}_{IML_k}$ *and* $\mathscr{P} \in \Sigma^{\iota}_{\mathcal{P}_{IMC}}$ *such that* $P \xrightarrow{\alpha} \mathscr{P}$ *can be derived from the rules in set* RLS_{IML_k} *of Def. 17, the following holds: (i) if* $\alpha \in \mathcal{A}_{IML_k}$ *and* $\mathscr{P} \neq []$ *then* $(\mathsf{range}\,\mathscr{P}) = \{0, \iota\}$, *(ii) if* $\alpha = \sqrt{}$ *then* $\iota \notin (\mathsf{range}\,\mathscr{P})$. $\qquad\qquad\square.$

Definition 18 (Formal semantics of IML_k**).** *The formal semantics of* IML_k *is the* RTS^{ι} $\mathcal{R}_{IML_k} =_{\mathrm{def}} (\mathcal{P}_{IML_k}, \mathcal{A}^{\vee}_{IML_k}, \rightarrowtail)$ *where* $\rightarrowtail \subseteq \mathcal{P}_{IML_k} \times \mathcal{A}^{\vee}_{IML_k} \times \Sigma^{\iota}_{\mathcal{P}_{IML_k}}$ *is the least relation satisfying the rules in set* RLS_{IML_k} *of Def. 17.* $\qquad\bullet$

Theorem 5. $\mathcal{R}_{IML_k}$ *is total and functional.*

Corollary 2. *For all* $P \in \mathcal{P}_{IML_k}, \alpha \in \mathcal{A}^{\vee}_{IML_k}$ *there exists a* unique $\mathscr{P}$ *such that* $P \xrightarrow{\alpha} \mathscr{P}$.

The following theorem establishes the formal correspondence between the RTS^{ι} semantics of IML_k and the semantics definition given in [15]. Notice that in this case the cumulative rate must be computed over *all* copies of all transitions from P to Q in the *multi*-relation $\dashrightarrow$ defined in [15].

Theorem 6. *For all* $P, Q \in \mathcal{P}_{IML_k}$, $\alpha \in \mathcal{A}_{IML_k}$, *and unique functions* $\mathscr{P}, \mathscr{P}' \in \Sigma_{\mathcal{P}_{IML_k}}$ *such that* $P \xrightarrow{\alpha} \mathscr{P}$ *and* $P \xrightarrow{\sqrt{}} \mathscr{P}'$ *the following holds: (i)* $(\mathscr{P}\,Q) = \iota$ *if and only if* $P \xrightarrow{\alpha} Q$; *(ii)* $(\mathscr{P}'\,Q) = \mathbf{rt}(P, Q)$. $\qquad\square$

6   Conclusions

In this paper we introduced *Rate Transition Systems* and we showed how they can be used as a unifying framework for the definition of the semantics of stochastic process algebras. *RTS*s facilitate the *compositional* definition of such semantics exploiting operators on the next state functions which are the functional counterpart of classical process algebra operators. We applied this framework to representative fragments of major stochastic process calculi including *TIPP*, *PEPA* and *IML* and showed how they solve the issue of transition multiplicity in a simple and elegant way[7]. Moreover, we showed how *RTS*s throw light on differences and similarities of different languages. For each calculus, we also proved the formal correspondence between its *RTS* semantics and its standard SOS one. It turned out that, in all cases we considered here, it is sufficient to use *functional RTS*s, i.e. *RTS* where the transition relation is indeed a function. General *RTS*s are however useful in translations of Interactive Markov Chains to Continuous Time Markov Decision Processes [18], or in the definition of the *RTS* semantics for the Stochastic π-calculus (see [9]). Future work includes the investigation of the nature and actual usefulness of general *RTS*s, and in particular their explicit representation of non-determinism, also in the context of behavioural relations, along the lines of [22].

---

[7] The approach has been applied also to *EMPA* but is not reported here due to space limitations. The details can be found in [11].

References

1. Aldini, A., Bernardo, M., Corradini, F.: A Process Algebraic Approach to Software Architecture Design. Springer, Heidelberg (to appear)
2. Baier, C., Hermanns, H., Katoen, J.-P., Haverkort, B.: Efficient computation of time-bounded reachability probabilities in uniform continuous-time Markov decision processes. Theoretical Computer Science 345, 2–26 (2005)
3. Bernardo, M., Gorrieri, R.: A tutorial on EMPA: A theory of concurrent processes with nondeterminism, priorities, probabilities and time. Theoretical Computer Science 202(1-2), 1–54 (1998)
4. Bravetti, M., Latella, D., Loreti, M., Massink, M., Zavattaro, G.: Combining Timed Coordination Primitives and Probabilistic Tuple Spaces. In: Kaklamanis, C., Nielson, F. (eds.) TGC 2008. LNCS, vol. 5474, pp. 52–68. Springer, Heidelberg (2009)
5. Van Hung, D., Chaochen, Z.: Probabilistic Duration Calculus for Continuous Time. Formal Aspects of Computing. The International Journal of Formal Methods 11, 21–44 (1999)
6. De Nicola, R., Katoen, J.-P., Latella, D., Loreti, M., Massink, M.: KLAIM and its Stochastic Semantics. Technical Report 6, Dipartimento di Sistemi e Informatica, Università di Firenze (2006),
   http://rap.dsi.unifi.it/~loreti/papers/TR062006.pdf
7. De Nicola, R., Katoen, J.-P., Latella, D., Loreti, M., Massink, M.: Model Checking Mobile Stochastic Logic. Theoretical Computer Science 382(1), 42–70 (2007),
   http://dx.doi.org/10.1016/j.tcs2007.05.008
8. De Nicola, R., Latella, D., Loreti, M., Massink, M.: MarCaSPiS: a Markovian Extension of a Calculus for Services. In: Hennessy, M., Klin, B. (eds.) Proceedings of the 5th Workshop on Structural Operational Semantics (SOS 2008), Reykjavik, Iceland, July 6, pp. 6–20 (2008); Preliminary Proceedings. Final Proceedings to appear as ENTCS by Elsevier
9. De Nicola, R., Latella, D., Loreti, M., Massink, M.: Rate-based Transition Systems for Stochastic Process Calculi. In: Marchetti, A., Matias, Y. (eds.) Automata, Languages and Programming - C. LNCS. Springer, Heidelberg (2009)
10. De Nicola, R., Latella, D., Massink, M.: Formal modeling and quantitative analysis of KLAIM-based mobile systems. In: Haddad, H., Liebrock, L., Omicini, A., Wainwright, R., Palakal, M., Wilds, M., Clausen, H. (eds.) Applied Computing 2005. Proceedings of the 20th Annual ACM Symposium on Applied Computing, pp. 428–435, Association for Computing Machinery - ACM (2005), ISBN 1-58113-964-0
11. De Nicola, R., Latella, D., Moreli, M., Massink, M.: On a Uniform Framework for the Definition of Stochastic Process Languages. Full Version. Technical report, Consiglio Nazionale delle Ricerche, Istituto di Scienza e Tecnologie dell'Informazione 'A. Faedo' (to appear, 2009)
12. Deng, Y., van Glabbeek, R., Hennessy, M., Morgan, C., Zhang, C.: Characterising testing preorders for finite probabilistic processes. In: IEEE Symposium on Logic in Computer Science, pp. 313–325. IEEE Computer Society Press, Los Alamitos (2007)
13. Gotz, N., Herzog, U., Rettelbach, M.: Multiprocessor and distributed systems design: The integration of functional specification and performance analysis using stochastic process algebras. In: Donatiello, L., Nelson, R. (eds.) SIGMETRICS 1993 and Performance 1993. LNCS, vol. 729. Springer, Heidelberg (1993)

14. Haverkort, B.: Markovian Models for Performance and Dependability Evaluation. In: Brinksma, E., Hermanns, H., Katoen, J.-P. (eds.) EEF School 2000 and FMPA 2000. LNCS, vol. 2090, pp. 38–83. Springer, Heidelberg (2001)
15. Hermanns, H.: Interactive Markov Chains. LNCS, vol. 2428, p. 129. Springer, Berlin (2002)
16. Hermanns, H., Herzog, U., Katoen, J.-P.: Process algebra for performance evaluation. Theoretical Computer Science 274(1-2), 43–87 (2002)
17. Hermanns, H., Herzog, U., Mertsiotakis, V.: Stochastic process algebras - between LOTOS and Markov chains. Computer Networks and ISDN Systems 30, 901–924 (1998)
18. Hermanns, H., Johr, S.: Uniformity by Construction in the Analysis of Nondeterministic Stochastic Systems. In: 2007 International Conference on Dependable Systems & Networks, pp. 718–728. IEEE Computer Society Press, Los Alamitos (2007)
19. Hillston, J.: A compositional approach to performance modelling. In: Distinguished Dissertation in Computer Science. Cambridge University Press, Cambridge (1996)
20. Klin, B., Sassone, V.: Structural Operational Semantics for Stochastic Process Calculi. In: Amadio, R.M. (ed.) FOSSACS 2008. LNCS, vol. 4962, pp. 428–442. Springer, Heidelberg (2008)
21. Knast, R.: Continuous-Time Probabilistic Automata. Information and Control 15, 335–352 (1969)
22. Zhang, L., Hermanns, H., Eisenbrand, F., Jansen, D.: Flow Faster: Efficient Decision Algorithms For Probabilistic Simulations. Logical Methods in Computer Science 4(6), 1–43 (2008)
23. Prandi, D., Quaglia, P.: Stochastic COWS. In: Krämer, B.J., Lin, K.-J., Narasimhan, P. (eds.) ICSOC 2007. LNCS, vol. 4749, pp. 245–256. Springer, Heidelberg (2007)
24. Priami, C.: Stochastic π-Calculus. The Computer Journal 38(7), 578–589 (1995)

A   Proof of Proposition 1

Proposition 1. *The transient behaviour of CTMC $C = (S, \mathbf{R})$ with $\mathbf{R}[\bar{s}, \bar{s}] > 0$ for some $\bar{s} \in S$ coincides with that of CTMC $\tilde{C} = (S, \tilde{\mathbf{R}})$, such that*

$$\tilde{\mathbf{R}}[s, s'] =_{\text{def}} \begin{cases} 0 & \text{if } s = s' \\ \mathbf{R}[s, s'] & \text{otherwise} \end{cases}$$

$\square$

Proof. Suppose $\mathbf{R}[\bar{s}, \bar{s}] > 0$ and let $(\pi \, \bar{s} \, t)$ be the probability that C is in state $\bar{s}$ at time t, $\mathbb{P}\{C(t) = \bar{s}\}$. For h small enough, the evolution of C in the period $[t, t + h)$ can be captured using $(\pi \, \bar{s} \, t)$ as shown below, letting $p_{\bar{s}}$ denote the probability that no transition from $\bar{s}$ is taken during the period $[t, t + h)$ and $p_{s,\bar{s}}$ denote the probability that a transition from s to $\bar{s}$ takes place during the period $[t, t + h)$[8]:

----

[8] Notice that, we do *not* require $s \neq \bar{s}$, as usually found in the literature (see, e.g. [14]).

$$\pi\,\bar{s}\,(t+h)$$

$=$ {Probability Theory; Definition of $p_{\bar{s}}$ and $p_{s,\bar{s}}$; h small}

$$(\pi\,\bar{s}\,t)\cdot\left(1-\sum_{s\in S}\mathbf{R}[\bar{s},s]\cdot h\right)+\sum_{s\in S}(\pi\,s\,t)\cdot\mathbf{R}[s,\bar{s}]\cdot h+o(t)$$

$=$ {Algebra}

$$(\pi\,\bar{s}\,t)-(\pi\,\bar{s}\,t)\cdot\sum_{s\in S\setminus\{\bar{s}\}}\mathbf{R}[\bar{s},s]\cdot h-(\pi\,\bar{s}\,t)\cdot\mathbf{R}[\bar{s},\bar{s}]\cdot h+$$

$$\sum_{s\in S\setminus\{\bar{s}\}}(\pi\,s\,t)\cdot\mathbf{R}[s,\bar{s}]\cdot h+(\pi\,\bar{s}\,t)\cdot\mathbf{R}[\bar{s},\bar{s}]\cdot h+o(t)$$

$=$ {Algebra}

$$(\pi\,\bar{s}\,t)-(\pi\,\bar{s}\,t)\cdot\sum_{s\in S\setminus\{\bar{s}\}}\mathbf{R}[\bar{s},s]\cdot h+\sum_{s\in S\setminus\{\bar{s}\}}(\pi\,s\,t)\cdot\mathbf{R}[s,\bar{s}]\cdot h+o(t)$$

Thus the evolution of C in the period $[t,t+h)$ does *not* depend on $\mathbf{R}[\bar{s},\bar{s}]$. And in fact, letting

$$\mathbf{Q_R}[s,s']\ =_{\mathrm{def}}\ \begin{cases}\mathbf{R}[s,s'],\text{if }s\neq s'\\[2mm]-\sum_{s''\in S\setminus\{s\}}\mathbf{R}[s,s''],\text{if }s=s'\end{cases}$$

we get $\pi\,\bar{s}\,(t+h)=(\pi\,\bar{s}\,t)+\left(\sum_{s\in S}(\pi\,s\,t)\cdot\mathbf{Q_R}[s,\bar{s}]\right)\cdot h+o(t)$ from which we get

$$\frac{d(\pi\,\bar{s}\,t)}{dt}=lim_{h\to 0}\frac{(\pi\,\bar{s}\,(t+h))-(\pi\,\bar{s}\,t)}{h}=\sum_{s\in S}\mathbf{Q_R}[s,\bar{s}]\cdot(\pi\,s\,t)$$

The vector $((\pi\,s\,t))_{s\in S}$ of the transient probabilities for C is thus characterised as the solution of the equation

$$\left(\frac{d(\pi\,s\,t)}{dt}\right)_{s\in S}=((\pi\,s\,t))_{s\in S}\mathbf{Q_R}\qquad\qquad\text{given }((\pi\,s\,0))_{s\in S}$$

which clearly coincides with the equation for the transient probabilities of $\tilde{C}$ observing that $\mathbf{Q_R}=\mathbf{Q}_{\hat{\mathbf{R}}}$.

Applying a Formal Method in Industry: A 15-Year Trajectory

Thierry Lecomte

ClearSy,
Aix en Provence, France
Thierry.lecomte@clearsy.com

Abstract. This article presents industrial experience of applying the B formal method in the industry, on diverse application fields (railways, automotive, smartcard, etc.). If the added value of such an approach has been demonstrated over the year, using a formal method is not the panacea and requires some precautions when introduced in an industrial development cycle.

Keywords: B formal method, deployment, industry.

1 Introduction

Historically, the B Method [1] was introduced in the late 80's to design correctly safe software. Promoted and supported by RATP[1], B and Atelier B, the tool implementing it, have been successfully applied to the industry of transportation. Figure 1 depicts the worldwide implementations of the B technology for safety critical software, mainly as automatic pilots for metros. Today, Alstom Transportation Systems and Siemens Transportation Systems (representing 80% of the worldwide metro market) are the two main actors in the development of B safety-critical software development. Both have a product based strategy and reuse as much as possible existing B models to develop future metros.

A more widely scope use of B appeared in the mid '90s, called *Event-B* [2], to analyze, study and specify not only software, but also whole systems. *Event-B* has been influenced by the work done earlier on Action Systems by the Finnish School (Action System however remained an academic project). *Event-B* is the synthesis between B and Action System. It extends the usage of B to systems that might contain software but also hardware and pieces of equipment. In that respect, one of the outcome of *Event-B* is the proved definition of systems architectures and, more generally, the proved development of, so called, "system studies" [7][10], which are performed before the specification and design of the software. This enlargement allows one to perform failure studies right from the beginning in a large system development. *Event-B* has been applied in many cases to various fields: certification of smartcard security policies (level EAL5+, Common Criteria), verification of Ariane 5 launcher

---

[1] Régie Autonome des Transports Parisiens : operates bus and metro public transport in Paris.

M. Alpuente, B. Cook, and C. Joubert (Eds.): FMICS 2009, LNCS 5825, pp. 26–34, 2009.

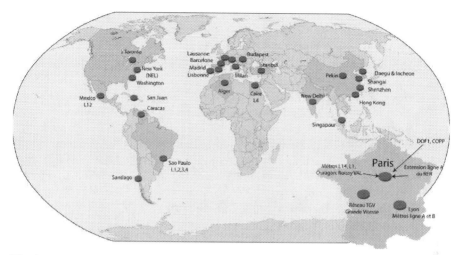

Fig. 1. Worldwide implementations of systems embedding software generated from B models

embedded flight software, generation of proven hardware specification [6], etc. *Event-B* has now its own modelling and proof platforms: Atelier B[2] and Rodin[3].

In this article, we try to make clear what the different usages of B are in industry, and to report on experienced added-value, in order to provide more arguments for and against formal methods.

2   The Genesis

First real success was Meteor line 14 driverless metro in Paris: Over 110 000 lines of B models were written, generating 86 000 lines of Ada. No bugs were detected after the proofs, neither at the functional validation, at the integration validation, at on-site test, nor since the metro lines operate (October 1998). The safety-critical software is still in version 1.0 in year 2009, without any bug detected so far.

At that time, because of demographic explosion in Paris and its suburb, it was decided to reduce the interval between trains (by using fully automated trains) in order to transport more passengers, as it is not possible or is very costly to modify existing infrastructures or to create bigger, specific trains and cars. No technique/technology/method was seen as mature enough to back the development off the embedded software. RATP spent several millions € for transforming a tool developed internally at Alsthom Transportation Systems into a CASE tool able to generate SIL4 compliant code, leading to the creation of Atelier B.

It was initially a one-man decision to fund the development of a prototype tool that would be used for building a software responsible for transporting safely millions passengers a year. This decision had many consequences on the organization of RATP, leading to have almost more people involved in the verification of the

---

[2] *http://www.atelierb.eu/*
[3] *http://sourceforge.net/projects/rodin-b_sharp/*

development process and documentation than engineers producing software on contracting company side. Even if Atelier B was not developed formally, this tool was subject to extensive verification and validation. In particular:

- the theorem prover was subject to external expertise,
- a dedicated tableau-based prover was build to validate most of the theorem prover mathematical rules,
- a committee was set up to demonstrate by hand unprocessed rules
- a mini automated prover was developed to verify the correctness of the dedicated tableau-based prover

The overall process was time and resource consuming but at the end it was accepted as a sound process. Several qualifications were operated by RATP on B software, that are today subcontracted to any V&V engineer. Thanks to the huge contribution on V&V methodology, B development cycle is perceived as a standard and doesn't require any more specific resources.

Siemens and Alstom claim today to develop most safety critical software with B. Siemens has also developed a useful technology, a tool able to generate semi-automatically refinements and implementations, leading to have safety-critical software developed for a cost similar to any other not-safety related software [3].

However, the "magic" of a 100% proven software also requires verifying that its formal specification complies with requirements written in natural language. As everyone knows, natural language is imprecise, ambiguous and requires frequently interpretation. Demonstrating that requirements and specification match is not an easy game, and is not only a question of traceability/coverage but more related to understanding. Except for trivial examples, most requirements are expressed with jargon/technical language which needs to be made explicit, transforming a 2 or 3 line sentence into a full page mathematical predicate. Compliancy in this case requires specialists and is highly subject to human error, requiring extensive validation/simulation at system level.

3 System Level Modeling

B was initially invented for modeling software. However it has appeared at several occasions that a 100% proven software is not a guaranty against failure, as the proof is related to the compliancy between specification and implementation, not to the correctness of the specification of the software regarding the system where it is plugged into. For example, one metro automatic pilot was not able to stop a train at a platform because of a specification error.

The idea of using B for modeling system level specification and to identify formally correct software specification then emerged.

3.1 Embedded Software

The invention of Event-B in the 90's coincided with the massive introduction of electronics onboard cars, leading to a cultural shock and serious difficulties to specify and maintain the electronic architecture of recent cars. Lack of methods and tools for validating distributed specification lead us to enter a 5 year close collaboration with the maintenance department of a car manufacturer. At that time, a sub-contracted diagnosis system was able to identity 40% of the faults, theoretically leading to change all removable electronic components to solve the problems. It was too late to operate on the design, so it was decided to set up a formal model of the 52 embedded functions of a car, covering comfort and safety-related functions, (software based, electronics, mecatronics, etc.). Models were developed from different sources of information such as driver manual, technical documents, diagrams, etc. Calling subcontractors providing components was also part of the modeling phase, in order to get a better understanding of the car behavior, being expected or not, especially in case of failure. This aspect is of paramount importance as the real specification of a car appears to be distributed over a large number of persons. Sometimes this specification is not reachable, for example in the case of a manufacturer not willing to share the internal of the devices he is producing. This lack of knowledge leads sometimes to misbehaviors or "self-emerging specification", resulting from the contribution of several devices put together on a car by independent teams. It was for example possible, in a special case, to lock a driver inside a car, even if he had the key to release and open the door.

In the case of our modeling, some of the 52 functions were abandoned because of the lack of information. The related model was in fact full of question marks and we were not able to answer these questions, even by testing the equipments. Hopefully these functions are all not related to safety.

The modeling was constituted of a flat 30 000 lines B model, principally used to make explicit the behavior of the car. No proof was conducted on it. Cause/consequences matrices were extracted from this model and lead to the construction of a excel file, providing hints on the equipment at fault on a diagnosed car. This approach was repeated on 4 different cars but sharing architecture and some equipment. Part of the modeling was reused from one car to the other, leading to cut modeling time by 3 between the first one and the last one.

The resulting documentation was then provided to the design department while explaining that this kind of information is required to maintain modern cars.

3.2 Platform Screen Doors

In France, RATP has used for years platform screen doors (PSD) that prevent customers to enter or to fall on tracks. Such a system was adopted by the METEOR driverless metro, as it dramatically improves trains availability. In order to offer higher quality services and more safety to its customers, RATP was trying to introduce this kind of protection system in several lines, automated or not. For practical reasons, trains and cars could not be modified with the introduction of PSD. Before starting to deploy a new PSD system in an entire line, RATP initiated a project aimed at developing a prototype PSD system for three stations of line 13 [5][8][9].

Once the train is at standstill, the controller should be able to detect train doors opening and closing, and then issue PSD opening and closing orders. These orders have to be securely issued (failure by elaborating a wrong opening order may lead to customers injury or death), and controller have to be designed, tested and validated in accordance with railway regulations (IEC 50126, 50128, 50129 in particular).

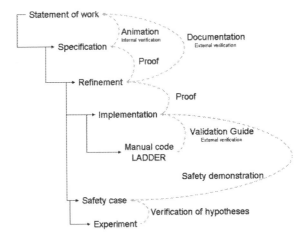

Fig. 2. Development and verification process

In order to reach the required safety level during project timescale, we decided to set up a development method aimed at reaching targeted reliability, and also ensuring traceability between the different stages of the projects in order to reduce the validation effort. This method was heavily based on the B formal method, and applied during most phases of the project.

Before any development activity, a formal functional analysis of the system was performed, to evaluate "completeness" and ambiguity freeness of the statement of work. The B method was used to:

-   Verify on the overall system (PSD + controller) that functional constraints and safety properties were verified (no possibility to establish forbidden connections between train and platform or between train and tracks).
-   Lead to the observation of dangerous system behaviour.

System and software specification were then formalized in B by the development team, taking into account only nominal behaviour for the sensors (in absence of perturbation). Models obtained from previous functional analysis (independent from any PSD controller architecture) were directly reused. The proposed architecture was modelled and inserted in these previous models. New architecture was successfully checked by proof to comply with functional specification of the system, including parts of the French underground regulations. Controller functions were then precisely modelled (train arrival, train detection, train departure, train door opening, train door closing, etc). In the meantime, an independent safety case[4] was developed in parallel by the security team, in order to precisely define how external perturbations may influence the behaviour of the PSD controller. Perturbations were given a priori or a posteriori frequencies, depending on availability of such data at RATP, and a mathematical model, independent from the B model, was set up in order to determine

---

[4] Safety oriented study that provides a convincing and valid argument that a system is adequately safe for a given application in a given environment.

quantitatively the security level of the system. A priori frequencies were verified during the eight month experiment. In case these frequencies were not verified and lower system security below SIL3 level, the PSD controllers would have to be redesigned considering this new information.

Specification documentation was partly elaborated from the system level models developed during this project. The composys[5] tool helps the modeller to add contextual information (comments, description, component name, etc) in B models that are used to generate in natural language the specification documentation describing the complete system. As events are associated to components and as variables are used within events (read/write), Composys computes relationships among components constituting the system being modelled, depending on how variables are read or modified. This document was used to check models with experts of the domain, unable to read and understand formal models.

The development of the software was based on the formal models, as B enables the production of source code, proven to comply with its specification. Siemens automaton can be programmed in the LADDER language but, unfortunately, requires entering program source code via its graphical interface (according to its certificate) to keep its SIL3 accreditation. A dedicated translation schema (from B to LADDER) was elaborated. B to LADDER state diagrams translation is straightforward and some optimisations were introduced in order to verify temporal constraints (cycle time in particular). During validation phase, one can determine which event of the B model corresponds to the path of the LADDER program for a cycle (a LADDER program is defined by logical equations and is analyzed in term of execution path). In case the source code is automatically generated by a qualified translator (as for automatic pilots, by Siemens and Alstom), no unit test is required, this testing phase being covered by the proof of the model.

In this project, as the source code was not generated automatically by such a translator, test was required and test specification was elaborated by usual means. Some months after the beginning of the project, we obtained a fully functional, tested and validated application. The process described above has enabled us to produce a 100% tested, error free (against its specification) software when running validation test bench for the first time. A dedicated test bench was designed to simulate major perturbations (sensors were emulated) and run during days, but no faulty behaviour was observed.

3.3 SmartCard

On the contrary of safety-critical systems where standards do not require to use formal methods to reach highest safety level, the microelectronics security standards, especially in the smart card domain, oblige circuits to be checked against formal methods for EAL5+ levels and higher. For EAL5+ devices, the security policy needs to be formally verified. Design modeling could make use of semi-formal methods and a table based traceability between specification and design documentation is sufficient. EAL6 and higher levels require (almost) fully use of formal methods at every phase. EAL constraints also propagate to subcontractors involved in the development

---

[5] http://www.composys.fr

as well as the technical/confidentiality organization (what is the use of inviolable smartcard if information on the PIN code generation process is easily reachable?).

We were involved in the first certifications of EAL5+ smartcard microcircuits in France, for different companies and in collaboration with different evaluation centers. The main reason for reaching this level was initially due to marketing. Our first evaluations were performed by independent experts that were not aware of B, its restrictions (well known in the railway, due to experience) and French government made some remarks on the resulting evaluation report, leading to the writing of a methodological guidelines for conducting evaluation on Event-B models.

Since then, smartcard microcircuits are regularly evaluated at EAL5+ level, based on an Event-B model of the security policy, with a far better confidence on the results. For a recent product, the evaluation was also performed in Germany by a TÜV, leading to acceptance but also contributing to improve the process (the remarks emitted by the evaluation center have been transmitted to the French government).

4   Animation and Documentation

Everyone has experienced difficulty to have third party person understanding a state of the art formal model. The mathematical language is at fault, as well as the text-based representation. To counter this, we have experimented two different approaches:

- Generation of documentation, based on the B model and on a dictionary provided by the user, in order to have sentences in natural language describing entities and behavior, as well as a static graphical representation of the relationships among the different entities. This approach is not error prone as you can make mistakes when writing the dictionary, but its main advantage is to make your modeling more understandable that could be evaluated and studied by a third party expert.
- Generation of a graphical animation of the system would help to understand and validate the dynamic part of the modeling, that could be tricky to assess when dealing with large models and complex/complicated enabling conditions for events. For example, a USB device was once modeled and proved correct until the model was animated and demonstrated not being compliant with the USB protocol (one guard was made too restrictive but it was not detected by proof).

In the case of the development of PSD, specification documentation was partly elaborated from the system level models developed during this project and documented with composys. This tool has no proof capabilities but, as an engineering tool, helps the modeller to add contextual information (comments, description, component name, etc) in B models that are used to generate in natural language the specification documentation describing the complete system. As events are associated to components and as variables are used within events (read/write), Composys computes relationships among components constituting the system being modelled, depending on how variables are read or modified.

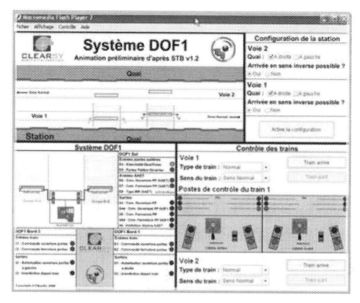

Fig. 3. An animated model submitted for a call for tender

Animation was used at several occasions, including during the writing of proposals where B models were developed and associated with a flash-based animation The resulting B model was animated [11] with the Brama animator[6], in order to verify on given scenarios that the model produced was corresponding to the real system we were modelling. This model animator was not part of the validation process, as this would require it to be qualified as a SIL3 software, but it helped us to check models against reality and to internally verify their suitability.

The animations were also used to make top managers happy and "intelligent", because usually they have to read thick documents (call for tender, proposals) and most of the time they mainly read the commercial part. Standalone animations allow for easily understanding the functional specification of a system and to play with the system, keeping in mind that the resulting software will be generated from the B model being animated. We finally discovered that this kind of deliverable was widely distributed among target service and could be more or less considered as gentle virus (we saw our animation used as screen-saver on many computers).

5 Conclusion

Formal methods have been considered for years as hobbies for PhD and academic people, by industry. Being in charge of disseminating the B method, we have experimented its introduction into several development processes, including ours. If B is well introduced in the railways domain, it has started to conquer microelectronics, due to the fact that this method has acquired maturity over the years. However it is important to

---

[6] *http://www.brama.fr*

determine how much and where to use a formal method within an existing organization. New tools and new practices are available to ease acceptance in industry.

References

1. Abrial, J.R.: The B-book: Assigning programs to meanings. Cambridge University Press, Cambridge (1996)
2. Abrial, J.R.: Rigorous Open Development Environment for Complex Systems: event B language (2005)
3. Burdy, L.: Automatic Refinement. In: Proceedings of BUGM at FM 1999 (1996)
4. Casset, L.: A formal specification of the Java byte code verifier using the B method. Lisbonne 99 (1999)
5. Sabatier, D., et al.: Use of the Formal B Method for a SIL3 System Landing Door Commands for line 13 of the Paris subway. In: Lambda Mu 15 (2006)
6. Benveniste, M., et al.: A Proved "Correct by Construction" Realistic Digital Circuit. In: RIAB, FMWeek (2009)
7. Sabatier, D., et al.: FDIR Strategy Validation with the B method. In: DASIA 2008 (2008)
8. Lecomte, T.: Safe and Reliable Metro Platform Screen Doors Control/Command Systems. In: FM 2008 (2008)
9. Lecomte, T., et al.: Formal Methods in Safety Critical Railway Systems. In: SBMF 2007 (2007)
10. Hoffmann, S., et al.: The B Method for the Construction of Micro-Kernel Based Systems. In: ZB 2007 (2007)
11. Lecomte, T., et al.: BRAMA: a New Graphic Animation Tool for B Models. In: ZB 2007 (2007)

What's in Common between Test, Model Checking, and Decision Procedures?

K.L. McMillan

Cadence Research Labs

Abstract. The interaction of proof search and counterexample search is at the heart of recent methods in decision procedures model checking. In this talk, we'll consider the relation between these methods and test.

When we set out to prove a mathematical conjecture, often our first step is try to construct a counterexample for the conjecture. When we fail to do this, our failure may suggest a lemma: some salient fact that explains our failure. Knowing this fact, we are then forced to look elsewhere for a counterexample, continuing in this way until (hopefully) our lemmas add up to a proof. Thus, proof and counterexample search are parallel processes that guide each other. We might say that to be good at finding counterexamples, you have to be good at proof, and *vice versa*.

This proof/counterexample duality is a thread that runs through much recent research in formal verification. In this talk, we'll follow this thread, and consider some of the implications of this idea for the future of verification, formal and otherwise.

Decision procedures. In decision procedures, both for Boolean SAT and SAT modulo theories (SMT), the duality is embodied in the DPLL mechanism [1]. Here, we attempt to construct a satisfying assignment (a counterexample to our conjecture) by assigning values to Boolean variables. When we reach a variable that has no feasible assignment, we deduce a new fact. This new fact rules out a class of possible counterexamples, forcing us to backtrack and reconsider earlier choices. This interaction counterexample search and deduction helps to focus both processes on relevant variables and relevant facts. Thus, we might say that DPLL is *relevance biased*. More recently, this mechanism has also been generalized to search in richer domains.

Model checking. In model checking, the proof/counterexample duality often appears in the form of "abstraction refinement". To avoid a combinatorial explosion, the model checker works in an abstract domain, which we can think of as a restricted language for expressing facts about the system state. When this language is insufficient to prove the desired property, the model checker generates a class of potential counterexamples. Refinement enriches the abstract domain to allow it to rule out this class [2]. Interestingly, the refinement process is typically based on a proof generated by a decision procedure using the DPLL mechanism described above. This proof can be factored into an appropriate form using a technique called Craig interpolation [4].

M. Alpuente, B. Cook, and C. Joubert (Eds.): FMICS 2009, LNCS 5825, pp. 35–36, 2009.

This latter observation has led to methods that generate proofs of system properties directly from interpolants, without using an abstract domain [5]. This is closer in spirit to the DPLL approach. We can think of these methods as generating tests for the system (potential counterexamples) and using the refutations of these tests to build the required proof artifacts (such as inductive invariants and procedure summaries).

Test. In test, a recent trend has been to use decision procedures to generate program inputs that exercise alternate branches in program traces [3]. We cannot quite describe this as a relevance-biased approach, since these testing tools do not derive general facts about the program that are relevant to a given property. However, we can observe a sort of convergence between testing methods and model checking. In the talk, we'll explore some ways in which model checking methods could be incorporated into test tools in order to focus test generation more on finding tests that violate particular properties.

Testing is in a sense searching for a counterexample. If it's true that to be good at counterexample search you must be good at proof, then it stands to reason that (relevance biased) methods of proof generation might be useful in test, even if ultimately no proofs are generated. Similarly, better test should lead to more efficient proof. It seems plausible that we will see a convergence of test, model checking and decision procedures, such that the difference between the first two will be more a matter of degree than of principle.

About the speaker. Ken McMillan is currently a research scientist at Cadence Berkeley Labs in Berkeley, California. He works in formal verification, primarily in model checking, decision procedures and compositional methods. He holds a BS in electrical engineering from the University of Illinois at Urbana (1984), an MS in electrical engineering from Stanford (1986) and a Ph.D. in computer science from Carnegie Mellon (1992). He is the author of the SMV symbolic model checker, and received the 1992 ACM doctoral dissertation award for his thesis on symbolic model checking. For his work in this area, he also received an SRC technical excellence award (1995), the ACM Paris Kannelakis award (1998), and the Alan Newell award from Carnegie Mellon (1998). His current research is focused on using Craig interpolation methods for software verification.

References

1. Biere, A., Heule, M., van Maaren, H., Walsh, T. (eds.): Handbook of Satisfiability. IOS Press, Amsterdam (2009)
2. Clarke, E.M., Grumberg, O., Jha, S., Lu, Y., Veith, H.: Counterexample-guided abstraction refinement for symbolic model checking. J. ACM 50(5), 752–794 (2003)
3. Godefroid, P., Klarlund, N., Sen, K.: DART: directed automated random testing. In: PLDI 2005, pp. 213–223. ACM, New York (2005)
4. McMillan, K.L.: An interpolating theorem prover. Theor. Comput. Sci. 345(1), 101–121 (2005)
5. McMillan, K.L.: Lazy abstraction with interpolants. In: Ball, T., Jones, R.B. (eds.) CAV 2006. LNCS, vol. 4144, pp. 123–136. Springer, Heidelberg (2006)

Verifying Cryptographic Software Correctness with Respect to Reference Implementations[*]

José Bacelar Almeida, Manuel Barbosa, Jorge Sousa Pinto, and Bárbara Vieira

CCTC / Departamento de Informática
Universidade do Minho
Campus de Gualtar, 4710-Braga, Portugal
{jba,mbb,jsp,barbarasv}@di.uminho.pt

Abstract. This paper presents techniques developed to check program equivalences in the context of cryptographic software development, where specifications are typically reference implementations. The techniques allow for the integration of interactive proof techniques (required given the difficulty and generality of the results sought) in a verification infrastructure that is capable of discharging many verification conditions automatically. To this end, the difficult results in the verification process (to be proved interactively) are isolated as a set of lemmas. The fundamental notion of natural invariant is used to link the specification level and the interactive proof construction process.

1 Introduction

Software implementations of cryptographic algorithms and protocols are at the core of security functionality in many IT products. However, the development of this class of software products is understudied as a domain-specific niche in software engineering.

The development of cryptographic software is clearly distinct from other areas of software engineering due to a combination of factors. First of all, cryptography is an inherently inter-disciplinary subject. The design and implementation of cryptographic software draws on skills from mathematics, computer science and electrical engineering. The assumption that such a rich body of research can be absorbed and applied without error is tenuous for even the most expert software engineer. Secondly, security is notoriously difficult to sell as a feature in software products, even when clear risks such as identity theft and fraud are evident. An important implication of this fact is that security needs to be as close to invisible as possible in terms of computational and communication load. As a result, it is critical that cryptographic software is optimised aggressively, without altering the security semantics. Finally, typical software engineers develop systems focussed on desktop class processors within computers in our offices and homes. The special case of cryptographic software is implemented on a

---

[*] This work was partially supported by the European Union under the FP7-STREP project CACE (Project Number 216499), and by the FCT-funded RESCUE project (PTDC/EIA/65862/2006).

M. Alpuente, B. Cook, and C. Joubert (Eds.): FMICS 2009, LNCS 5825, pp. 37–52, 2009.

much wider range of devices, from embedded processors with very limited computational power, memory and autonomy, to high-end servers, which demand high-performance and low-latency. Not only must the cryptographic software engineers understand each platform and the related security requirements, they must also optimise each algorithm with respect to each platform since each will have vastly different performance characteristics.

CACE (Computer Aided Cryptography Engineering [5]) is an European Project that targets the lack of support currently offered to cryptographic software engineers. The central objective of the project is the development of a tool-box of domain-specific languages, compilers and libraries, that supports the production of high quality cryptographic software. The aim is that specific components within the tool-box will address particular software development problems and processes; and combined use of the constituent tools is enabled by designed integration between their interfaces. The project started in 2008 and will run for three years.

This paper stems from CACE - Work Package 5, which aims to add formal methods technology to the tool-box, as a means to increase the degree of assurance than can be provided by the development process. We describe promising early results obtained during our exploration of existing verification techniques and tools used to construct high-assurance software implementations for other domains. Specifically, we present our achievements in using an off-the-shelf verification tool to reason about the functional correctness of a C implementation of the RC4 encryption scheme that is included in the well-known open-source library openSSL [15].

Contribution. The main contribution of this paper is to report on the application of the off-the-shelf Frama-c verification platform to verifying correctness of a real-world example of a cryptographic software implementation: the widely used C implementation of the RC4 stream cipher available in the openSSL library. We focus on functional correctness, which is a critical use-case for verification tools when applied to cryptographic software. The (conceptual) specifications of cryptographic schemes are very often presented as pseudo-code algorithms, which may be easy to transcribe into a high-level programming language. However, given that cryptographic implementations are typically optimised for high efficiency, the best implementation is unlikely to be the most readable one. For this reason, we formalise the property of functional correctness of the RC4 implementation in terms of input/output behavioural equivalence to another (more readable) C implementation of the same algorithm. We then explore techniques to prove such an equivalence, which we believe may be of independent interest.

Paper Organisation. Sections 2 and 3 give background on deductive verification and RC4 in openSSL. Section 4 introduces the method used to prove equivalence between the reference and practical implementations of RC4, and Sections 5 and 6 describe the formalisation of loop refactorings in Coq, based on the notion of *natural invariant*. Section 7 presents related work and Section 8 concludes the paper.

2   Background: Deduction-Based Program Verification

The techniques employed in this paper are based on Hoare Logic [12], brought to practice through the use of *contracts* – specifications consisting of preconditions and postconditions, annotated into the programs. In recent years, verification tools based on contracts have become more and more popular, as their scope evolved from toy languages to very realistic fragments of languages like C, C#, or Java.

In a nutshell, a verification infra-structure consists of a verification conditions generator (VCGen for short) and a proof tool, which may be either an automatic theorem prover or an interactive proof assistant. The VCGen reads in the annotated code (which contains contracts and other annotations meant to facilitate the verification, such as loop invariants and variants) and produces a set of proof obligations known as *verification conditions*, that will be sent to the proof tool. The correctness of the VCGen guarantees that, if all the proof obligations are valid, then the program is correct with respect to its specification. Depending on the specified properties, the verification conditions may, or may not, be automatically provable.

The concrete tools we have used in this work were `Frama-c` [3], a tool for the static analysis of C programs that contains a multi-prover VCGen [10]; and a set of proof tools that included the Coq proof assistant [18], and the Simplify [9] and Ergo [7] automatic theorem provers. C programs are annotated using the ANSI-C Specification Language (ACSL [3]). Both `Frama-c` and ACSL are work in progress; we have used the latest (Lithium) release of `Frama-c`.

`Frama-c` contains the `gwhy` graphical front-end that allows to monitor individual verification conditions. This is particularly useful when combined with the possibility of exporting the conditions to various proof tools, which allows users to first try discharging conditions with one or more automatic provers, leaving the harder conditions to be studied with the help of an interactive proof assistant. An additional feature of `Frama-c` that we have found useful is the declaration of Lemmas. Unlike axioms, which require no proof, lemmas are results that can be used to prove goals, but give themselves origin to new goals. In the proofs we developed, it was often the case that once an appropriate lemma was provided, all the verification conditions could be automatically discharged, leaving only the difficult lemma to be proved in Coq.

3   The RC4 Cipher and Its Implementation in openSSL

RC4 is a symmetric cipher designed by Ron Rivest at RSA labs in 1987. It is a proprietary algorithm, and its definition was never officially released. Source code that allegedly implements the RC4 cipher was leaked on the internet in 1994, and this is commonly known as ARC4 due to trademark restrictions. In this work we will use the RC4 denomination to denote the definition adopted in literature [16]. RC4 is widely used in commercial products, as it is included as one of the recommended encryption schemes in standards such as TLS, WEP

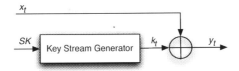

Fig. 1. Block diagram of the RC4 cipher

and WPA. In particular, an implementation of RC4 is provided in the pervasively used open-source library openSSL, which we selected as the case study for this paper.

In cryptographic terms, RC4 is a synchronous stream cipher, which means that it is structured as two independent blocks, as shown in Figure 1. The security of the RC4 cipher resides in the strength of the key stream generator, which is initialized with a secret key SK. The key stream output is a byte[1] sequence k_t that approximates a perfectly random bit string, and is independent of plaintext and ciphertext. The encryption operation consists simply of XOR-ing each plaintext byte x_t with a fresh keystream byte k_t. Decryption operates in an identical way. The key stream generator operates over a state which includes a permutation table $S = (S[l])_{l=0}^{l=255}$ of (unsigned) byte-sized values, and two (unsigned) byte-sized indices i and j. We denote the values of these variables at time t by S_t, i_t and j_t. The state and output of the key stream generator at time t (for $t \geq 1$) are calculated according to the following recurrence, in which all additions are carried out modulo 256.

$$i_t = i_{t-1} + 1$$
$$j_t = j_{t-1} + S_{t-1}[i_t]$$
$$S_t[i_t] = S_{t-1}[j_t]$$
$$S_t[j_t] = S_{t-1}[i_t]$$
$$k_t = S_t[S_t[i_t] + S_t[j_t]]$$

The initial values of the indices i_0 and j_0 are set to 0, and the initial value of the permutation table S_0 is derived from the secret key SK. The details of this initialisation are imaterial for the purpose of this paper, as they are excluded from the analysis.

We present in Appendix A the C implementation of RC4 included in the openSSL open-source. The function receives the current state of the RC4 key stream generator (key), and two arrays whose length is provided in parameter len. The first array contains the plaintext (indata), and the second array will be used to return the ciphertext (outdata). We note that this implementation is much less readable than the concise description provided above, as it has been optimised for speed using various tricks, including macro inlining and loop unrolling.

---

[1] We adopt the most widely used version of RC4 which operates over byte-sized words, which is also the one implemented in openSSL.

```
unsigned char RC4NextKeySymbol(RC4_KEY *key) {
  unsigned char tx,ty;

  key->x=(key->x+1) % 256;
  tx=key->data[key->x];
  key->y=(tx+key->y) % 256;
  ty=key->data[key->y];
  key->data[key->x]=ty;
  key->data[key->y]=tx;
  return key->data[(tx+ty) % 256];
}

void RC4(RC4_KEY *key, const unsigned long len,
         const unsigned char *indata, unsigned char *outdata) {
  int i=0;
  while(i<len) { outdata[i]=indata[i] ^ RC4NextKeySymbol(key); i++; }
}
```

Fig. 2. RC4 specification

4   Functional Correctness of Code Refactoring

It is typical of cryptographic software that specifications are given as algorithms, rather than using the notion of an abstract model. The programmer is free to improve the code, say by introducing optimizations or internal reorganizations (e.g. to improve efficiency, maintainability or to satisfy non-functional security properties), as long as the input-output behaviour is the same as that prescribed by a reference implementation. In software engineering, such a transformation is usually known as *code refactoring*.

To illustrate this point, recall the description of the RC4 algorithm provided in Section 3. A direct transcription of this specification to a C implementation could look something like the code in Figure 2. Although this implementation is quite readable, and arguably verifiable by inspection, it was created without the slightest consideration for efficiency. This stands in contrast with the openSSL implementation of RC4 (see Appendix A) where readability (and the inherent assurance of correctness) was sacrificed to achieve better performance.

This example supports the domain-specific motivation for the discussion presented in this section: the natural way to obtain assurance that an implementation of a cryptographic algorithm is correct, is to verify that it is functionally equivalent to another (more readable) implementation of the same algorithm. We have investigated how this goal can be achieved for the particular case of RC4, by identifying refactoring steps that may require a proof of equivalence in order to establish the correctness of different RC4 implementations. We describe these refactoring steps in the remainder of this section. In the next section we present our approach to verifying the identified class of equivalence relations using an off-the-shelf tool such as Frama-c. The results we obtain are, of course,

```
void RC4(RC4_KEY *key, const unsigned long len,
               const unsigned char *indata, unsigned char *outdata) {
  unsigned char keystream[len];

  int i=0;
  while(i<len) { keystream[i] = RC4NextKeySymbol(key); i++; }

  i=0;
  while(i<len) { outdata[i]=indata[i] ^ keystream[i]; i++; }
}
```

Fig. 3. RC4 implementation with key pre-processing

not only applicable to implementations of other cryptographic algorithms, but also to other application domains where similar program transformations may be employed.

A simple refactoring to capture key pre-processing. The first example we present of a possible refactoring of the RC4 specification in Figure 2 is suggested by a common optimisation performed when using stream ciphers. Indeed, one of the ways of speeding up the throughput of stream cipher processing is to compute (a portion of) the key stream before the plaintext is available (or the ciphertext if one is decrypting). This means that the encryption operation to be performed on-the-fly is then reduced to simple masking using an XOR operation, which can be done extremely fast. For sychronous ciphers such as RC4, the number of key stream bits that can be pre-computed can be arbitrarily large, as this is totally independent of the encrypted data. The version of RC4 presented in Figure 3 moves in this direction by separating the key stream generation process from the plaintext masking (or ciphertext unmasking process). In the next section we will discuss a technique that can be used to prove equivalence beween the programs in Figures 2 and 3 using a verification infrastructure like that discussed in Section 2.

A sequence of refactorings leading to the openssl implementation. We now discuss a more elaborate sequence of refactoring steps that permit reaching the openSSL implementation of RC4 in Appendix A, departing from the reference implementation in Figure 2. The first refactoring step, leading to the RC4 function in Figure 4, top, is not very interesting from a verification point of view. It consists of a number of simple transformations whose validity can be proven with some effort using Frama-c: (1) removing the auxiliary function by inlining the corresponding code in the main function body; (2) rearranging local variables to match those in the openSSL implementation; (3) applying the transitivity property of assignments in C to combine two statements; and (4) replacing modular operations by their equivalent bit-wise operations. A macro is also introduced to improve readability.

```
void RC4(RC4_KEY *key, const unsigned long len,
     const unsigned char *indata, unsigned char *outdata)
{
  unsigned char x,y,tx,ty, *d;
  int i;

  x = key->x; y = key->y; d = key-> data;

  i=0;
  while(i<len) { RC4LOOP(indata,outdata,i); i++; }

  key->x=x; key->y=y;
}
```

```
void RC4(RC4_KEY *key, const unsigned long len,
         const unsigned char *indata, unsigned char *outdata)
{
  unsigned char x,y,tx,ty, *d;
  int i;

  x = key->x; y = key->y; d = key-> data;

  i= (int)(len>>3L);
  while(i>0) {
    RC4LOOP(indata,outdata,0);
    RC4LOOP(indata,outdata,1);
    RC4LOOP(indata,outdata,2);
    RC4LOOP(indata,outdata,3);
    RC4LOOP(indata,outdata,4);
    RC4LOOP(indata,outdata,5);
    RC4LOOP(indata,outdata,6);
    RC4LOOP(indata,outdata,7);
    indata+=8; outdata+=8; i--;
  }

  i=(int)(len&0x07);
  while(i>0) {RC4LOOP(indata,outdata,i); i--; }

  key->x=x; key->y=y;
}
```

Fig. 4. RC4 refactoring steps 1 (top) and 2 (bottom)

The next refactoring steps, leading to the version shown in Figure 4, bottom, are more interesting examples of transformations involving loop refactorings. Concretely, the main loop is first separated into two loops with the same body, which are sequentially composed to realise the original number of iterations. The first loop is then modified by explicitly composing the original body with itself 8 times, and altering the increments accordingly.

The final refactoring steps, leading to the `openssl` version of RC4 in Appendix A, are introduced to achieve additional speed-ups. Firstly, pointer arithmetic is used to reduce the range of indexing operations, and loop counting is inverted. Then, different control flow constructions are applied: all `while` loops are reformulated using the `break` statement to remove the final backward jump, and `if` constructions are introduced to detect termination cases. Again, these refactoring steps can be handled in `Frama-c` with some effort, but they do not require non-trivial proof steps that justify a detailed presentation.

In the remainder of this paper we concentrate on presenting a technique that can be used to prove the equivalence of the different versions of the RC4 function that spring from the specific loop transformations outlined in the second step above.

Equivalence by Composition. We now formalise a notion of program equivalence that permits dealing with the refactoring paradigm introduced above. The required notion of program equivalence is based on Hoare logic, using a program composition technique inspired by self-composition, a technique for reasoning axiomatically about non-interference properties of programs [2]. The general technique introduced here sets the grounds for the work presented in the next section, where we explore the technical details involved in proving program equivalence relations such as those arising from the refactorings described above for RC4.

The basic principle underlying self-composition can be adapted to the current context: given two terminating programs C_1 and C_2, they can be combined by first renaming the variables in one of the programs so that they use distinct name spaces, and then composing the programs sequentially. Given some program C, let C^s be the program that is equal to C except that every variable x is renamed to a fresh variable x^s.

Let V be the set of variables occurring in both programs. The idea that we want to capture is that if the programs are executed from indistinguishable states with respect to V, they terminate in states that are also indistinguishable. C_1 and C_2 will be defined as equivalent if every execution of the composed program $C_1; C_2^s$, starting from a state in which the values of corresponding variables are equal, terminates in a state with the same property. This can be expressed as the following Hoare logic total correctness specification, that can be expressed in ACSL.

$$\left[\bigwedge_{x \in V} x = x^s\right] C_1; C_2^s \left[\bigwedge_{x \in V} x = x^s\right]$$

Weaker notions of equivalence can be handled by taking V to be a subset of $Vars(C_1) \cap Vars(C_2)$.

5   Proving Equivalence Using Natural Invariants

Is this section we elaborate on the general approach that we adopt to prove the equivalence between a refactored version of a function such as those in Figure 4, with respect to the originating function, in this case the reference implementation in Figure 2. In order to establish this equivalence using a deductive framework such as `Frama-c`, we need to:

- create a composed program which aggregates the two versions of the original program we aim to prove functionally equivalent;
- annotate the composed program with appropriate contracts and loop invariants;
- discharge the resulting proof obligations.

Moreover, we would like to overcome these steps with a reasonable degree of automation. Here, *reasonable* essentially means that we intend to take the maximum advantage from the fact that we are dealing with program refactorings, which admittedly share most of its control structure. Our strategy for tackling these problems consist in: (1) extracting a relational specification directly from the program code; (2) annotating the program with invariants derived from the specification; (3) generating specific lemmas justifying the most significant refactorings; and (4) using an automatic first-order theorem prover to discharge the proof-obligations. The generated lemmas, which constitute the (small) nontrivial part of the proof, must then be justified using an interactive theorem prover.

To illustrate this methodology, we consider a simple *While-language* with integer expressions and arrays. Its syntax is given by:

$$P ::= \{P\} \mid \textbf{skip} \mid P_1; P_2 \mid V := E_{int} \mid A[E_{int}] := E_{int}$$
$$\mid \textbf{if } (E_{bool}) \textbf{ then } P_1 \textbf{ else } P_2 \mid \textbf{while } (E_{bool}) \; P$$
$$E_{int} ::= Const_{int} \mid E_{int} \; op \; E_{int} \mid A[E_{int}] \mid \dots$$
$$E_{bool} ::= true \mid false \mid E_{bool} \wedge E_{bool} \mid E_{bool} \vee E_{bool} \mid E_{int} \; opRel \; E_{int}$$

For simplicity we do not include any form of variable declaration. Instead, we consider a fixed `State` type to keep track of all the variable values during the execution of the program. Integer variables are interpreted as (unbound) integers and arrays as functions from integers to integers (no size/range checking). We also adopt the usual axioms for array access and update operations.

$$\text{access} : (Z \to Z) \times Z \to Z$$
$$\text{update} : (Z \to Z) \times Z \times Z \to (Z \to Z)$$
$$\text{access}(\text{update}(a, k, x), k) = x$$
$$\text{access}(\text{update}(a, k', x), k) = \text{access}(a, k) \qquad \text{, if } k \neq k'.$$

The `State` type is defined as the cartesian product of the corresponding interpretation domains (each variable is associated with a particular position). We also consider an equivalence relation $\equiv$ that captures two extensionally equal states. Integer and boolean expressions are interpreted in a particular state, that is $[\![e_{Int}]\!] : State \to Z$, $[\![e_{Bool}]\!] : State \to B$. We take the standard definition for the big-step semantics of a program as its *natural specification*. Concretely:

$$\mathsf{spec}_{\mathbf{skip}}(s, s') = s \equiv s'$$

$$\mathsf{spec}_{\{P\}}(s, s') = \mathsf{spec}_P(s, s')$$

$$\mathsf{spec}_{P_1;P_2}(s, s') = \exists s'',\ \mathsf{spec}_{P_1}(s, s'') \wedge \mathsf{spec}_{P_2}(s'', s')$$

$$\mathsf{spec}_{v:=E}(s, s') = s' \equiv s\{v \leftarrow [\![E]\!](s)\}$$

$$\mathsf{spec}_{a[E_1]=E_2}(s, s') = s' \equiv s\{a \leftarrow \mathsf{update}(a, [\![E_1]\!](s), [\![E_2]\!](s))\}$$

$$\mathsf{spec}_{\mathbf{if}\ (C)\ \mathbf{then}\ P_1\ \mathbf{else}\ P_2}(s, s') = ([\![C]\!]s \wedge \mathsf{spec}_{P_1}(s, s')) \vee (\neg[\![C]\!](s) \wedge \mathsf{spec}_{P_2}(s, s'))$$

$$\mathsf{spec}_{\mathbf{while}\ (C)\ P}(s, s') = \exists n,\quad \mathsf{loop}^n_{C,\mathsf{spec}_P(s,s')}(s, s') \wedge \neg[\![C]\!](s')$$

where $\mathsf{loop}^n_{C,R}(s, s')$ is the inductively defined relation

$$\mathsf{loop}^0_{C,R}(s, s') \Longleftarrow s \equiv s'$$

$$\mathsf{loop}^{S(n)}_{C,R}(s, s') \Longleftarrow \exists s'',\ \mathsf{loop}^n_{C,R}(s, s'') \wedge [\![C]\!](s'') \wedge R(s'', s')$$

The relation $\mathsf{loop}^n_{C,R}(s, s')$ denotes the loop specification for the body R under condition C. In this definition we have made explicit the *iteration rank* (iteration count) in superscript – in fact, we will see that it is often convenient to consider it explicitly in the proofs. Nevertheless, when omitted, it should be considered as existentially quantified. Also, we will omit subscripts (both in loop and spec) when the corresponding programs are clear from the context. From the loop relation we recover what we call the loop's *natural invariant* as:

$$\mathrm{Inv}_{loop}(s) = \mathsf{loop}_{C,R}(s@\mathrm{Init}, s)$$

where C and R are the loop's condition and body, respectively, and $s@\mathrm{Init}$ denotes the snapshot of the loop's initial state.

Expressiveness and Relative Completeness. Natural invariants depend on a sufficiently expressive assertion language that should allow defining new inductive relations. This corresponds essentially to Cook's expressiveness criteria in his relative completeness result for Hoare Logic [8]. In fact, from the definition of spec we can easily recover the *strongest liberal predicate* as

$$\mathrm{slp}(S, P) = \{s' \mid P(s) \wedge \mathsf{spec}_S(s, s')\}$$

An immediate consequence of this observation is that we might conduct the verification of an arbitrary Hoare triple logically, namely

$$\{P\}S\{Q\} \quad \text{iff} \quad \mathrm{slp}(S, P) \supseteq Q \quad \text{iff} \quad P(s) \wedge \mathsf{spec}_S(s, s') \wedge Q(s').$$

Note that these requirements surpass the realm of first-order logic. Thus, when the target verification tool is a first-order theorem prover, we shall rely on a weak axiomatisation of these predicates (in our case, we consider an axiom for each constructor and a simple inversion principle). This observation clarifies why we need to supplement the first-order theory with additional lemmas. Moreover, it also shows that failure in verification is not necessarily caused by limitations in the first-order theorem provers. When full-fledged inductive reasoning is needed, we resort to Coq's higher-order logic capabilities to interactively prove specific lemmas. Fortunately, it is possible to identify a set of general lemmas that can be proven once-and-for-all, and that permit justifying interesting refactorings.

General Properties. We call *plain theory* to the first-order theory resulting from the program specification and the corresponding weak axiomatization of loop predicates. A consequence of the limitations of first-order theory/provers mentioned above is that the plain theory is insufficient to establish the adequacy of even the most trivial refactoring (the identity refactoring) when the programs use loops. To illustrate what is missing, we need to walk the reader through the proof of the following spec properties:

Proposition 1. *For every program fragment P and states $s_1, s_2, s_1', s_2',$*

- spec *preserves* $\equiv$, *i.e.* $s_1 \equiv s_2 \wedge s_1' \equiv s_2' \wedge \mathsf{spec}_P(s_1, s_1') \Rightarrow \mathsf{spec}_P(s_2, s_2')$.
- spec *is deterministic, i.e.* $\mathsf{spec}_P(s, s_1') \wedge \mathsf{spec}_P(s, s_2') \Rightarrow s_1' \equiv s_2'$.

The proof follows straight by induction on the program P using the following lemma

Lemma 1. *Let $R(s, s')$ be a deterministic relation on states, and C a boolean condition. Then, $\mathsf{loop}_{C,R}(s, s')$ is deterministic whenever $\neg[\![C]\!](s')$.*

This in turn is a consequence of the following two assertions:

$$s_1 \equiv s_2 \wedge \mathsf{loop}_{C,R}^{n_1}(s_1, s_1') \wedge \neg[\![C]\!](s_1') \wedge \mathsf{loop}_{C,R}^{n_2}(s_2, s_2') \wedge \neg[\![C]\!](s_2') \Longrightarrow n_1 = n_2$$

$$s_1 \equiv s_2 \wedge \mathsf{loop}_{C,R}^{n}(s_1, s_1') \wedge \mathsf{loop}_{C,R}^{n}(s_2, s_2') \Longrightarrow s_1' \equiv s_2'$$

Both of these statements are directly proved by a simple induction (on $\max(n_1, n_2)$ in the first case, and on n in the second). The first statement establishes the *synchronization* of both executions and the second their *determinism*. Augmenting the plain theory with these lemmas is mandatory to perform even the most basic reasoning.

This factorization strategy, in which we detach the synchronization and determinism properties, underlies our proposed paradigm for reasoning about multiple executions of the same (or related) program fragments. Moreover, we can strengthen the synchronization lemma by observing that it only depends on the equivalence between fragments of the initial state, namely those that affect the loop's condition. The determinism lemma can itself be rephrased replacing state equivalence by an arbitrary predicate.

Justifying Loop Refactorings. For the sake of presentation, we restrict our attention to specifications obtained from single loops with loop-free bodies. That is, we consider natural invariants of the form:

$$\mathsf{loop}_{C,\mathsf{spec}(P)}(s, s')$$

where P contain no loops. This scenario is enough to illustrate the applicability of the proposed strategy in tackling the sort of program refactorings needed for establishing correctness of the RC4 `openSSL` implementation.

The simplest loop refactoring that we can address using our technique is *loop unrolling*, where we detach instances of the loop-body. We find this refactoring in the optimisations described in the previous sections. This sort of transformation is justified by the loop's inversion lemma:

$$\forall n \; s \; s', \; \mathsf{loop}_{C,R}^{S(n)}(s, s') \Longrightarrow \exists s'', \quad \mathsf{loop}_{C,R}^{n}(s, s'') \wedge [\![C]\!](s'') \wedge R(s'', s').$$

This relatively simple class of refactorings can then be handled directly by the plain theory augmented with synchronization and determinism lemmas.

For more interesting refactorings, we may need to formulate specific lemmas to justify them. Let us illustrate this by a *loop-fusion* refactoring: we consider the equivalence between two consecutive loops (loops 1 and 2) and one single *fused* loop (loop 3). This is applicable to the RC4 pre-processing optimisation presented in the previous section. Let us denote the inductive predicates of these loops by $\mathsf{loop}_1, \mathsf{loop}_2$ and loop_3, respectively. We assume, for simplicity, that all the loops share the same control structure (loop condition and associated state). This means that we are able to prove *mixed* synchronization lemmas such as, for all $n_1 \; n_2 \; s_1 \; s_2 \; s_1' \; s_2'$,

$$\pi^C(s_1) \equiv \pi^C(s_2) \wedge \mathsf{loop}_1^{n_1}(s_1, s_1') \wedge \neg[\![C]\!](s_1') \wedge \mathsf{loop}_2^{n_2}(s_2, s_2') \wedge \neg[\![C]\!](s_2') \Longrightarrow n_1 = n_2.$$

Again, the proof is a straightforward generalisation of the single loop version. Once this result is established, one can move to the proof of the main lemma that can be used to justify the fusion refactoring:

$$\forall n \; s_1 \; s_2 \; s_1' \; s_1'' \; s_2',$$
$$s_1 \equiv s_2 \wedge \mathsf{loop}_1^n(s_1, s_1'') \wedge \mathsf{loop}_2^n(s_1'', s_1') \wedge \mathsf{loop}_3^n(s_2, s_2') \Longrightarrow s_1' \equiv s_2'.$$

The advantage of our method is that, since this lemma is based on simple properties concerning the three loop bodies, which are all non-recursive, it can be easily discharged by automatic provers.

6   Implementation Details

We have tested the proposed methodology in checking the correctness of the RC4 `openSSL` implementation (shown in appendix). The specification predicates were extracted manually, and included in the ACSL code as inductive definitions. These definitions are allowed by the last revision of the ACSL language (version 1.4), but we remark that when the target verification tool is a first-order prover they are translated to a weak axiomatization (as described in Section 5). Additional lemmas were also included in the ACSL code and proved by the Coq proof assistant. For that purpose, we have developed a library that includes a full formalization of natural invariants as presented in the last section. This library makes extensive use of the Coq's module system [6] in order to structure the development. As a rule, we embed each lemma and respective proof in a functor parametrized by the basic facts it depends on. In particular, we have defined functors for deriving synchronization, determinism and loop fusion lemmas. All the facts required by these functors are non-iterative, and thus are easily discharged by the automatic provers. In this way, we are able to treat this library as a catalog of refactorings that can be used on demand during the verification process — we emphasise that there is no need to conduct further interactive proofs, unless this catalog is extended to cover a new class of loop refactorings.

7 Related Work

Natural Invariants provide an explicit rendition of program semantics. In [13] a similar encoding of program semantics in logical form can be found, which advocates the use of second-order logic as appropriate to reason about programs, since it allows to capture the inductive nature of the input-output relations for iterative programs. To some extent, our use of Coq's higher-order logic may be seen as an endorsement of that view. However, we have made an effort to combine the strength of higher-order logic reasoning with facilities made available by automatic first-order provers.

Our "proof-by-composition" technique is reminiscent of the self-composition approach for verifying non-interference[2]. Terauchi and Aiken [17] identified problems in applying it, arguing that automatic tools (software model checkers like SLAM [1] and BLAST [11]) are not powerful enough to verify this property over programs of realistic size. To compensate for this, the authors propose a program transformation technique, which incorporates the notion of security level downgrading using *relaxed non-interference* [14]. Our work proposes an alternative solution since it enriches the uderlying first-order theory with lemmas that overcome the identified limitations.

Relational Hoare Logic [4] has also been used to prove the soundness of program analyses and optimising transformations. Its scope is thus similar to our proofs-by-composition setting. The main difference is the fact that we do not need to move away from traditional Hoare Logic, which allows us to rely on standard available verification tools.

8 Conclusions

In this paper we have presented a methodology for verifying correctness of implementations with regard to reference implementations, an important concern in domains such as the verification and certification of cryptographic software implementations. We have focused on proposing strategies and techniques allowing us to maximize the benefits of using well established and publicly available tools, such as `Frama-c`, first-order automatic theorem provers and the Coq proof assistant. The approach can be summed up as follows

1. Program equivalences in general can be expressed (for terminating programs) as Hoare triples using a composition technique that simulates the execution of two programs by a single program. Such triples can be written in an interface specification language like ACSL and fed to a standard VCGen like `Frama-c`.
2. However, program equivalences are difficult verification challenges by nature, and automatic proof is, on its own, of little help. Resorting to an interactive proof tool to conduct inductive proofs involving loops is inevitable.
3. Natural invariants are good candidates for establishing the connection between the interface specification language and the proof assistant: on one hand, all the interactive reasoning is transferred to the inductive predicates that form the invariant; on the other hand, the invariant can be annotated into the specification files to be fed through the VCGen. We remark that these invariants (and some standard lemmas) can be generated mechanically.
4. Concluding the verification process is then a matter of identifying the relevant refactoring and instantiating the corresponding lemma. Once equipped with these lemmas an automatic prover is able to discharge the remaining proof obligations.
5. Once recognized, a new refactoring might be included by defining a new functor responsible for instantiating the corresponding lemma. It will require a once-and-for-all formal proof asserting the refactoring correctness (proved interactively in Coq).

This approach was put to practice to prove (as a sequence of refactoring steps) the equivalence between a reference implementation of an open-source cryptographic algorithm and the realistic implementation included in the appendix. Other applications that we are developing for this approach based on natural invariants include proofs of information flow security properties, using the self-composition technique, and related properties such as the absence of error propagation in stream ciphers.

References

1. Ball, T., Rajamani, S.K.: The slam project: debugging system software via static analysis. In: POPL 2002: Proceedings of the 29th ACM SIGPLAN-SIGACT symposium on Principles of programming languages, pp. 1–3. ACM, New York (2002)
2. Barthe, G., D'Argenio, P.R., Rezk, T.: Secure information flow by self-composition. In: CSFW, pp. 100–114. IEEE Computer Society, Los Alamitos (2004)
3. Baudin, P., Filliâtre, J.-C., Marché, C., Monate, B., Moy, Y., Prevosto, V.: ACSL: ANSI/ISO C Specfication Language. In: CEA LIST and INRIA, 2008. Preliminary design (version 1.4), December 12 (2008)
4. Benton, N.: Simple relational correctness proofs for static analyses and program transformations. In: Jones, N.D., Leroy, X. (eds.) POPL, pp. 14–25. ACM, New York (2004)
5. Computer Aided Cryptography Engineering. EU FP7, http://www.cace-project.eu/

6. Chrzaszcz, J.: Implementation of modules in the Coq system. In: Basin, D., Wolff, B. (eds.) TPHOLs 2003. LNCS, vol. 2758, pp. 270–286. Springer, Heidelberg (2003)
7. Conchon, S., Contejean, E., Kanig, J.: Ergo: a theorem prover for polymorphic first-order logic modulo theories (2006)
8. Cook, S.A.: Soundness and completeness of an axiom system for program verification. SIAM J. Comput. 7(1), 70–90 (1978)
9. Detlefs, D., Nelson, G., Saxe, J.B.: Simplify: a theorem prover for program checking. J. ACM 52(3), 365–473 (2005)
10. Filliâtre, J.-C., Marché, C.: The Why/Krakatoa/Caduceus platform for deductive program verification. In: Damm, W., Hermanns, H. (eds.) CAV 2007. LNCS, vol. 4590, pp. 173–177. Springer, Heidelberg (2007)
11. Henzinger, T.A., Jhala, R., Majumdar, R., Sutre, G.: Lazy abstraction. In: POPL 2002: Proceedings of the 29th ACM SIGPLAN-SIGACT symposium on Principles of programming languages, pp. 58–70. ACM, New York (2002)
12. Hoare, C.A.R.: An axiomatic basis for computer programming. Communications of the ACM 12, 576–580 (1969)
13. Leivant, D.: Logical and mathematical reasoning about imperative programs. In: POPL, pp. 132–140 (1985)
14. Li, P., Zdancewic, S.: Downgrading policies and relaxed noninterference. In: POPL 2005: Proceedings of the 32nd ACM SIGPLAN-SIGACT symposium on Principles of programming languages, pp. 158–170. ACM Press, New York (2005)
15. The OpenSSL Project, http://www.openssl.org
16. Schneier, B.: Applied cryptography: protocols, algorithms, and source code in C, 2nd edn. Wiley, New York (1996)
17. Terauchi, T., Aiken, A.: Secure information flow as a safety problem. In: Hankin, C., Siveroni, I. (eds.) SAS 2005. LNCS, vol. 3672, pp. 352–367. Springer, Heidelberg (2005)
18. The Coq Development Team. The Coq Proof Assistant Reference Manual – Version V8.2 (2008), http://coq.inria.fr

A   openSSL Implementation of RC4

```
typedef struct rc4_key_st { unsigned char x,y,data[256];} RC4_KEY;

void RC4(RC4_KEY *key,const unsigned long len,
         unsigned char *indata, unsigned char *outdata) {

  register unsigned char *d,x,y,tx,ty;
  int i;
  x=key->x;
  y=key->y;
  d=key->data;

#define LOOP(in,out) \
  x=((x+1)&0xff); \
  tx=d[x]; \
  y=((tx+y)&0xff); \
  d[x]=ty=d[y]; \
  d[y]=tx; \
  (out) = d[((tx+ty)&0xff)]^ (in);
#define RC4_LOOP(a,b,i) LOOP(a[i],b[i])

  i=(int)(len>>3L);
  if (i) {
    while(1) {
      RC4_LOOP(indata,outdata,0);
      RC4_LOOP(indata,outdata,1);
      RC4_LOOP(indata,outdata,2);
      RC4_LOOP(indata,outdata,3);
      RC4_LOOP(indata,outdata,4);
      RC4_LOOP(indata,outdata,5);
      RC4_LOOP(indata,outdata,6);
      RC4_LOOP(indata,outdata,7);
      indata+=8;
      outdata+=8;
      if (--i == 0) break;}}
  i=(int)(len&0x07);
  if(i) {
    while(1) {
      RC4_LOOP(indata,outdata,0); if (--i == 0) break;
      RC4_LOOP(indata,outdata,1); if (--i == 0) break;
      RC4_LOOP(indata,outdata,2); if (--i == 0) break;
      RC4_LOOP(indata,outdata,3); if (--i == 0) break;
      RC4_LOOP(indata,outdata,4); if (--i == 0) break;
      RC4_LOOP(indata,outdata,5); if (--i == 0) break;
      RC4_LOOP(indata,outdata,6); if (--i == 0) break;}}
  key->x=x;
  key->y=y;
}
```

Towards an Industrial Use of FLUCTUAT on Safety-Critical Avionics Software*

David Delmas[1], Eric Goubault[2], Sylvie Putot[2], Jean Souyris[1], Karim Tekkal[2], and Franck Védrine[2]

[1] Airbus France S.A.S., 316, route de Bayonne, 31060 TOULOUSE Cedex 9, France
`Firstname.Lastname@airbus.fr`
[2] CEA LIST, Laboratory for the Modelling and Analysis of Interacting Systems, Point Courrier 94, Gif-sur-Yvette, F-91191 France
`Firstname.Lastname@cea.fr`

Abstract. Most modern safety-critical control programs, such as those embedded in fly-by-wire control systems, perform a lot of floating-point computations. The well-known pitfalls of IEEE 754 arithmetic make stability and accuracy analyses a requirement for this type of software. This need is traditionally addressed through a combination of testing and sophisticated intellectual analyses, but such a process is both costly and error-prone. FLUCTUAT is a static analyzer developed by CEA-LIST for studying the propagation of rounding errors in C programs. After a long time research collaboration with CEA-LIST on this tool, Airbus is now willing to use FLUCTUAT industrially, in order to automate part of the accuracy analyses of some control programs. In this paper, we present the IEEE 754 standard, the FLUCTUAT tool, the types of codes to be analyzed and the analysis methodology, together with code examples and analysis results.

1 Introduction

For a decade, Airbus has been implementing formal techniques developed by academia into its own verification processes, for some avionics software products. So far, the most successful technique has been abstract interpretation based static analysis [5,6]. It is currently used industrially on several avionics software products developed at Airbus to compute safe upper-bounds of stack consumption with AbsInt StackAnalyzer, and worst-case execution time with AbsInt aiT WCET [24,23].

More static analyzers could be transferred soon. For instance, ASTRÉE [7] is a credible candidate for an industrial use in the near future [8,22], in order to prove the absence of run-time errors on control programs. Indeed, such programs perform a lot of floating-point computations, so that the absence of floating-point

---

* This work is supported by FP7 European project INTERESTED, ITEA 2 European project ES_PASS, a grant from the DIGITEO foundation, and the french DPAC (Direction des Programmes Aéronautiques Civils).

M. Alpuente, B. Cook, and C. Joubert (Eds.): FMICS 2009, LNCS 5825, pp. 53–69, 2009.
© Springer-Verlag Berlin Heidelberg 2009

overflow or other invalid operation has to be guaranteed. But proving freedom from run-time errors is not enough: the issue of the precision of computations has to be addressed also. This is typically the kind of properties for which FLUC-TUAT is designed. For this reason, Airbus is willing to use FLUCTUAT within its industrial process.

1.1 Numerical Computations in Control Programs

All control programs are based on control theory, which describes the physical data that are manipulated, together with control algorithms, in the realm of (ideal) real numbers. Even if the control algorithms are correct by design in real number computations, we have to prove that the imprecision due to finite-precision implementation has negligible effects on the system, for instance, introduces negligible errors compared to the imprecision of the computer I/O, on which bounds are generally available. This view is complementary, but not equivalent to the view taken in particular in robust control theory. Robust control theory deals with control algorithms which are in some sense "robust" to perturbations of input signals and to uncertainties in parameters of the controlled system but not to "computation" perturbation, i.e. the fact that finite-precision machines do have subtle discrete semantics which perturb the control algorithm along the full history of computation.

Take for instance, a flight control computer. It reads inputs from pilot controls (side sticks and pedals) and other sensors and aircraft systems or functions (such as the autopilot), and computes commands for actuators of control surfaces. This has been achieved using fixed-point arithmetic until the 1990s, but the later fly-by-wire generations have switched to floating-point representation. The main difference between both formats is the nature of errors. Fixed-point numbers yield absolute errors, whereas floating-point yield relative errors. Besides, the IEEE 754 standard provides engineers with a precise specification of floating-point data formats and basic operations, which makes it easier to assess accuracy systematically. Moreover, more and more microprocessors implementing a native Floating-Point Unit can be embedded.

1.2 Accuracy and Sensitivity Analyses

Control software is usually developed in a model-based approach. Most of the source code is generated automatically from high-level synchronous data-flow specifications. The computations to be performed are described by system designers at model-level in a graphical stream language such as SCADE [9] or Simulink [16], by means of external basic blocks. These basic operators implement the elementary calculations. They are usually available in some external library including logical, temporal and numerical operators. This toolbox can be either provided together with the modelling tool, or implemented by the user in a lower-level programming language, in order to meet his specific needs exactly. The latter case occurs typically for safety-critical avionics software that have to be certified according to the DO-178B/ED-12B aeronautical international standard. In this context, assessing the accuracy and stability of all numerical library operators is a key point in the overall numerical precision analysis. We need to analyze very precisely, for each operator:

1. the potential loss of accuracy;
2. the potential propagation of errors from inputs to outputs (i.e. sensitivity).
3. the behavior of the underlying algorithm:
   a. bounding the number of iterations of an iterative algorithm when it may depend on the accuracy;
   b. proving that the algorithm actually computes outputs close to what is expected, both in real and floating-point numbers (functional proof).

This need has been addressed so far through a combination of testing and intellectual analyses. In this paper, we aim at describing a way to automate this analysis using the FLUCTUAT tool. Therefore, we first present the IEEE 754 standard and the FLUCTUAT tool, then we state the analysis method and demonstrate it on examples similar to some of Airbus's library operators[1]. We will show mostly the use of FLUCTUAT for points 1 and 2 above, but also for 3.a and 3.b in Section 4.3.

2   The IEEE-754 Standard

The IEEE-754 standard [17] defines the format of floating-point numbers and the basic arithmetic operations on every processor supporting it. The standard defines the float format (8 bits for the exponent, 23 bits for the mantissa and 1 bit for the sign) and the double format (11 bits for the exponent, 52 bits for the mantissa and 1 bit for the sign). It also makes a distinction between several kinds of floating point numbers, which we describe for double precision numbers:

- the normalized numbers have a non-null, non-maximal exponent and, 53 relevant bits in the mantissa (the upper bit is implicitly 1) : $f = 2^{exp-2^{11-1}+1} \times (1.0 + m/2^{52})$, where exp is the exponent and m the mantissa,
- the denormalized numbers have a null exponent, a non-null mantissa and $1 + \lfloor \log_2(m) \rfloor$ relevant bits in the mantissa : $f = 2^{-2^{11-1}+2} \times (m/2^{52})$,
- $+0$ (resp. -0) has a null exponent, a null mantissa and a positive (resp. negative) sign,
- plus and minus infinities have a maximal exponent, a null mantissa,
- NaN (Not a Number) has a maximal exponent, a non-null mantissa. The upper bit of the mantissa differentiates "Signaling NaN" from "Quiet NaN".

The standard also specifies four possible rounding modes: round to nearest (and in case of a tie, round to nearest even mantissa) which is the default mode, round to minus infinity, round to plus infinity, round to zero. The atomic arithmetic operations $+$, $-$, $\times$ /, and $\sqrt{}$ are exactly rounded, that is their result is the real result rounded to the nearest floating-point number, according to the chosen rounding mode. Some common pitfalls due to the use of finite precision may

---

[1] For obvious confidentiality reasons, no real embedded code can be shown.

induce high relative errors or problematic behavior : among them, we can cite representation errors (for example on seemingly innocent constants such as 0.1), absorption (when adding two numbers of very different amplitudes), cancellation (when subtracting two very close numbers), unstable tests (when the real and float control flows are different, with a discontinuity between the two flows), or a drift in computation that will eventually cause large errors. We give here a few examples of these :

Representation error and computation drift

```
float time = 0.0; int ct = 0; while (++ct < 20000) time += 0.1;
```

The user could expect that the successive errors should cancel out and so that `time` at the end of the loop is close to the real value 2000 . It is not the case, and $(\texttt{time} - 2000.0)/\texttt{time} = 2.7 \times 10^{-4}$, since the initial error on the representation of 0.1 is always the same, and then, for all `time` between any $[2^n, 2^{n+1}[$, all computations are rounded in the same direction.

Invariant and safety The following example comes from [20].

```
double modulo(double x, double mini, double maxi)
  { double delta = maxi-mini; double decl = x-mini;
     double q = decl/delta; return x - ((int) q)*delta; }
```

does not return a number $\in [mini, maxi]$, since when $decl/delta$ is rounded up to a power of 2, like 1.0, the result is $<$ `mini`. Such a case occurs one time every 2^{54} – e.g. `modulo(179.99999999999998, -180, 180) < -180` –, but it may be a source of crash for a system.

Absorption and cancellation Consider the function $f(x, y) = 333.75y^6 + x^2(11x^2y^2 - y^6 - 121y^4 - 2) + 5.5y^8 + x/(2y)$ proposed by Rump: computed in float $f_f(77617, 33096) = 1.172603...$, in double $f_d(77617, 33096) = 1.1726039400531...$ We would thus think that the computation is correct, however in real numbers $f(77617, 33096) = -0.82739$. This is due to a catastrophic cancellation during the computation.

Moreover, compilers can transform the code in order to optimize the final binary code, in such a way that source-level analysis might be unsound. We will not discuss this issue in detail here, but workarounds consist in, mainly, analyzing compilation patterns and parameterize the static analyzer or partially rewrite the C code so that it agrees with the binary (evaluation order etc.); using a certified compiler [18]; or analyze the binary directly (see for instance [19] for a description of a version of FLUCTUAT which directly analyzes relocatable assembly code) or conjointly with the source code, through a "compilation of invariants", see for instance [21]. However, in Airbus' process, no unsound optimisation is performed by the compiler, and the compiled code can be safely traced back to the source code, as imposed by the DO-178B standard.

3 The FLUCTUAT Tool

3.1 General Description

FLUCTUAT [15] is a static analyzer by abstract interpretation of ANSI C programs, that focuses on numerical properties. For that, it computes ranges of values that can be taken, for all possible executions, at all control points of the program, with two different semantics, the idealized one in real numbers, and the implemented one in finite precision numbers (here IEEE 754 floating-point numbers and machine integers). It bounds the difference between the values taken by variables with these two semantics, and decomposes it on its provenance on the control points of the program, allowing the user to determine which parts of the program mainly contribute to the rounding error.

A graphical interface (see Figure 4) allows in particular to visualize, at the end of the program and for each variable, the errors committed in the program as a graph, on which the user can quickly identify the main sources of errors.

3.2 Specific Abstract Domains Based on Affine Arithmetic

FLUCTUAT relies on weakly-relational abstract domains that use affine forms [12,14,11] for the computation of values and errors on variables.

Abstract domain for idealized value in real numbers. Affine arithmetic is a more accurate extension of interval arithmetic, introduced in 93 [3], that takes into account linear correlation between variables. The real value of a variable x is represented by an affine form $\hat{x}$:

$$\hat{x} = x_0 + x_1\varepsilon_1 + \ldots + x_n\varepsilon_n,$$

where $x_i \in \mathbb{R}$ and the *noise symbols* ε_i are independent symbolic variables with unknown value in $[-1, 1]$. The coefficients $x_i \in \mathbb{R}$ are the *partial deviations* to the center $x_0 \in \mathbb{R}$ of the affine form. Indeed, these deviations express uncertainties on the values of variables, for example when inputs are given in a range of values. The sharing of the same noise symbols between variables expresses *implicit dependency*.

The joint concretization of these affine forms is a center-symmetric polytope, that is a zonotope. These zonotope-based abstract domains provide an excellent trade-off between computational cost and accuracy. We refer the reader to [12,14] for a full description of the abstract domain based on these forms.

In practice, these affine forms are themselves computed with floating-point coefficients, but the computation is made sound by over-approximating the rounding error committed on these coefficients and agglomerating this error in new noise terms.

Abstract domain for floating-point value and difference with real value. The abstract domain implemented in FLUCTUAT which we used for the experimentations presented here, extends these affine forms for the computation of the floating-point value of variables and for the difference between the real and floating-point computation, in the following model :

$$f^x = (\alpha_0^x + \bigoplus_i \alpha_i^x \varepsilon_i) + (e_0^x + \bigoplus_l e_l^x \eta_l + \bigoplus_i m_i^x \varepsilon_i),$$

where

- f^x is the floating-point abstract value for variable x,
- $\alpha_0^x + \bigoplus_i \alpha_i^x \, \varepsilon_i$ is the affine form that models the real value of x, i being the control points of the program,
- e_0^x is the center of the error,
- η_l are noise symbols that express the dependency between the errors, so that $e_l^x \, \eta_l$ expresses the rounding error committed at point l of the program, and its propagation through further computations,
- $m_i^x \, \varepsilon_i$ expresses the propagation of the uncertainty on value at point i, on the error term; it allows to model dependency between errors and values.

A new noise symbol is created for each new rounding error introduced by the computations. Thus, at the end of the program, for each visible variable, we can associate each error term of its affine error form to the location in the program that introduced it. This information is drawn on an error graph.

3.3   Use and Main Features of FLUCTUAT

We introduce in this section some features of FLUCTUAT that will be exemplified in the following sections.

Directives. FLUCTUAT comes along with a language of directives to be added in the source code by the user. The first kind of directives allows to specify values of variables, possibly with initial errors. For example `double x = DBETWEEN(0,1);` will specify that x is a double precision variable which can take a value between 0 and 1, whereas `double x = DOUBLE_WITH_ERROR(0,1,-0.01,0.01);` will specify that is has in addition an error in [-0.01,0.01], for example due to the use of an imperfect sensor to measure that value. Also, one can, in a loop, bound the derivative between successive inputs, which is useful in some cases to get plausible behavior. Note also that we have recently made a further step in taking into account a model of a continuous environment in our analysis, using a guaranteed integrator to bound the behavior of the continuous environment. This is out of the scope of this paper, but more details can be found in [2]. Also note that in some cases, we use the `BUILTIN` directives to construct sub-domains on which to analyze a given function (as in Section 4.3) which allows for improving precision of the analysis by a "manual" disjunctive analysis. In that case, we collect back the values that variables can take on the full domain using directive `res=DCOLLECT(subres,res);` (res is the result of the analyzed function that we construct by collecting results on subdomains: subres).

The second kind of directives allows the user to print more information than just the values and graphs of errors at the end of the program. Specifying `DPRINT(x)` in the source code will make the analyzer print the value and error of double precision variable x each time it meets the directive, allowing the user to follow the evolution of x in the program. If specifying `DSENSITIVITY(x)` at some point of the program, the sensibility of variable x to inputs of the program will be displayed : indeed, the abstract domains of FLUCTUAT are particularly well suited to such sensitivity analysis, by constructing linearized forms on the inputs. Also, using heuristics based on these same linearized forms, the analyzer can generate scenarii that allow to reach a value close to the maximal (or minimal) bound on some variable, and then run it.

Parameters of the analysis. Many parameters allow to tune the analysis, they can be set via the graphical interface. Among them, some allow to tune the trade-off between accuracy and computation in the fixpoint computation for loops, for instance the initial unfolding of loops, the number of cyclic unfoldings (useful in some examples to compute the fixpoint of a more contractant function), and the number of iterations before extrapolating the result (useful to reach a fixpoint in finite time in all cases).

When in presence of highly non-linear computations, it can be needed to subdivide some inputs for a more accurate computation, which can be done automatically.

Also, symbolic execution can be used, in some cases where the analysis gives large bounds, to confirm the behavior around some particular input values. The symbolic execution mode is based on the same abstract semantics as for the static analysis mode, but follows the abstract trace starting with input variables having as values the midpoint of their input ranges, and as errors, their full error range as specified through the corresponding directives. Symbolic execution can thus also be combined with subdivision (regular, for the time being) to have sample values in the input range.

4   Automating the Accuracy Analysis of Basic Operators with FLUCTUAT

4.1   Families of Basic Operators

Synchronous control programs, among which fly-by-wire, are built with several types of operators:

Pure boolean/integer operators. All inputs and outputs have boolean or integer types, and outputs at time t only depend on inputs at time t. Algorithms use no remanent data, and perform no floating-point computations. Typical such operators are logic gates and boolean switches.

Pure temporal operators. All inputs and outputs have boolean or integer types. Outputs at time t depend on inputs at ticks 0, 1, ..., t-1, t of the synchronous clock. Algorithms perform no floating-point computation, but use remanent data. Such operators include delays, timers, flip-flops, triggers, input confirmation operators, etc.

Pure numerical operators. Most inputs and outputs are real-valued. Outputs at time t only depend on inputs at time t. Algorithms perform floating-point computations, but use no remanent data. Main types are sum, product, comparison, conversion and interpolation operators. Well-known examples are divisions, square roots, trigonometric and transcendental functions.

Both numerical and temporal operators. Typical such recursive operators are digital filters, and signal integrators, derivators and speed limiters.

This paper focuses on numerical operators, be they temporal or not. Previous work has addressed functional verification of operators using theorem-proving techniques [1], but floats could not be handled through weakest precondition calculus.

In the examples we will give, note that the algorithms used for embedded operators are somewhat specific. For instance, the source codes for pure numerical operators contain hardly any loop at all, and no unbounded loop if any, as worst-case execution time and timing determinism are key constraints for safety-critical control programs. The same constraint applies for temporal numerical operators, although there is always an implicit main loop implementing the reactive nature of the control program, which will be emulated in the examples on recursive operators such as digital filters. These temporal numerical operators can be used on a very long period of time (i.e. on a large number of iterations) and we analyze them for any potential number of iterations, see Section 4.4.

4.2   The Analysis Process

Building the analysis project. The user selects a set of C source files through the GUI. The source code should be compilable/linkable, but for directives useful to the analysis (see Section 3.3), that provide the tool with:

- hypotheses on the environment of the program:
    - ranges of input variables (real or floating-point) values;
    - ranges of errors on input variables;
    - bounds on inputs variables speed.
- union or intersection strategies to:
    - fine-tune the analysis process;
    - build irregular "custom" subdivisions for input ranges.
- requirements for printing relevant information.

Parametrizing the analysis. Directives help tune the analysis locally, whereas analysis options allow for global parametrisation. The main choices for the purpose of analyzing basic operators are:

- abstract semantics: relational or non-relational static analysis versus symbolic execution;
- initial and cyclic unfolding of loops (mainly for recursive operators);
- refinement of bitwise operations when such operations are used;
- regular subdivisions of input variable ranges (in case we want very precise results on non-linear computations).

Exploitation of results. The tool warns about possible:

- run-time errors, and their source in the analyzed program: the user has to make sure they cannot occur in his application, due to thresholds or closed-loop control. This can be for instance achieved performing a global analysis with ASTRÉE. When possible, the program should be fixed for the tool not to issue such warnings.
- unstable tests (when the floating-point and the real control flows may be different): the user must make sure they have no impact on the values computed by his program. In particular, he must check these tests cannot create discontinuities in the set of output values.

Static analyses may also yield infinite or abnormally large ranges or errors on output variables (the analyzer points to the main sources of errors). In this case, the user should switch to the symbolic execution mode of the tool, in order to make sure the analyzed program is not trivially unstable. More generally, the precision of the static analysis should be assessed through worst-case generation[2] and symbolic execution with (possibly many) subdivisions. The static analysis parameters should be tuned until results can be compared to that of symbolic execution.

4.3 Analyzing Interpolation Operators

An arctangent approximation. Using rational functions to approximate the arctangent function is a good trade-off between efficiency and precision. For instance, one may choose the Padé approximant of order $(2, 2)$:

$$\frac{\arctan(x)}{x} \sim \frac{15 + 4x^2}{15 + 9x^2} = 1 - \frac{x^2}{3 + \frac{9}{5}x^2}$$

Using this approximation on the interval $[0, 1]$ provides a method for approximating $\arctan(x)$ for all x in $\mathbb{R}$, via the identities:

$$\arctan(x) = -\arctan(-x) = \frac{\pi}{2} - \arctan(\frac{1}{x})$$

Let us derive a straightforward implementation for the arctangent operator:

```
const double Pi=3.141592653589793238;
double PADE_2_2(double x) {          double ARCTAN_POS(double x) {
  double x_2=x*x;                      if (x>1) return Pi/2-ARCTAN_0_1(1/x);
  return 1-x_2/(3+9./5*x_2);           else      return ARCTAN_0_1(x); }
}
                                     double ARCTAN(double x) {
double ARCTAN_0_1(double x) {          if (x<0) return -ARCTAN_POS(-x);
    return x*PADE_2_2(x);              else      return ARCTAN_POS(x); }
}
```

Now we may run an accuracy analysis of the ARCTAN operator for the complete range of double precision floating-point numbers:

---

[2] FLUCTUAT is able to deliver its best guess for input values of a program, so that to maximize or minimize some output variable, see [13].

```
double x = DBETWEEN(-DBL_MAX, DBL_MAX);
double y = ARCTAN(x);
```

The analysis takes 10 ms and 16 MB, and ensures $y \in [-1.57, 1.57]$. This interval is of course very satisfactory, as the expected output range for an arctangent approximation is $]-\frac{\pi}{2}, \frac{\pi}{2}[$. The computed over-approximation of the error interval for y is $[-4.83 \times 10^{-16}, 4.83 \times 10^{-16}]$. This error interval is an over-approximation of the difference between the algorithm result in the real field and the algorithm result in floating-point arithmetic. It does not take into account the difference between the implementation and the real arithmetic function $arctan$. However, this model error can often be tackled with the tool (see paragraph "a glimpse on functional proofs" at the end of this section for the sine implementation). A side-remark is the fact that the π constant cannot be represented exactly as it is declared in the code with Pi: the representation error is found by FLUCTUAT to be in $[1.214 \times 10^{-16}, 1.249 \times 10^{-16}]$.

Now we want to perform a sensitivity analysis on function ARCTAN. Because this analysis does not cope with unstable tests nor subdivisions, for the time being, we need to run separate analyses on the $]-\infty, -1[$, $[-1, 0]$, $[0, 1]$ and $]1, \infty[$ subintervals. Besides, sensitivity has little meaning for very large inputs, we thus restrict ourselves to $[-10^4, -1[\cup [-1, 0] \cup [0, 1] \cup]1, 10^4]$.

The analysis for the restricted range $[0,1]$ takes 10 ms and 16 MB, and ensures that $|\frac{\Delta y}{\Delta x}| \leq 0.788$. For $]1, 10^4]$, we replace DBETWEEN(0,1) with DBETWEEN(DSU-CC(1), 1.e4) where DSUCC(x) (resp. DPREC(x)) stands for the next (resp. previous) floating-point number after (resp. before) x. The analysis costs are unchanged. FLUCTUAT ensures that $|\frac{\Delta y}{\Delta x}| \leq 3.12 \times 10^{-08}$. The results for $]-10^4, -1[$ (resp. $[-1, 0]$) are the same (resp. as for $[0, 1]$).

As a conclusion, FLUCTUAT helps us prove that the implementation in floating-point numbers of this approximation of the arctangent function:

1. introduces only negligible errors;
2. cannot amplify errors on inputs.

An interpolated sine. Embedded programs classically use interpolation tables to approximate trigonometric functions, such as the sine of an angle expressed in degrees. For instance, one may build an array of 361 doubles providing approximations of the sine function for every half degree:

$$\forall k = 0, 1, \ldots 360, \left| T[k] - \sin\left(\frac{k}{2}\right) \right| < 10^{-4},$$

and implement an approximation of sine by interpolating between the points of this table for angles between 0 and 180 degrees and using the identities

$$\forall x \in \mathbb{R}, \forall k \in \mathbb{Z}, \sin(x) = -\sin(-x) = \sin(x + 360k) = \sin\left(x - 360 \left\lfloor \frac{x + 180}{360} \right\rfloor \right)$$

Let us, as for the arctangent, try to run an analysis for the full range of double numbers, for the following naïve implementation of the sine operator:

```
extern const double T[361];
double SIN_0_180(double x) {
 double dx, i_dx, v_inf;
 double v_sup; int i;
 dx=2*x; i=dx; i_dx=i;
 v_inf=T[i]; v_sup=T[i+1];
 return v_inf + (dx - i_dx)
         * (v_sup - v_inf); }


double SIN_180(double x) {
 if (x<0)
  return -SIN_0_180(-x);
```

```
 else
  return SIN_0_180(x); }


double SIN_POS(double x) {
 if (x>180) return SIN_180(x
      -360.*(int)((x+180.)/360.));
 else        return SIN_180(x); }


double SIN(double x) {
 if (x<0) return -SIN_POS(-x);
 else      return SIN_POS(x); }
```

The analysis takes only 1.52 seconds and 24 MB. FLUCTUAT issues infinite values and errors for the result of the sine function, and warns that the (int)((x+180.)/360.) cast may be undefined. Indeed this implementation uses a conversion from double to int, so it is only valid for inputs x such that $\left\lfloor \frac{|x|+180}{360} \right\rfloor$ can be represented in the type int. In our 32 bits case, this is the $]-773094113100, 773094113100[$ interval. This is not an issue, provided that call contexts for SIN in the whole control program are guaranteed to fall into this last interval, for instance through a global static analysis with ASTRÉE.

The analysis costs for the reduced domain are unchanged, but its result is still disappointing: the computed over-approximation of the value (and error) interval for the result of the sine algorithm in floating-point numbers is $[-3.09 \times 10^{12}, 3.09 \times 10^{12}]$, whereas it is $[-1.5, 1.5]$ in the real-number semantics. Besides, FLUCTUAT warns the user that the program test in function SIN_180 is unstable. The warning also stresses that "real is bottom" in the (x<0) branch, which means that whenever the floating-point execution takes this branch, the real execution executes the (x>=0) branch. This requires careful attention.

At this point, we realize we may be faced with the pitfall described in Section 2 with the modulo example. As a matter of fact, whenever x is very close to (but smaller than) a number of the form $180 + 360 \times k$, for some $k \in \mathbb{N}$, then a rounding error occurs when evaluating expression (x+180.)/360. in floating-point arithmetic. The result is rounded to the double representing $k + 1$. In all such cases, the x - 360.*(int)((x+180.)/360.) expression has value close to (though below) 180 in the reals, but close to (though below) -180 in the floats.

In such a case, expression $T[i + 1]$ in function SIN_0_180 attempts to access array T out of bounds, as signalled by FLUCTUAT. Thus, we need to fix our naïve implementation of the sine operator. We add a 362nd array element, such that $T[0] = T[360] = T[361] = \sin(0) = \sin(\pm 180) = 0$.

Now we have fixed the implementation, we subdivide the input ranges enough for FLUCTUAT to perform a very accurate analysis on every subinterval defined by the interpolation table. For instance, on the $[-180, 180]$ range, using 720 subdivisions, a four hour / 20 MB analysis ensures $y \in [-1.0004, 1.0004]$ with errors in $[-1.75 \times 10^{-2}, 1.75 \times 10^{-2}]$.

Such a large relative error is unacceptable, especially considering the interpolation table has been chosen to ensure a 10^{-4} accuracy. In order to decide whether this is due to an issue in the implementation or to a lack of precision of the static analysis, we switch to the symbolic execution mode of FLUCTUAT with same range and subdivisions, thus choosing a sample of inputs in the input range. As a result, we get a useful (though unsound for the whole range of values) estimate of the error range for y: $[-1.05 \times 10^{-16}, 1.05 \times 10^{-16}]$. This result is a good hint that the accuracy of the implementation is not at stake. We thus look for a more precise way to perform the static analysis: we write a new main function implementing a custom irregular subdivision, with a singleton for every interpolation point of the interpolation table:

$$[-180, 180.5[= \bigcup_{i=-360}^{360} \left\{ \frac{i}{2} \right\} \cup \left] \frac{i}{2}, \frac{i+1}{2} \right[$$

```
double x=-180., y=0., xi, yi; int i;
for (i=-360; i<=360; i++) {
  xi = i*0.5;   yi = SIN(xi);
  x = DCOLLECT(x, xi);   y = DCOLLECT(y, yi);
  xi = DBETWEEN(DSUCC(i*0.5), DPREC((i+1)*0.5)) ;
  yi = SIN(xi); x = DCOLLECT(x, xi);   y = DCOLLECT(y, yi); }
```

The static analysis is run with no (tool-generated) subdivision, but unrolling the main loop 720 times. It takes 97.39 seconds and 36 MB, and ensures $x \in [-1.8 \times 10^2, 1.805 \times 10^2]$ and $y \in [-1.0, 1.0]$ with errors in $[-4.97 \times 10^{-16}, 4.97 \times 10^{-16}]$.

Over 99% of the error range originates from instruction dx=2*x. Next comes expression v_inf + (dx - i_dx) * (v_sup - v_inf). The rest are negligible representation errors within the interpolation table. Such a result is satisfactory: the imprecision generated by the floating-point implementation is negligible compared to the accuracy of the interpolation table.

Now we may also run sensitivity analyses for all $[\frac{i}{2}, \frac{i+1}{2}[$ subintervals of the $[-180, 180[$ range. Each (separate) analysis takes 20 MB and runs (at most) for 0.71 second. Merging the 720 results, we can guarantee $|\frac{\Delta y}{\Delta x}| \leq 0.0176$. This is of course a very satisfactory result, as we are approximating a real-valued sine function expressed in degrees, i.e. such that

$$\left| \frac{d}{dx} \left(\sin \left(\frac{180}{\pi} x \right) \right) \right| = \left| \frac{180}{\pi} \cos \left(\frac{180}{\pi} x \right) \right| \leq \frac{180}{\pi} \sim 0.0175$$

A glimpse on approximate functional proofs. As previously indicated, we can use FLUCTUAT to check that the approximate operator satisfies, in real and in floating-point numbers, some properties close to classical properties of the real sin function. For example here:

$$\sin(x) = -\sin(-x) = sin(180 - x) \quad \sin(x)^2 + \sin(x - 90)^2 = 1$$

We basically replace the body of the loop calling the SIN function on subintervals of length $\frac{1}{2}$ by the following:

```
xi = DBETWEEN(DSUCC(i*0.5+90), DPREC((i+1)*0.5+90)) ;
s1 = SIN(xi); c1 = SIN(xi-90);
z1 = s1 + SIN(-xi); z4 = s1-SIN(180-xi);
z6 = s1*s1+c1*c1-1.0;
```

FLUCTUAT proves the following in 111 seconds and 40.96 Mb (for x in [90,180]): $z1 \in [-4.337 \times 10^{-18}, 4.337 \times 10^{-18}]$ in reals and $z1 \in [-5.44 \times 10^{-16}, 5.44 \times 10^{-16}]$ in floating-point numbers, $z4 \in [-4.34 \times 10^{-18}, 4.34 \times 10^{-18}]$ in reals and $z4 \in [-4.34 \times 10^{-16}, 4.34 \times 10^{-16}]$ in floating-point numbers, $z6 \in [-1.32 \times 10^{-4}, 1.21 \times 10^{-4}]$ with negligible error (within $[-8.44 \times 10^{-16}, 7.93 \times 10^{-16}]$). Moreover FLUCTUAT finds out that the worst-case for the value of z6 is at iterate 74, and more precisely, it delivers as best guess for reaching the maximum of $z6$: $x = 127.5$. Asking FLUCTUAT to check this value, it gives $z6 = 1.21 \times 10^{-4}$ confirming the supremum bound found by static analysis. A simple analysis shows that this is due to an error less than 10^{-4} on the corresponding table entries. This shows that our algorithm for the sine function is actually most probably computing something quite close to the sine function, with the 10^{-4} absolute precision expected, mostly due to the implementation even in infinite precision (the interpolation table), and not to its finite precision implementation.

4.4   Analyzing Recursive Operators

Analyzing a set of order 2 filters conjointly. Consider the code of Figure 1. It implements a linear filter of order 2, run N times with at each iteration a new unknown input E within [0,1], independent of the previous inputs.

We find the results summarized in Table 1. The first columns of the table indicate respectively the number of cyclic unfolding and the number of iteration at which we begin to widen (instead of using the join operator). These are essential parameters to tune the accuracy of the analysis. We then give the time

```
double E, E0, E1, S0, S1, S;
int i;
E=DBETWEEN(0,1.0);
E0=DBETWEEN(0,1.0);
for (i=1;i<=N;i++) {
  E1 = E0;    E0 = E;
  E = DBETWEEN(0,1.0);
  S1 = S0;    S0 = S;
  S = 0.7*E-E0*1.3+E1*1.1
          +S0*1.4-S1*0.7;
  DPRINT(S);  }
DSENSITIVITY(S);
```

Fig. 1. A linear order 2 filter

```
double E, E0, E1, S0, S1, S;
double A1, A2, A3, B1, B2; int i;
A1 = DBETWEEN(0.5, 0.8);
A2 = DBETWEEN(-1.5,-1);
A3 = DBETWEEN(0.8,1.3);
B1 = DBETWEEN(1.39,1.41);
B2 = DBETWEEN(-0.71,-0.69);
E=DBETWEEN(0,1.0);E0=DBETWEEN(0,1.0);
for (i=1;i<=N;i++) {
  E1 = E0;    E0 = E;
  E = DBETWEEN(0,1.0);
  S1 = S0;    S0 = S;
  S = A1*E+E0*A2+E1*A3+S0*B1+S1*B2;
  DPRINT(S); }
DSENSITIVITY(S);
```

Fig. 2. A set of order 2 filters

of analysis on a laptop PC (1Gb memory, Pentium Duo 1.66GHz), the maximal amount of memory used, and the ranges the analysis gives for the floating-point value of the output S of the filter, and for its imprecision error:

Table 1. Results on the order 2 filter of Fig. 1

c. unfold	widen. thresh.	time	mem.	S (float)	S (error)
10	50	41 s	53 Mb	$[-6.30; 7.96]$	$[-5.13 \times 10^{-14}; 5.15 \times 10^{-14}]$
30	50	167 s	53 Mb	$[-5.18; 6.84]$	$[-3.23 \times 10^{-14}; 3.25 \times 10^{-14}]$
60	50	418 s	53 Mb	$[-5.12; 6.78]$	$[-3.11 \times 10^{-14}; 3.14 \times 10^{-14}]$

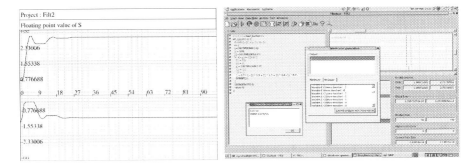

Fig. 3. Floating-point values along the iterations   **Fig. 4.** Fluctuat screen at the end of the analysis

Completely unfolding the loop on 100 iterations confirms that the bounds found by the analysis are fairly precise (see Figure 3): S is found to be in [-1.09, 2.76] with error in $[-1.15 \times 10^{-14}, 1.17 \times 10^{-14}]$. Still, there is room for improvement. We are currently experimenting a new "global" union which would find [-3.61,5.28] instead of [-6.30,7.96] in the case of a cyclic unfolding of 10, and [-3.00,4.67] instead of [-5.12,6.78] in the case of a cyclic unfolding of 60. Note that these results are just a bit less precise (for the floating-point range) than what the specialized abstract domain for filters of [10] delivers, while also giving precise bounds for the implementation error as well as their origins.

Consider the code of Figure 2 now. It is the same order 2 filter, but with uncertain coefficients. These coefficients might look as narrow intervals, but a manual calculation reveals that the poles of the Z-transform of this filter have a module in [0.932,0.975], thus close to instability (the filter would be unstable if the norm could go above one).

FLUCTUAT finds the results shown in Table 2. On the first line, we see the results for the full static analysis for N unknown, the second and third line show the results of the loop completely unfolded on the first 200 iterations (hence the analysis is particularized to N=200), first without subdividing coefficients B1 and B2, and then, subdividing them. We can see that the results of the static analysis (i.e. [post]fixpoint calculation) are not too much over-approximated compared to the results of the unfolded loop, which, as could be seen on the evolution

Table 2. Results on the order 2 filter of Fig. 2

#B1&B2	c.	widen.	time	mem.	S (float)	S (error)
1, 1	200	20	1242 s	65 Mb	$[-15.1; 16.6]$	$[-7.9 \times 10^{-14}; 7.9 \times 10^{-14}]$
1, 1	200	no	21 s	57 Mb	$[-5.63; 7.13]$	$[-2.93 \times 10^{-14}; 2.93 \times 10^{-14}]$
10, 10	200	no	2943 s	57Mb	$[-4.81; 6.33]$	$[-2.61 \times 10^{-14}; 2.61 \times 10^{-14}]$

graph, are quite stable on the last iterations, so should not be far from the actual invariant[3]. As in Table 1, we indicate the number of cyclic unfolding, the widening threshold, time and memory usage, and floating-point/error range for the output S. First column indicates how much we subdivide coefficients B1 and B2 : FLUCTUAT can also deliver automatically estimates for coefficients A1, A2, A3, B1 and B2 in their input ranges such that the corresponding output reaches a value close to the bounds previously delivered by the static analysis (using here 10 subdivisions on B1 and 10 subdivisions on B2). For the upper bound, it finds B1=1.41, B2=-0.69, A1=0.8, A2=-1 and A3=1.3, along with input values for successive iterates of E, when we unfold the loop for 200 iterations. When the filter is executed with these values, S is found to be equal to 5.34.

For the lower bound, it finds B1=1.408, B2=-0.71, A1=0.5, A2=-1.5 and A3=0.8. In that case, S is found to be equal to -0.75. This gives an idea of the quality of the invariants found.

5   Conclusions and Future Work

In this paper, we have shown how FLUCTUAT can be used to automate part of the accuracy analysis of basic numerical operators of control programs. We have shown extremely precise results could be obtained in a quite systematic way, which should ease the work of engineers in charge of this task.

The next step, for such a research prototype, is its industrial use within operational development teams. This requires some extra work. First, an "industrial" version of the tool is needed: this phase has already been prepared through a DIGITEO[4] grant and plans are currently made for creating a service oriented spinoff company, together with partial transfer to publishing companies, such as ABSINT and ESTEREL (through the European project INTERESTED). Also, depending on the verification strategy of operational end-users, FLUCTUAT may need to be qualified as a verification tool, according to the DO-178B/ED-12B aeronautical international standard. If such is the case, Airbus will conduct qualification activities matching the targeted context. Detailed information on the principles and architecture of the tool will be needed from the tool provider,

---

[3] This could also be analyzed by a modified version of the ASTREE analyzer, implementing a specific extension of the abstract domain of [10], with comparable, but slighly less precise results.

[4] DIGITEO is a French research foundation devoted to complex software-intensive systems, regrouping such institutions as Ecole Polytechnique, CEA, INRIA, Supelec, Paris XI, ENS Cachan, Centrale etc. see http://www.digiteo.fr.

in order to anticipate DO-178C extended qualification objectives for such formal tools. There again, work has started thanks to the support from DIGITEO.

Further work on the accuracy analysis of basic operators could be to interoperate FLUCTUAT with FRAMA_C (http://frama-c.cea.fr) or ASTRÉE. The latter could be used to compute over-approximated ranges for input variables of all operators on the complete program, and the former could then restrict its accuracy analyzes to these sound input intervals. In the cases where the local value analysis with FLUCTUAT is more precise than the global analysis with ASTRÉE, invariants computed by the former may be re-injected to improve the precision of the analysis of the latter.

Beyond local accuracy analyses of basic operators, FLUCTUAT can also be used to perform very accurate analyses on C code generated from sets of SCADE sheets. First steps have been made in that direction with the successful study of a complex program relying on set of linear recursive filters of orders varying from 3 to 8. Outside the scope of the cooperation with Airbus, CEA-LIST has also had successful experiences with other industrialists such as Hispano-Suiza and IRSN, see [15], and a 33KLoC C program implementing a critical function for Astrium's Automated Transfer Vehicle, see [4]. This should be further investigated, in order to assess the accuracy of some critical independent system-level aircraft functions.

References

1. Baudin, P., Delmas, D., Duprat, S., Monate, B.: Proving temporal properties at code level for basic operators of control/command programs. In: Proceedings of ERTS 2008, SIA (2008)
2. Bouissou, O., Goubault, E., Putot, S., Tekkal, K., Vedrine, F.: Hybridfluctuat: a static analyzer of numerical programs within a continuous environment. In: Computed Aided Verification conference, CAV 2009, Grenoble, France. LNCS, vol. 5643, pp. 620–626. Springer, Heidelberg (2009)
3. Comba, J.L.D., Stolfi, J.: Affine arithmetic and its applications to computer graphics. In: Anais do VI Simpósio Brasileiro de Computação Gráfica e Processamento de Imagens (SIBGRAPI 1993), October 1993, pp. 9–18 (1993)
4. Conquet, E., Cousot, P., Cousot, R., Goubault, E., Ghorbal, K., Lesens, D., Putot, S., Turin, M.: Space software validation using abstract interpretation. In: Proceedings of DASIA (2009)
5. Cousot, P.: Abstract interpretation based formal methods and future challenges. Informatics, 138–156 (2001)
6. Cousot, P., Cousot, R.: Basic concepts of abstract interpretation. In: IFIP Congress Topical Sessions, pp. 359–366 (2004)
7. Cousot, P., Cousot, R., Feret, J., Mauborgne, L., Miné, A., Monniaux, D., Rival, X.: The astrée analyzer. In: Sagiv, M. (ed.) ESOP 2005. LNCS, vol. 3444, pp. 21–30. Springer, Heidelberg (2005)
8. Delmas, D., Souyris, J.: Astrée: From research to industry. In: Riis Nielson, H., Filé, G. (eds.) SAS 2007. LNCS, vol. 4634, pp. 437–451. Springer, Heidelberg (2007)
9. Dormoy, F.-X.: Scade 6 a model based solution for safety critical software development. In: Embedded Real-Time Systems Conference (2008)

10. Feret, J.: Static analysis of digital filters. In: Schmidt, D. (ed.) ESOP 2004. LNCS, vol. 2986, pp. 33–48. Springer, Heidelberg (2004)
11. Ghorbal, K., Goubault, E., Putot, S.: The zonotope abstract domain taylor1+. In: Computed Aided Verification conference, CAV 2009, Grenoble, France. LNCS, vol. 5643, pp. 627–633. Springer, Heidelberg (2009)
12. Goubault, E., Putot, S.: Static analysis of numerical algorithms. In: Yi, K. (ed.) SAS 2006. LNCS, vol. 4134, pp. 18–34. Springer, Heidelberg (2006)
13. Goubault, E., Putot, S.: Under-approximations of computations in real numbers based on generalized affine arithmetic. In: Riis Nielson, H., Filé, G. (eds.) SAS 2007. LNCS, vol. 4634, pp. 137–152. Springer, Heidelberg (2007)
14. Goubault, E., Putot, S.: Perturbed affine arithmetic for invariant computation in numerical program analysis. CoRR, abs/0807.2961 (2008)
15. Goubault, E., Putot, S., Baufreton, P., Gassino, J.: Static analysis of the accuracy in control systems: Principles and experiments. In: Leue, S., Merino, P. (eds.) FMICS 2007. LNCS, vol. 4916, pp. 3–20. Springer, Heidelberg (2008)
16. Hunt, Lipsman, Rosenberg, Coombes, Osborn, Stuck: A Guide to MATLAB, 2e: for Beginners and Experienced Users. Cambridge University Press, Cambridge (2006)
17. IEEE 754 standard for floating-point arithmetic. Floating-Point Working Group of the Microprocessor Standards Subcommittee of the Standards Committee of the IEEE Computer Society. Work in Progress (2004)
18. Leroy, X.: Formal certification of a compiler back-end, or: programming a compiler with a proof assistant. In: 33rd ACM symposium on Principles of Programming Languages, pp. 42–54. ACM Press, New York (2006)
19. Martel, M.: Validation of assembler programs for dsps: a static analyzer. In: PASTE 2004: Proceedings of the 5th ACM SIGPLAN-SIGSOFT workshop on Program analysis for software tools and engineering, pp. 8–13. ACM, New York (2004)
20. Monniaux, D.: The pitfalls of verifying floating-point computations. ACM Trans. Program. Lang. Syst. 30(3), 1–41 (2008)
21. Rival, X.: Symbolic transfer functions-based approaches to certified compilation. In: Leroy, X. (ed.) 31st Symposium on Principles of Programming Languages, pp. 1–13. ACM, New York (2004)
22. Souyris, J., Delmas, D.: Experimental assessment of astrée on safety-critical avionics software. In: Saglietti, F., Oster, N. (eds.) SAFECOMP 2007. LNCS, vol. 4680, pp. 479–490. Springer, Heidelberg (2007)
23. Souyris, J., Le Pavec, E., Himbert, G., Borios, G., Jégu, V., Heckmann, R.: Computing the worst case execution time of an avionics program by abstract interpretation. In: 5th Intl. Workshop on Worst-Case Execution Time (WCET) Analysis, Dagstuhl, Germany (2007)
24. Thesing, S., Souyris, J., Heckmann, R., Randimbivololona, F., Langenbach, M., Wilhelm, R., Ferdinand, C.: An abstract interpretation-based timing validation of hard real-time avionics software. In: DSN (2003)

Dynamic State Space Partitioning
for External Memory Model Checking*

Sami Evangelista[1] and Lars Michael Kristensen[2]

[1] Computer Science Department, Aarhus University, Denmark
evangeli@cs.au.dk
[2] Department of Computer Engineering, Bergen University College, Norway
lmkr@hib.no

Abstract. We describe a dynamic partitioning scheme usable by model
checking techniques that divide the state space into partitions, such as
most external memory and distributed model checking algorithms. The
goal of the scheme is to reduce the number of transitions that link states
belonging to different partitions, and thereby limit the amount of disk
access and network communication. We report on several experiments
made with our verification platform ASAP that implements the dynamic
partitioning scheme proposed in this paper.

1   Introduction

Model checking [3] is a technique used to prove that finite-state systems match
behavioral specifications. It is based on a systematic exploration of all reachable
states in the search for illegal behaviors violating the specification. Despite its
simplicity, its practical application is subject to the well-known state explosion
problem [17]: the state space may be far too large to be explored in reasonable
time or to fit within the available memory.

Most techniques devised to alleviate the state explosion problem can be classi-
fied as belonging to one of two families. The first family of techniques reduce the
part of the state space that needs to be explored in such a way that all properties
of interest are preserved. Partial order reduction [9] which limits redundant interleavings is an example of such a technique. More pragmatic approaches do not
reduce the state space, but make a more economical use of available resources, or
augment them, in order to extend the range of problems that can be analyzed.
State compression [11], distributed verification [16], and disk-based verification
[4] belong to this second family of techniques.

In the field of external memory and distributed verification, it is common to
divide the state space into *partitions* (although some external and distributed
algorithms do not rely on such a partitioning, e.g., [4,10]). For example, in the
distributed algorithm of [16], each process involved in the verification is responsible for storing and visiting all the states of a partition. Whenever a process
generates a state that does not belong to the partition it is responsible for, it

---

* Supported by the Danish Research Council for Technology and Production.

M. Alpuente, B. Cook, and C. Joubert (Eds.): FMICS 2009, LNCS 5825, pp. 70–85, 2009.
© Springer-Verlag Berlin Heidelberg 2009

sends it to its owner such that the state can be stored and its successor states can be explored. An important component of this algorithm is the *partition function* (known to all processes) which is used to map states to partitions. In the ideal case, the partition function should have two properties. Firstly, it should generate as few *cross transitions* as possible. Cross transitions link two states of different partitions and thus systematically generate messages over the network. Secondly, it should distribute states evenly into partitions to ensure that all processes have the same workload. A hash function based on the bit string used to represent states may achieve an optimal distribution, but generates many cross transitions due to the insensitivity of hashing to locality.

To address this problem, we introduce a dynamic partitioning scheme based on the idea of *partition refinement*. Initially, there is a single partition in which the partition function maps all states. Then, whenever a partition has to be split up — for instance because its size exceeds memory capacity — it is divided into sub-partitions and the partition function is refined accordingly. To represent a partition function that can change over time we introduce the idea of *compositional partition functions*. Refinement is done by progressively considering new components of the state vector (descriptor) in the partition function, e.g., variables or communication channels. For instance, after a first refinement step, a state will be mapped to one of the partitions $p_1, \ldots, p_n$ depending only on the value of its ith component in the state vector. Then, if p_1 has to be refined, we consider an additional component of the state vector. As refinement is applied on a single partition at a time, partitions $p_2, \ldots, p_n$ will remain unchanged.

Our intuition is to take advantage of the fact that events typically modify a small number of components in the state vector. Thus, if a partition function is based only on a few components of the system and does not consider others, events that do not modify these components will not generate cross transition, and hence disk accesses or network communications will be limited. However, we replace the objective of a uniform distribution of states into partitions by a less ambitious one: partitions may be of different sizes, but we can ensure an upper bound on their size. Even though this does not have any consequence with an external memory algorithm, it may impact a distributed algorithm in that processes may not receive the same amount of workload.

The refinement algorithm has been implemented in the ASAP [18] tool, on top of the external algorithm of [1]. We report the results of several experiments showing that we were able to significantly decrease the number of disk accesses. More importantly, our algorithm improves the algorithm of [1] such that it performs well on classes of models where it previously performed poorly.

Structure of the paper. In the next section, we briefly recall the principle of the two partitioning based algorithms of [16] and [1] that will be the basis of our work. Section 3 presents related work. Our dynamic scheme based on partition refinement is introduced in Section 4 followed in Section 5 by different heuristics to support the refinement. The experiments conducted with our verification tool are presented in Section 6. Finally, Section 7 concludes this paper. We assume the reader is familiar with the principle of state space exploration.

Definitions and notations. We assume a universe of system states $\mathcal{S}$, an initial state $s_0 \in \mathcal{S}$, a set of events $\mathcal{E}$, an enabling function $en : \mathcal{S} \to 2^{\mathcal{E}}$, and a successor function $succ : \mathcal{S} \times \mathcal{E} \to \mathcal{S}$. We want to explore the state space implied by these parameters, i.e., the triple (R, T, s_0) such that $R \subseteq \mathcal{S}$ is the set of reachable states and $T \subseteq R \times R$ is the set of transitions defined by:

$$R = \{s_0\} \cup \{ s \in \mathcal{S} \mid \exists s_1, \ldots, s_n \in \mathcal{S} \text{ with } s = s_n \land$$
$$\forall i \in \{0, \ldots, n-1\} : \exists e_i \in en(s_i) \text{ with } succ(s_i, e_i) = s_{i+1}\}$$
$$T = \{(s, s') \in R \times R \mid \exists e \in en(s) \text{ with } succ(s, e) = s'\}$$

2 Partitioning the State Space

Algorithm 1 (left) shows the algorithm of [1] that mimics a distributed search using external storage, and the distributed algorithm of [16] (right) which is the basis of most work in the field of parallel and distributed model checking. Both algorithms rely on a partitioning function $part : \mathcal{S} \to \{1, \ldots, N\}$ which partitions the set of visited states and the queue of unprocessed states into $\mathcal{V}_1, \ldots, \mathcal{V}_N$ and $\mathcal{Q}_1, \ldots, \mathcal{Q}_N$, respectively.

In the external algorithm (ll. 1–10), only a single partition i is loaded in memory at a time. The visited states of partition i are stored in memory in $\mathcal{V}_i$, and its unprocessed states reside in the queue $\mathcal{Q}_i$. All other partitions $j \neq i$ are not stored in memory, i.e., $\mathcal{V}_j = \emptyset$, but stored on disk files $\mathcal{F}_j$. Queues are also stored on disk, although, for the sake of simplicity of our presentation, we assume here that they are kept in main memory. Initially, all structures and files are empty. The algorithm inserts the initial state s_0 in the appropriate queue $part(s_0)$ (l. 4). Then, as long as one of the queues contains a state, the algorithm selects the longest queue i (l. 6), loads the associated partition from disk file $\mathcal{F}_i$ to memory in $\mathcal{V}_i$ (l. 7) and starts expanding the states in queue $\mathcal{Q}_i$ using procedure $search_i$ (l. 8) which will be explained below. When the $search_i$ procedure does not have any new state to expand for this partition, it writes back the partition to disk file $\mathcal{F}_i$ and empties $\mathcal{V}_i$ (ll. 9–10). Selecting the longest queue is mainly a heuristic to perform few partition switches (writing back $\mathcal{V}_i$ in disk file $\mathcal{F}_i$ and selecting a new partition).

In the distributed algorithm (ll. 11–19), data structures are kept in the memory of the N processes involved in the state space exploration. Each process i owns a partition $\mathcal{V}_i$ and a queue of unprocessed states $\mathcal{Q}_i$ that it has to explore. Both structures are initially empty, and the process that owns the initial state puts it in its queue (ll. 16–17). As long as termination is not detected (l. 18), the process expands the states in its local queue using procedure $search_i$ (l. 19). Termination occurs when all queues and communication channels are empty.

The common part of both algorithms is the $search_i$ procedure that expands all the states queued in $\mathcal{Q}_i$ until it becomes empty. Each state s removed from $\mathcal{Q}_i$ (l. 22) is checked to be in partition $\mathcal{V}_i$. This check is performed since a state in $\mathcal{Q}_i$ may have been inserted in $\mathcal{Q}_i$ because it was a destination state of a cross transition. If s has not been met before it is inserted into $\mathcal{V}_i$ (l. 24) and then expanded (ll. 25–29). During the expansion, we compute all the successors s' of

---

Algorithm 1. Two search algorithms based on state space partitioning

```
 1: (* external algorithm of [1] *)           11: (* distributed algorithm of [16] *)
 2: for i in 1 to N do                         12: execute proc₁ ‖ … ‖ procₙ
 3:     Qᵢ := ∅ ; Vᵢ := ∅ ; Fᵢ := ∅            13:
 4: Q_part(s₀).enqueue(s₀)                      14: procedure procᵢ is
 5: while ∃i : ¬Qᵢ = ∅ do                      15:     Qᵢ := ∅ ; Vᵢ := ∅
 6:     i := longestQueue()                     16:     if part(s₀) = i then
 7:     Fᵢ.load(Vᵢ)                             17:         Qᵢ.enqueue(s₀)
 8:     searchᵢ()                               18:     while ¬ termination() do
 9:     Vᵢ.unload(Fᵢ)                           19:         searchᵢ()
10:     Vᵢ := ∅
```

```
20: procedure searchᵢ is    (* search procedure common to both algorithms *)
21:     while Qᵢ ≠ ∅ do
22:         s := Qᵢ.dequeue()
23:         if s ∉ Vᵢ then
24:             Vᵢ.insert(s)
25:             for e in en(s), s' = succ(s, e) do
26:                 j := part(s')
27:                 if i = j then       (* local transition *)
28:                     if s' ∉ Vᵢ then Qᵢ.enqueue(s')
29:                 else  Qⱼ.enqueue(s')  (* cross transition *)
```

---

s and determine the partition j they belong to (l. 26), using function *part*. If $i = j$ the transition from s to s' is a *local transition*. We can simply check if s' is in memory in table V_i and put it the in queue Q_i if needed. Otherwise, this is a cross transition, and the partition of state s' is not available in memory (it is stored on disk or belongs to another process). We thus unconditionally put it in Q_j. For the external algorithm of [1] this is implemented by enqueueing the state in the memory queue Q_j (and possibly writing s' in the disk file associated with Q_j), whereas for the distributed algorithm of [16] it implies to pack the state in a message and send it to the owner of the appropriate partition, i.e., process j. Upon reception, the state is enqueued by the receiving process in Q_j.

The performance of these algorithms depends to a large extent on the partition function *part*. In the distributed algorithm, cross transitions highly impact the number of messages exchanged and thereby indirectly the execution time. For the external algorithm, partition swaps, and hence disk accesses, are generated by cross transitions. Although this objective is more specific to the distributed algorithm, function *part* should also distribute states evenly among partitions so that processes receive a comparable workload.

3   Related Work

Stern and Dill [16], Bao and Jones [1] and Garavel et al. [8] left open the problem of the partition function. They used in their experiments a standard hash function taking as input the entire state vector. The importance of the partition function was stressed in [12]. Assuming that the system to be verified is a set of communicating processes, the partition function proposed in [12] only hashes the part of the state vector describing a selected process p. Thus, only when that part changes, i.e., the search algorithm explores events in p, is a cross transition generated. Compared to a global hash function, this scheme efficiently reduces the number of messages exchanged (up to a factor of 5) and, hence, the execution time (up to a factor of 3). The downside is a degraded distribution of states over the nodes of the network.

The dynamic partitioning in [13] groups states into *classes* and partitions consist of a set of classes. When memory becomes scarce, the partition function is modified by reassigning some classes of the overflowing partition to other partitions. The function mapping states to classes can be a local hash function as in [12]. The results of this dynamic partitioning strategy in term of message exchanges and verification time are comparable to the ones of [12]. The main advantage is that no knowledge of the system is necessary: run-time information is used to keep the partitioning balanced and, indeed, we generally observed in our experiments (to be discussed in Sect. 6) a good distribution of states.

An efficient partitioning algorithm based on abstraction and refinement of the state space is introduced in [2]. However, the state space has to be first constructed in order to define the partition function meaning that this approach mainly targets off-line model checking.

In structured duplicate detection [19] as used in external graph search, an abstraction of the state space is used to determine when to load/unload partitions from/to disk. However, this approach seems hard to apply in the context of model checking due to the difficulty of defining an abstract graph from a complex specification. Close to that idea is the work of Rangarajan et al. [15]. The algorithm they propose first explores a sample of the state space. This sample is abstracted into a higher level graph using a single variable v of the system. An abstracted state aggregates all states having the same value of v. A partition function can then be constructed from this abstracted graph. The algorithm can reiterate this process on all variables to improve the quality of the function. The underlying principle is the same as in [12] and [13]: only when the selected variable is modified can a cross transition be generated. The experiment made in [15] shows that this method can significantly outperform the local hash partitioning implemented in PSPIN [12].

We propose a way to dynamically (i.e., during state space exploration) modify the partition function by progressively taking into account more components of the underlying system. Our work can be seen as an extension of [15] since some of the ideas we develop were briefly mentioned in [15] – like the one of considering several variables of the system to define the partition function. Another contribution of our dynamic approach is that it can still guarantee an upper bound on the size of any partition loaded in memory which previous approach like [12,13,15] could not. From now on, we focus on the external algorithm of [1] although the proposed method and the heuristics in Sect. 5 can, to a large extent, be applied also to distributed model checking.

Algorithm 2. The partition refinement procedure

1: **procedure** $refine_i$ **is**
2:     update partition function $part$: partition i is divided into $i_1, \ldots, i_n$
3:     **for** $s \in \mathcal{V}_i$ **do** { $s.write(\mathcal{F}_{part(s)})$ }
4:     **while** $\neg\ \mathcal{Q}_i.isEmpty()$ **do** { $s := \mathcal{Q}_i.dequeue()$; $\mathcal{Q}_{part(s)}.enqueue(s)$ }
5:     $\mathcal{V}_i := \emptyset$; $\mathcal{F}_i := \emptyset$; **go to line 6 of Algorithm 1**

---

4   Dynamic Partitioning Based on Refinement

Our dynamic partitioning scheme is based on the principle of *partition refinement*. The algorithm starts with a single partition to which all states are initially mapped. If the state space is small enough to be kept in main memory the algorithm acts as a standard RAM algorithm. Otherwise, whenever the partition $\mathcal{V}_i$ currently loaded in memory exceeds the memory capacity, procedure $refine_i$ of Algorithm. 2 is triggered. It firsts updates the partition function $part$ (l. 2) in such a way that each state that was previously mapped to partition i is now mapped to a new partition $j \in \{i_1, \ldots, i_n\}$. Then, it writes the states in $\mathcal{V}_i$ to disk files $\mathcal{F}_{i_1}, \ldots, \mathcal{F}_{i_n}$ (l. 3) and reorganizes the queue $\mathcal{Q}_i$ in the same way (l. 4). Once this reorganization is finished, the table $\mathcal{V}_i$ and the disk file $\mathcal{F}_i$ are emptied (l. 5), and the search can restart by picking a new partition. Note that partition i is the only one to be reorganized; all other partitions remain unchanged.

Our focus is now on the implementation of line 2 of procedure $refine_i$. We describe in the rest of this section how our algorithm uses a *compositional partition function* that can change during the state space exploration. We propose a way to dynamically refine the partition function by gradually considering more components of the state vector of the system being analyzed.

A compositional partition function can be represented as a *partitioning diagram*. Figure 1 is the graphical representation of a diagram D. Rounded boxes represent terminal nodes and branching nodes are drawn using circles. The nodes are labeled either with a partition, e.g., p_0, p_1, or with a *branching function* of which the domain is the universe of states $\mathcal{S}$ and the codomain can be deduced from the labels of its outgoing arcs: $g : \mathcal{S} \to \{t, f\}$, $h : \mathcal{S} \to \{a, b, c\}$ and $i : \mathcal{S} \to \{0, 1, 2\}$. This diagram induces a partition function part_D mapping states to partitions. Starting from the root g of this diagram, we successively apply to the state the different functions labeling the branching nodes of the diagram until reaching a terminal node, i.e., a partition. The branches to follow are given by the labels of the outgoing edges from branching nodes. Below is a few examples of application of part_D:

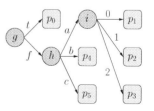

Fig. 1. A compositional partitioning diagram D

$$\mathsf{part}_D(s) = p_0 \;\Leftrightarrow\; g(s) = t$$
$$\mathsf{part}_D(s) = p_5 \;\Leftrightarrow\; g(s) = f \wedge h(s) = c$$
$$\mathsf{part}_D(s) = p_3 \;\Leftrightarrow\; g(s) = f \wedge h(s) = a \wedge i(s) = 2$$

Three functions (g, h and i) are used to decide if a state belongs to partition p_3. Hence we say that partition p_3 is *dependent* on functions g, h and i.

The following definition formalizes the notion of partitioning diagrams. Note that the definition of the edge set E implies that partitions are the terminal nodes of the diagram and that functions are branching nodes.

Definition 1 (Compositional partitioning diagram (CPD)). *A Compositional partitioning diagram is a tuple $D = (V, E, r_0, \mathcal{F}, \mathcal{P})$ such that:*

- *$G = (V, E)$ is a directed acyclic graph with vertices $V = \mathcal{F} \cup \mathcal{P}$ and edges E, and $r_0 \in V$ is the only root node of G;*
- *$\mathcal{F} = \{f_i : \mathcal{S} \to \mathcal{L}_i\}$ is a set of branching functions;*
- *$\mathcal{P} \subseteq 2^{\mathcal{S}}$ is a set of state partitions;*
- *$E \subseteq \mathcal{F} \times \mathcal{L} \times V$ (with $\mathcal{L} = \cup_i \mathcal{L}_i$), such that for all $f_i \in \mathcal{F}, l \in \mathcal{L}_i$ there exists exactly one $v' \in V$ such that $(f_i, l, v') \in E$.*

A CPD determines a partition function as formalized in the following definition.

Definition 2 (Compositional partition function). *Let $D = (V, E, r_0, \mathcal{F}, \mathcal{P})$ be a CPD. The function $\mathsf{part} : V \times \mathcal{S} \to \mathcal{P}$ is defined by:*

$$\mathsf{part}(v, s) = \begin{cases} v & \text{if } v \in \mathcal{P} \\ \mathsf{part}(v', s) & \text{if } v \in \mathcal{F}, \text{where } (v, v(s), v') \in E \end{cases}$$

The compositional partition function $\mathsf{part}_D : \mathcal{S} \to \mathcal{P}$ is defined by:

$$\mathsf{part}_D(s) = \mathsf{part}(r_0, s)$$

Refinement of a CPD consists of replacing a terminal node representing a partition by a new branching node. Thus, a state s that was previously mapped to the refined partition is now redirected to a new sub-partition according to the value of $g(s)$ where g is the function labeling the new branching node.

Our refinement algorithm assumes the global system can be viewed as a set of distinct *components* $C_1 \in \mathcal{D}_1, \ldots, C_n \in \mathcal{D}_n$ and that a state of the system is obtained from the state of these components, i.e., $\mathcal{S} = \mathcal{D}_1 \times \ldots \times \mathcal{D}_n$. This naturally capture systems with a statically defined state vector (e.g., DVE systems [5], Petri nets). However, as the partition function dynamically evolves as the search progresses, this constraint could easily be relaxed. We denote by f_{C_i} the function that from a given state s returns the value of component C_i. During the refinement of partition p, the partition diagram is modified as follows. The algorithm first inspects the diagram to determine the functions F on which partition p is dependent. These functions label the branching nodes on the path from the root to the terminal node associated with p in the diagram. Then it picks a function $f_{C_i} \notin F$. Each of its outgoing branches leads to a new partition. At last, p_i is replaced in the diagram by the branching node f_{C_i}. We shall use the term *candidate component* (or simply candidate), to denote a component that can be used to refine a partition, i.e., any component C_i such that the refined partition is not already dependent on f_{C_i}.

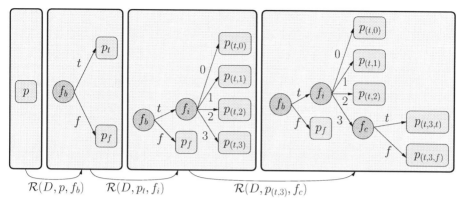

Fig. 2. A dynamic compositional diagram D

Figure 2 shows the graphical representation of a compositional partition diagram D that dynamically evolves as described above. We assume the following components are part of the underlying system: $b \in \{t, f\}$, $c \in \{t, f\}$ and $i \in \{0, 1, 2, 3\}$. Initially, there is a single partition p and all states are mapped to that partition. As p exceeds the allowed size, it is refined into p_t and p_f after the selection of the boolean component b to be used for the refinement. States already visited with $b = t$ are put in partition p_t and states with $b = f$ are put in p_f. Later, partition p_t becomes too large. Since this partition is already dependent on function f_b it would not make sense to refine it using component b: all states of p_t would be redirected to the same partition. Hence, the algorithm selects to refine it using component i. Partition p_t is thus split in $p_{(t,0)}$, $p_{(t,1)}$, $p_{(t,2)}$ and $p_{(t,3)}$ and states that were previously in p_t, i.e.,with $b = t$, are redirected to one of these according to the value of component i. Note that p_f is unchanged. Thus, states that satisfy $b = f$ will still be mapped to this partition whatever the value of their other components.

The definition below formalizes this idea of partition refinement.

Definition 3 (Partition refinement). *Let $D = (V, E, r_0, \mathcal{F}, \mathcal{P})$ be a CPD. The refinement $\mathcal{R}(D, f, p)$ of D with respect to $f : \mathcal{S} \to \mathcal{L}_f$ and $p \in \mathcal{P}$ is the CPD $D' = (V', E', r'_0, \mathcal{F}', \mathcal{P}')$ with:*

- *$\mathcal{F}' = \mathcal{F} \cup \{f\}$;*
- *$\mathcal{P}' = \mathcal{P} \setminus \{p\} \cup \mathcal{P}_{\mathcal{L}_f}$, where $\mathcal{P}_{\mathcal{L}_f} = \{p_l \mid l \in \mathcal{L}_f\}$ and $p_l = \{s \in p \mid f(s) = l\}$;*
- *$E' = E \setminus \{(v, l, q) \in E \mid q = p\} \cup \{(f, l, p_l) \mid l \in \mathcal{L}_f\} \cup \{(v, l, f) \mid (v, l, p) \in E\}$;*
- *$r'_0 = f$ (if $r_0 = p$), and $r'_0 = r_0$ (otherwise).*

The motivation behind this dynamic partitioning scheme is to benefit as much as possible from system properties. Usually, realistic systems are composed of many components, and events only modify a small fraction of them leaving others unchanged. Our refinement algorithm tries to minimize cross transitions by only selecting for each partition a few components to depend on. Let us consider, for instance, the last step in the evolution of the compositional diagram of Fig. 2.

All the states of partition $p_{(t,2)}$ have in common that $b = t \wedge i = 2$. Hence, from any state of this partition, an event that does not change the value of b or i will not generate a cross transition.

Clearly, the way the component is selected during a refinement step largely impacts the number of cross transitions it will cause. For instance, the worst choice would be to select a global variable updated by all events. In that case, any transition from a state of the resulting partitions will be a cross transition.

5 Selection of Candidate Components

We propose in this section several heuristics to efficiently select components to be used as a basis for the refinement. We classify these in two categories. *Static heuristics* perform an analysis of the model or sample the state space to order components. Then, during the search, the next component is always chosen according to that predetermined order. Hence along two different paths (of same length) of the partitioning diagram, we always find the same components in the same order. With *dynamic heuristics*, the component selected is chosen during the refinement step on the basis of data collected on-the-fly during the search.

Static Heuristics

Heuristic **SA***: Static Analysis.* With this first heuristic, the algorithm tries to predict from a static analysis of the model the modification frequency of components. The analysis performed is simple. We count for each state component, the number of events that modify it and order components accordingly in increasing order. Some weights may also be associated with events as we did in our implementation for the DVE language. For example, events nested in loops can be assigned a high weight as we can reasonably assume that their execution will occur frequently.

Heuristic **SS***: Static Sample.* Heuristic SA from above is based on a static analysis of the model and as such assumes a uniform distribution of event executions. However, in practice, this assumption is not always valid. Some events are typically executed only a few times, e.g., initialization events, whereas some will generate most of the state transitions. With heuristic SS, we attempt tackle this problem by first exploring a sample of the state space. An array of integers indexed by state components is maintained and each time an event is executed, the counters of all modified components are incremented. State components are then ordered according to the values of their counters, lowest values first. It is very important to perform a randomized search in order to explore a reasonably representative sample of the state space. A breadth-first search, for instance, would only explore the states of the first levels of the state space, and these usually share very few characteristics with the states we can find at deeper levels (and hence different executable events).

Dynamic Heuristics

Heuristic **DR***: $\underline{D}$ynamic $\underline{R}$andomized* This strategy picks out a component randomly from a set of candidates. The purpose of this strategy is only to serve as a baseline to assess the other dynamic strategies below.

Heuristic **DE***: $\underline{D}$ynamic $\underline{E}$vent execution* Heuristic DE is the dynamic equivalent of the heuristic SA: the array of integers specifying, for each component, the number of modifications of that component, is maintained as the state space exploration progresses. During a refinement step, the algorithm selects, among candidates, the one which has, until now, been the least frequently modified.

Heuristic **DD***: $\underline{D}$ynamic $\underline{D}$istribution.* The previous heuristics do not consider how well states are distributed among sub-partitions during a refinement step. This may, however, have important consequences in subsequent steps. Suppose that a partition p is refined in two sub-partitions, the first one, p_1, receiving 95% of the states of p, and the second one, p_2, receiving 5% of these states. Then, it is likely that during the next expansion step of partition p_1, new states will be added to p_1 which will cause it to exceed the maximal allowed size and hence to be refined. We can thus reasonably consider the first refinement to be useless. As refinement steps are costly — it entails writing back to disk each state in the partition currently loaded in memory — these refinements should be avoided as much as possible.

With heuristic DD, the refinement procedure simulates all possible refinements by computing for each state s of the partition to be refined the values $f_{C_{i_1}}(s)$, ..., $f_{C_{i_k}}(s)$, where $f_{C_{i_1}}, \ldots, f_{C_{i_k}}$ are the partition functions for the candidate components. This indicates how good the state distributions induced by the different candidates are. Then, the algorithm picks the component that achieves the lowest standard deviation, that is, the most even distribution of states among partitions. Applying $f_{C_{i_1}}, \ldots, f_{C_{i_k}}$ on all states does not incur a major time penalty. In the worst case (if all components are candidates), this is equivalent to compute a hash value on the entire state vector, which is usually negligible compared to the later writing of the state in the sub-partition file. In our experiments, we observed that, when heuristics DE and DDE (that extends DE with this "simulation" process, see below) exhibited comparable performances in term of disk accesses, the execution times were roughly the same.

Heuristic **DDE***: $\underline{D}$ynamic $\underline{D}$istribution and $\underline{E}$vent execution.* This last heuristic combines the idea of heuristics DD and DE: we prefer candidates that achieve a good state distribution and which is not frequently modified. During a refinement step, the following metric is computed for each candidate C_i:

$$h(C_i) = updates[i] \cdot std(C_i) \tag{1}$$

where $updates[i]$ is the number of modifications of component i recorded so far and $std(C_i)$ is the standard deviation in the sizes of sub-partitions obtained if component C_i is chosen for refinement. The algorithm picks the candidate having the lowest value.

6 Experiments

The PART algorithm of [1] as well as our dynamic partitioning technique have been implemented in the ASAP model checking platform [18]. We report in this section on experimental results obtained with this implementation. Additional data from the experiments can be found in [7].

Application of refinement to DVE systems. All models we have used are written in the DVE language and comes from the BEEM database [14]. We did not experiment with models belonging to the categories "Planning and scheduling" and "Puzzles" that are mostly toy examples having few common characteristics with real-life models. In the DVE language, the system is described as a set of automata synchronizing through communication channels and global variables. Communications can either be synchronous or asynchronous. An automaton is described as a set of states, local variables, and guarded events. To use our refinement algorithm, we considered as components each of the following items: the state of an automaton, i.e., its program counter; a variable (global or local); and the content of a communication channel. Arrays were considered as components although this obviously was not a good solution in some cases. We plan to refine that in a future implementation. Since the domain of variables can be very large and cannot be defined a priori, we used for each component C_i the component function $f_i = h_i(C_i) \bmod p$ where h_i is a hash function from $\mathcal{D}_i$ (the domain of component C_i), to $\mathbb{N}$ and p is the maximum number of sub-partitions we want a partition to be refined in (p was set to 20 in our implementation).

Experimental context. Apart from our refinement technique, we also implemented the static and dynamic partitioning schemes of [12] and [13] both using a local hash function that only refers to the part of the state vector corresponding to a specific process of the system. In our implementation of [13], a partition is split in two sub-partitions when it exceeds memory capacity: half of the classes that comprises the partition are put in a new partition. The process used for hashing was selected after an initial sampling of the state space. We selected the process which achieved both a uniform state distribution and a low number of cross transitions using heuristic h in Equation 1 from the previous section. The initial sampling was stopped after 100,000 states had been visited. This represents from 10% of the state space to less than 0.2% for the largest instances.

We experimented with PART using different partitioning schemes on 35 instances of the BEEM database having from $1 \cdot 10^6$ to $60 \cdot 10^6$ states. Since instances of the same model often have similar state spaces, we only kept for each model the instance with the largest state space. During each run we gave the PART algorithm the possibility to keep in memory at most 2% of the state space[1]. Half of this amount was given to the memory buffer of the state queue (remember that PART stores the queue on disk) and half was given to the partition loaded in memory. Hence, each partition could contain at most 1% of the total state space size. With static partitioning, it is impossible to put an upper bound on

---

[1] Other sizes were experimented: 10%, 5% and 1%. Due to lack of space, these experiments have been left out in this section, but can be found in [7].

a partition size. Therefore, assuming the distribution of states upon partitions might be unfair, we configured the static schemes with 256 partitions to guarantee (to the extend possible) that a partition will not contain more than 1% of the state space. For dynamic partitioning strategies, when a partition exceeded this capacity, it was automatically split using refinement with our algorithm or by reassigning classes of states to partitions with the algorithm of [13]. As noted earlier, the algorithm of [13] cannot guarantee an upper bound on a partition size: when a partition contains a single class it cannot be further reorganized.

Experimental results. Table 1 shows the result of our experiments. Due to lack of space, we only report the data for 14 representative instances, but still provide the average over the 35 instances experimented[2]. We performed 10 runs per instance, each with a different partitioning strategy. Each column provides data for a single run. For static and dynamic settings, GHC stands for "Global Hash Code": the partition function is the global hash function modulo the number of partitions; and LHC stands for "Local Hash Code": only the part of the state vector corresponding to a specific process is hashed, that is, the algorithms of [12] (in the static setting) and [13] (in the dynamic setting). Dynamic + Compositional is our refinement algorithm with the different heuristics proposed in Section 5: SA (Static + Analysis), SS (Static + Sample), DR (Dynamic + Randomized), DE (Dynamic + Event execution), DD (Dynamic + Distribution) and DDE (Dynamic + Distribution and Event execution). For heuristic SS, we performed exactly the same preliminary search as the one performed for strategies with LHC: we stopped the search after the visit of 100,000 states. For each instance, rows CT and IO provide the number of cross transitions and disk accesses performed (both for the queue and for disk partitions). Absolute values are given for column Static - GHC. Other values are relative to this one. The ϵ symbol is used to denote values less than 0.001. Best values have been highlighted in bold.

We first observe that, for most instances, heuristic DR performs worse than other heuristics. We found no instances where heuristic DR generated fewer cross than heuristics SS and DE. This confirms our initial intuition on the impact of the candidate's choice made during refinement.

Heuristic SS and heuristic DE (the dynamic equivalent of SS) exhibit comparable performances. This indicates that the preliminary randomized search often provides a very good sample of the state space. We only observed a notable difference for a few instances, especially the largest ones for which the sample was too small to be representative enough (e.g., `train-gate.7` and `collision.4`).

In [6], we observed that PART (using a global hash function to partition the state space) is not designed for long state spaces, i.e., state spaces with many levels, which should also hold for the distributed algorithm of [16]. To illustrate that, let us consider the extreme case where the graph is a long sequence of states. Using a good hash function we can assume the probability of a transition to be a cross transition is close to $\frac{N-1}{N}$ (where N is the number of partitions). Hence, with this state space structure, most transitions will immediately be followed by a partition swap. With a distributed algorithm, the search will consist of

---

[2] The complete table can be found in [7].

Table 1. Performance of PART with different partitioning schemes

	Static		Dynamic		Dynamic + Compositional					
	GHC	LHC	GHC	LHC	SS	SA	DR	DE	DD	DDE
	bopdp.3				*1,040,953 states*			*2,747,408 transitions*		
CT	2.7 M	0.091	0.965	**0.078**	0.223	0.300	0.311	0.183	0.256	0.306
IO	39 M	**0.148**	1.008	0.189	0.311	0.243	0.324	0.370	0.323	0.304
	brp.6				*42,728,113 states*			*89,187,437 transitions*		
CT	88 M	0.281	0.899	0.277	**0.040**	0.083	0.286	0.042	0.170	0.049
IO	5.9 G	0.346	1.057	0.292	0.132	0.130	0.979	0.123	**0.046**	0.082
	collision.4				*41,465,543 states*			*113,148,818 transitions*		
CT	112 M	0.088	0.969	0.087	0.078	0.030	0.255	**0.011**	0.131	0.056
IO	1.5 G	0.183	1.135	0.235	0.178	0.220	0.395	**0.176**	0.211	0.294
	firewire_link.5				*18,553,032 states*			*59,782,059 transitions*		
CT	59 M	0.262	0.981	0.254	0.054	0.050	0.173	**0.010**	0.346	0.017
IO	788 M	2.282	0.971	0.869	0.224	**0.190**	0.488	0.220	0.715	0.206
	firewire_tree.5				*3,807,023 states*			*18,225,703 transitions*		
CT	18 M	0.111	0.983	0.109	0.114	0.190	0.153	**0.065**	0.195	0.138
IO	141 M	**0.177**	0.969	0.461	2.148	0.323	0.665	0.757	0.248	0.287
	fischer.6				*8,321,728 states*			*33,454,191 transitions*		
CT	33 M	0.109	0.966	**0.107**	0.474	0.470	0.629	0.474	0.683	0.468
IO	130 M	**0.478**	1.221	0.547	0.896	0.915	0.980	0.874	0.855	0.840
	iprotocol.7				*59,794,192 states*			*200,828,479 transitions*		
CT	196 M	0.276	0.958	0.152	**0.003**	0.114	0.319	0.004	0.170	0.021
IO	2.6 G	1.390	1.090	0.634	**0.190**	0.220	1.383	0.209	0.784	0.211
	msmie.4				*7,125,441 states*			*11,056,210 transitions*		
CT	10 M	0.048	0.852	**0.047**	0.204	0.794	0.528	0.211	0.448	0.253
IO	97 M	**0.315**	0.925	0.419	0.603	1.013	0.739	0.545	0.797	0.556
	pgm_protocol.8				*3,069,390 states*			*7,125,121 transitions*		
CT	6.3 M	0.273	0.932	0.268	**0.024**	0.110	0.208	**0.024**	0.286	0.025
IO	255 M	0.447	0.800	0.303	**0.100**	0.145	0.373	**0.100**	0.185	0.102
	plc.4				*3,763,999 states*			*6,100,165 transitions*		
CT	6.0 M	0.018	0.985	0.017	ϵ	ϵ	0.073	ϵ	0.104	0.001
IO	1.3 G	0.085	1.251	0.107	0.030	**0.018**	0.393	0.030	0.110	0.020
	rether.7				*55,338,617 states*			*61,198,113 transitions*		
CT	60 M	0.040	0.980	**0.039**	0.042	0.049	0.183	0.051	0.106	0.093
IO	3.7 G	0.170	1.150	0.244	0.151	**0.128**	0.383	0.164	0.198	0.217
	synapse.7				*10,198,141 states*			*19,893,297 transitions*		
CT	19 M	0.301	0.970	0.297	0.014	0.012	0.238	**0.010**	0.451	0.015
IO	161 M	0.792	1.096	0.778	0.372	0.396	0.659	**0.325**	0.768	0.369
	telephony.7				*21,960,308 states*			*114,070,470 transitions*		
CT	111 M	0.245	0.976	**0.239**	0.450	0.450	0.495	0.447	0.708	0.505
IO	619 M	0.838	1.110	0.854	0.958	0.972	1.272	0.977	**0.715**	1.263
	train-gate.7				*50,199,556 states*			*106,056,460 transitions*		
CT	105 M	0.028	0.976	**0.027**	0.359	0.270	0.566	0.212	0.783	0.224
IO	1.7 G	**0.105**	1.332	0.142	0.392	0.498	1.771	0.318	0.751	0.321
	Average on 35 models									
CT	1.000	0.255	0.962	0.236	0.163	0.206	0.327	**0.152**	0.419	0.179
IO	1.000	0.504	1.050	0.496	0.458	0.423	0.661	0.411	0.531	**0.393**

a long series of message exchanges with processes constantly waiting for new states. A partition function that exploits model structure can fill that gap. For instances `brp.6`, `iprotocol.7`, `pgm_protocol.8`, `plc.4`, and `rether.7` that have long state spaces (up to almost 8000 levels for `plc.4`), all partitioning strategies based on the model structure significantly outperform strategies Static - GHC and Dynamic - GHC with respect to both cross transitions and disk accesses. Also, except for `rether.7`, compositional partitioning performs significantly better than partitioning based on a local hash code.

For `firewire_tree.5`, heuristic DE generates, after refinements, unfair state distributions which leads to most time being spent on reorganizing partitions. Thus, although it is the one that generates the fewest cross transitions, this has little consequences on the overall number of disk accesses. Heuristics DD and DDE that try to distribute states equally among partitions largely outperforms DE on that instance. This observation can be generalized to most instances experimented: heuristic DE is the one that minimizes cross transitions, but not necessarily disk accesses. It would be interesting to experiment with the two heuristics in a distributed environment. In [13] it is advised to delete states after a reorganization rather than sending them to its new owner which is claimed to be too expensive. This comes at the cost of possibly revisiting states that have been deleted. Intuitively, since heuristic DE performs more refinements it should cause the deletion and revisit of more states than DDE and, hence, generate more cross transitions and message exchanges. It is therefore not immediately clear which one should be preferred in a distributed setting.

Although we see some correlation between the number of cross transitions and disk accesses, this is not always the case. Firstly, for the reason that explains the bad performances of heuristic DE for instance `firewire_tree.5`: disk accesses are also triggered by partition refinements. Secondly, because the consequences of cross transitions largely depend on the stage of the search they occur at: as the search progresses, partitions contain more and more states which increases the cost of swapping. Finally, it suffices that one cross transition leads to a state of partition j when queue $\mathcal{Q}_j$ is empty to guarantee that partition j will eventually be loaded in memory. All subsequent cross transitions do not affect the algorithm. Hence, a large number of cross transitions linking two partitions is not necessarily a bad thing.

Synchronizations in models `telephony` and `fischer` are realized through global arrays modified by most events. As the refinement procedure currently implemented considers arrays as single components, our algorithm is not really efficient in these cases. A better management of arrays should improve this. This remark applies to most mutual exclusion algorithms we have experimented with.

Table 1 indicates that our refinement algorithm outperforms the partitioning algorithms of [12] and [13] although only slightly. However, the experiment reported here is quite unfair to our algorithm as no memory limit was (and could be) given to strategies Static - LHC and Dynamic - LHC whereas our refinement algorithm works within a bounded amount of RAM. Table 2 gives for all instances of Table 1 and for these two partitioning schemes, the proportion

Table 2. Ratio of overflowing states (given by Eq. 2) with static (S-LHC) and dynamic (D-LHC) partition functions of [12] and [13] based on local hash code

	S-LHC	D-LHC		S-LHC	D-LHC
bopdp.3	0.677	0.677	msmie.4	0.939	0.939
brp.6	0.735	0.735	pgm_protocol.8	0	0
collision.4	0.722	0.722	plc.4	0	0
firewire_link.5	0	0	rether.7	0.550	0.192
firewire_tree.5	0.785	0.785	synapse.7	0.090	0.035
fischer.6	0.969	0.969	telephony.7	0.827	0.827
iprotocol.7	0	0	train-gate.7	0.950	0.950

$$\sum_{p \in \text{partitions}} \frac{\max(\text{size of partition } p - \text{ memory limit per partition}, 0)}{\text{state space size}} \qquad (2)$$

of overflowing states (see Eq. 2 of Table 2) where, again, the memory limit per partition that was given to our algorithm is 1% of the total number of states.

When the algorithm could stay within allowed memory, LHC based partitioning is clearly outperformed by a refinement based partition function. This is evidenced by Table 1 showing that for models firewire_link.5, iprotocol.7, pgm_protocol.8, plc.4 and synapse.7, refinement based partitioning generates — sometimes considerably — fewer cross transitions and disk accesses. In contrast, when LHC based partitioning performed better it usually meant that it used more memory than what was given to our refinement algorithm. This is especially the case for models fischer.6, msmie.4 and train-gate.7.

7   Conclusions and Future Work

We have proposed in this paper a dynamic partitioning algorithm for external and distributed model checking, and extensively experimented with the disk-based algorithm of [1]. Our algorithm is based on the key idea of partition refinement. The search starts with a single partition and as memory becomes scarce, partitions are refined using new components of the analyzed system. Different heuristics have been proposed to appropriately select components during refinement steps. This scheme allows us to efficiently limit cross transitions at the cost of possibly generating unequal state distributions upon partitions compared to a partition function hashing the global state vector. However, our algorithm can still guarantee an upper bound on the size of any partition loaded in memory which previous approach like [12,13,15] could not. In addition to this, we have presented a common framework for external and distributed algorithms based on partitioning.

Our framework and results are also valid in the context of distributed memory verification. However, the choice of the heuristic is still an open question. Heuristic DE was apparently the best regarding cross transitions, but may not be the most appropriate as it can generate unfair state distributions and consequently more refinements that imply the deletion (and revisit) of more states. As part of a future work, we therefore plan to explore heuristics specifically designed for a distributed context.

References

1. Bao, T., Jones, M.: Time-Efficient Model Checking with Magnetic Disk. In: Halbwachs, N., Zuck, L.D. (eds.) TACAS 2005. LNCS, vol. 3440, pp. 526–540. Springer, Heidelberg (2005)
2. Bourahla, M., Benmohamed, M.: Efficient Partition of State Space for Parallel Reachability Analysis. In: AICCSA 2005, p. 21. IEEE Computer Society, Los Alamitos (2005)
3. Clarke, E.M., Grumberg, O., Peled, D.: Model Checking. MIT Press, Cambridge (1999)
4. Dill, D.L., Stern, U.: Using Magnetic Disk Instead of Main Memory in the Murϕ Verifier. In: Vardi, M.Y. (ed.) CAV 1998. LNCS, vol. 1427, pp. 172–183. Springer, Heidelberg (1998)
5. DVE Language, http://divine.fi.muni.cz/page.php?page=language
6. Evangelista, S.: Dynamic Delayed Duplicate Detection for External Memory Model Checking. In: Havelund, K., Majumdar, R., Palsberg, J. (eds.) SPIN 2008. LNCS, vol. 5156, pp. 77–94. Springer, Heidelberg (2008)
7. Evangelista, S., Kristensen, L.M.: Dynamic State Space Partitioning for External and Distributed Model Checking. Technical report, DAIMI – Aarhus University (2009), http://www.cs.au.dk/~evangeli/doc/ss-partitioning.pdf
8. Garavel, H., Mateescu, R., Smarandache, I.: Parallel State Space Construction for Model-Checking. In: Dwyer, M.B. (ed.) SPIN 2001. LNCS, vol. 2057, pp. 217–234. Springer, Heidelberg (2001)
9. Godefroid, P.: Partial-Order Methods for the Verification of Concurrent Systems. LNCS, vol. 1032. Springer, Heidelberg (1996)
10. Holub, V., Tuma, P.: Streaming State Space: A Method of Distributed Model Verification. In: TASE 2007, pp. 356–368. IEEE Computer, Los Alamitos (2007)
11. Holzmann, G.J.: State Compression in Spin: Recursive Indexing and Compression Training Runs. In: SPIN 1997 (1997)
12. Lerda, F., Sisto, R.: Distributed-Memory Model Checking with SPIN. In: Dams, D.R., Gerth, R., Leue, S., Massink, M. (eds.) SPIN 1999. LNCS, vol. 1680, pp. 22–39. Springer, Heidelberg (1999)
13. Lerda, F., Visser, W.: Addressing Dynamic Issues of Program Model Checking. In: Dwyer, M.B. (ed.) SPIN 2001. LNCS, vol. 2057, pp. 80–102. Springer, Heidelberg (2001)
14. Pelánek, R.: BEEM: Benchmarks for Explicit Model Checkers. In: Bošnački, D., Edelkamp, S. (eds.) SPIN 2007. LNCS, vol. 4595, pp. 263–267. Springer, Heidelberg (2007)
15. Rangarajan, M., Dajani-Brown, S., Schloegel, K., Cofer, D.D.: Analysis of Distributed Spin Applied to Industrial-Scale Models. In: Graf, S., Mounier, L. (eds.) SPIN 2004. LNCS, vol. 2989, pp. 267–285. Springer, Heidelberg (2004)
16. Stern, U., Dill, D.L.: Parallelizing the Murphi Verifier. In: Grumberg, O. (ed.) CAV 1997. LNCS, vol. 1254, pp. 256–278. Springer, Heidelberg (1997)
17. Valmari, A.: The State Explosion Problem. In: Reisig, W., Rozenberg, G. (eds.) APN 1998. LNCS, vol. 1491, pp. 429–528. Springer, Heidelberg (1998)
18. Westergaard, M., Evangelista, S., Kristensen, L.M.: ASAP: An Extensible Platform for State Space Analysis. In: ATPN 2009. LNCS, vol. 5606, pp. 303–312. Springer, Heidelberg (2009)
19. Zhou, R., Hansen, E.A.: Structured Duplicate Detection in External-Memory Graph Search. In: AAAI 2004, pp. 683–689. AAAI Press/The MIT Press (2004)

Compositional Verification of a Communication Protocol for a Remotely Operated Vehicle[*]

Alwyn E. Goodloe[1] and César A. Muñoz[2]

[1] National Institute of Aerospace
100 Exploration Way, Hampton, VA 23666, USA
Alwyn.Goodloe@nianet.org
[2] National Aeronautics and Space Administration
Langley Research Center, Hampton, VA 23681, USA
Cesar.A.Munoz@nasa.gov

Abstract. We present the specification and verification, in PVS, of a protocol intended to facilitate communication in an experimental remotely operated vehicle used by NASA researchers. The protocol is defined as a stack-layered composition of simpler protocols. It can be seen as the vertical composition of protocol layers, where each layer performs input and output message processing, and the horizontal composition of different processes concurrently inhabiting the same layer, where each process satisfies a distinct requirement. We formally prove that the protocol components satisfy certain delivery guarantees. Then, we demonstrate compositional techniques that allow us to prove that these guarantees also hold in the composed system. Although the protocol itself is not novel, the methodology employed in its verification extends existing techniques by automating the tedious and usually cumbersome part of the proof, thereby making the iterative design process of protocols feasible.

1 Introduction

A Remotely Operated Aircraft (ROA) is a distributed system where its critical components are dispersed between the airborne vehicle and the ground station. When flying, commands from the ground-based pilot are broadcast to the aircraft and telemetry data from the aircraft are broadcast to the ground station. Hence, communication between the air and ground components is critical for the safe operation of the vehicle. We present the formal verification, in the Prototype Verification System (PVS) [15], of a communications protocol designed for use in AirSTAR [2], a dynamically scaled experimental aircraft designed and built by NASA's Langley Research Center (LaRC) for use as a testbed for research on software health management and flight control. This protocol is formed from

---

[*] This work was supported by the National Aeronautics and Space Administration under NASA Cooperative Agreement NNX08AE37A awarded to the National Institute of Aerospace. This work was done while the second author was resident at the National Institute of Aerospace. Authors are in alphabetical order.

M. Alpuente, B. Cook, and C. Joubert (Eds.): FMICS 2009, LNCS 5825, pp. 86–101, 2009.
© Springer-Verlag Berlin Heidelberg 2009

the composition of several simpler protocols structured as a protocol stack. The verification approach presented in this paper is compositional allowing us to verify invariants of each component in the stack separately and then lifting those invariants to the composed system. We automate most of the proofs using PVS's proof scripting language. This promotes the iterative design of systems as laborious proofs need not be repeated by hand at each design iteration.

The mathematical development presented in this paper has been formally verified in PVS. This development is electronically available from `http://research.nianet.org/fm-at-nia/IVHM`.

2   Protocol Requirements

A ROA platform consists of an airborne vehicle and a ground station. Flight commands are sent from the ground station to the vehicle and telemetry data are sent from the aircraft to the ground station. Developments in both the design and application of ROAs have led to a number of innovations in wireless communication in this domain. For instance, a flock of ROAs may employ ad-hoc networking to imbue the collection with a routing capability allowing for sophisticated communication. AirSTAR, on the other hand, has a simple organization with one vehicle in the air and a single ground station, where the pilots are rarely out of visual sight of the aircraft and this is unlikely to change over the life of the aircraft. The aircraft currently uses a very simple communication scheme in which all broadcast messages are treated alike. Flight commands are time sensitive in the sense that if a message is lost or corrupted in transit, then it should not be resent because it would be considered stale by the time a new copy arrives. We call this requirement the *weak delivery requirement*. On the other hand, engineers and researchers on the ground need to receive all data produced by the aircraft in order to analyze aircraft performance as well as to plan future aircraft flights. Hence, the protocol should guarantee that all telemetry data broadcast is eventually delivered. We call this requirement the *guaranteed delivery requirement*.

We have been asked to design and formally verify a simple protocol that would satisfy these requirements without adding unneeded complexity such as routing. Since the requirements of weak and guaranteed delivery are in some sense orthogonal to each other, we structure the solution as two different protocols: the *weak delivery protocol* (WDP) and the *guaranteed delivery protocol* (GDP). The differences between WDP and GDP are similar to the differences between the User Datagram Protocol (UDP) and the Transmission Control Protocol (TCP) of the Internet protocol suite. However, WDP and GDP are considerably smaller, simpler, and more verifiable than UDP and TCP, which are considered to be too complex to be used in AirSTAR. In addition to these two protocols, other protocols are needed to support the communication between the aircraft and the ground station. In particular, we also consider a *link layer* that performs error detection and multiplexes WDP and GDP messages into the physical communication medium.

In this paper, we focus on *functional correctness*. Our correctness criteria for guaranteed delivery is that messages are received in the order they are sent. A liveness property says that the messages will eventually arrive. In the case of weak delivery, the correctness criteria states that every message received was in the sequence of messages that were sent. The protocol underwent several iterations and we employed a methodology that accommodated such evolution.

3   Protocol Stack

A collection of protocols is structured in a *protocol stack*, where each layer handles a different aspect of message processing. As a message moves down the stack, each layer performs some processing and adds packet headers. As a message moves up the stack, the corresponding packet headers are removed. Because there is no network layer for routing, the layers of our protocol stack roughly correspond to the application layer, transport layer, link layer, and physical layer. Given that the physical layer is concerned with the details of the communication hardware, we do not model it in our analysis. Instead, we model the communication medium, which we refer to as the *ether*.

At the top layer of our protocol stack is the application layer. All messages sent and received from the application layer are presumed to be sent via WDP or GDP depending on required message delivery guarantees. In other words, we assume that the application chooses between the WDP and GDP protocol when sending a message. The next layer down corresponds to the transport layer and it is here that the core of the GDP and WDP protocols reside. WDP simply sends a message, but provides no guarantee that the message ever arrived at its destination. Hence messages may be lost or corrupted in transit and are never resent. GDP is designed to provide its user with a guarantee that any message sent is eventually received. The link layer is the next layer in our protocol stack. Note that the GDP and WDP protocols directly interface with the link layer as there is no network layer. The *link layer* performs error detection and multiplexes the messages from the WDP and GDP layers. The ether models two communication channels over which messages are sent and received.

The proposed protocol stack is illustrated in Figure 1. The protocol stack can be viewed both vertically and horizontally. Vertically, each layer performs a specific transformation on a message, adding headers as it traverses down the stack and removing headers as it traverses up the stack. Horizontally, we see that GDP and WDP lie at the same layer, but they behave differently as they satisfy different requirements. These may be viewed as disjoint components occupying the same layer in the stack, but possess no shared state. On the other hand, the two layers interact with the same link layer. Consequently, the link layer is shared between the WDP and GDP components. Each protocol in the stack typically has a sender and receiver process. A message processed by the sender at one node should be processed by the receiver at the destination node.

In our model of the protocol stack, the protocol layers are connected using First In First Out (FIFO) queues. This structure is depicted in Figure 1, where

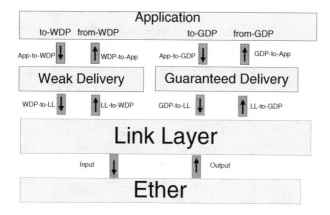

Fig. 1. Protocol stack

each queue is represented as a small rectangle with an arrow pointing in the direction of the information flow with a label naming the queue attached. Ignoring
the details of the application layer, we model the messages to be sent by WDP
and GDP by a pair of sequences `to-GDP` and `to-WDP`. At the receiving process,
the messages are placed in the pair of sequences `from-GDP` and `from-WDP`. Note
that the ether is not a protocol layer, but a model of the transport medium.

4   Protocol Specification

A specification of the protocol stack described in the previous section has been
constructed using PVS, which provides a rich specification language and a powerful theorem prover. The use of a theorem prover, as opposed to a model checker,
allows for a specification that is more abstract than an implementation, but concrete enough to provide a detailed description of the design amenable to rapid
prototyping. In the following, we give an overview of the specification of each
layer of the protocol stack.

4.1   Ether

The ether is specified as a pair of multisets (bags) that represent, respectively,
input and output communication channels.

$$\text{Ether} = \text{input} : \text{bag}[\text{LinkFrame}] \ \times \ \text{output} : \text{bag}[\text{LinkFrame}],$$

where `LinkFrame` is defined in Section 4.2. Our specification of the ether considers the fact that messages may be duplicated, corrupted, or dropped in the
physical layer or while in transit. The possible actions are defined by the type
`EtherAction` as follows:

```
DropIn(linkframe:LinkFrame) : DropIn? +
DupIn(linkframe:LinkFrame) : DupIn? +
NoiseIn(linkframe:LinkFrame) : NoiseIn?
```

where the constructor is defined left of the colon and a recognizer for the type defined to the right of the colon. The ether state machine, in effect, perturbs the ether by taking the current state and the action to perform and returns a transformed ether with a frame either corrupted, dropped, or duplicated. The PVS code for dropping a frame on the inbound was :

```
next(s:Ether,a:EtherAction) :Ether =  CASES a OF
    DropIn(linkframe) : s WITH [ `ether`input :=
        remove(linkframe,s`ether`input) ]
    . . .
```

which returns a new ether state with the value `linkframe` removed from the ether's input channel. Note the back-quote symbol is the PVS field access operator. In our models, the state machines are functional, but above this layer the model is relational. In this case, the relation

```
ether?(s,n:Ether) : bool = ∃(a: EtherAction) : n = next(s,a),
```

non-deterministically selects a valid action for the state machine to execute.

4.2   Link Layer

The link layer is intended to serve as an interface between the protocol stack and the communication medium, since we abstracted away the physical layer, as well as to provide common services needed by the protocols that lay at the next higher layer. The link layer also performs error detection, which in our model assumes the use of a check-sum. Furthermore, the link layer multiplexes messages sent from the WDP and GDP layers wrapping them in a common header, and demultiplexes them on the receiving side removing this header and sending the unwrapped frame to the appropriate protocol for processing.

A link layer frame is composed of a check-sum and either a GDP or WDP frame:

```
LinkFrame = cs: CheckSum × frame: Frame,
```

where the type `Frame` can be thought of as a disjoint sum of WDP and GDP frames. We do not model the details of performing a check-sum, but instead treat this functionality in an abstract way. The type `LinkInterface` is a 4-tuple formed from the four queues GDP-to-LL, WDP-to-LL, LL-to-GDP, and LL-to-WDP. The type `Link` is a tuple formed from the `LinkInterface` and the `Ether`. Hence, the type `Link` represents the state of all information entering and leaving the link layer.

The link layer functionality is represented by a transition function that, given the current `Link` and the action to perform, yields the next state, where the possible actions are: *send* a WDP message, *send* GDP message, and *receive* a message. If sending a WDP or GDP message, the sate machine removes a frame from the corresponding GDP-to-LL or WDP-to-LL queue, forms a link layer frame as the product of that frame and its check-sum, and places the result in the ether's input channel. If receiving a message, a LinkFrame is removed from the ether's output channel, the check-sum is verified and if invalid, the packet is dropped. Otherwise, the protocol checks if the packet is a GDP or WDP frame, strips off the check-sum, and places the message on the appropriate LL-to-GDP or LL-to-WDP queue. The state machine receive actions are expressed in PVS as follows:

```
Receive(linkframe) : IF  member(linkframe,s'ether'output)  THEN
  IF ¬ checksum?(linkframe) THEN
   s WITH [ 'ether'output := remove(linkframe,s'ether'output]
  ELSE CASES linkframe'frame OF
    GDP(gdpframe) :  s WITH [
      'link'll_to_gdp := enqueue(gdpframe,s'link'll_to_gdp),
      'ether'output := remove(linkframe,s'ether'output) ],

    WDP(wdpframe) : s WITH [
      'link'll_to_wdp := enqueue(wdpframe,s'link'll_to_wdp),
      'ether'output := remove(linkframe,s'ether'output) ]
    ENDCASES
  ENDIF
```

4.3   Weak Delivery Protocol

The Weak Delivery Protocol is extremely simple and so is its model. The type WDP is a 5-tuple formed from the two sequences to-WDP and from-WDP, the two queues App-to-WDP and WDP-to-App, and the LinkInterface. Sending a message is modeled as removing a message from the App-to-WDP queue and adding it to the WDP-to-LL queue. Receiving a message is modeled as removing a message from LL-to-WDP queue and adding it to the WDP-to-App queue.

4.4   Guaranteed Delivery Protocol

The Guaranteed Delivery Protocol shall satisfy the guaranteed delivery requirement. Following the standard solution to this problem, GDP is designed as a sliding-window protocol [19]. Discussions with the AirSTAR engineers revealed a communication pattern that led us to adapt a sliding-window protocol with block acknowledgment developed by Gouda [7, 8]. Although an informal proof may be found in the literature, ours appears to be the first attempt at a formal mechanical proof of the protocol.

Each GDP message has a sequence number that acts as an identifier. The receiver replies with a message acknowledging the receipt of a contiguous block of sequence of numbers. The sender and receiver maintain bounded windows, also called *windows*. The sender window `ackd` contains the messages sent that are waiting for a block acknowledgment. The receiver window, called `rcvd`, contains the messages received but not yet delivered to the application layer. The upper bounds of the sender's and receiver's windows are called, respectively, `sw` and `rw`. Each window entry has two fields: a data field and a Boolean mask field. The `ackd` mask field is set to false when that message is sent and true when an acknowledgment is received. The `rcvd` mask field is set to true when a message is received. The data in the buffers may be viewed as being indexed by the sequence numbers, although in the actual specification some amount of machinery is needed to map an unbounded range of sequence numbers to a bounded buffer.

The sender maintains the following pointers. The variable `ns` is a pointer to the sequence number of the next data item to be sent and the variable `na` is a pointer to the first sequence number that has yet to be acknowledged. That is, sequence numbers below `na` have all been acknowledged as received by the sender, but sequence number `na` has not yet been acknowledged. An invariant $na \leq ns \leq na + sw$ is maintained by the sender indicating that the window of sent but not acknowledged data is of size at most `sw`. The sender will not send messages with a sequence number greater than $na + sw$ until data message `na` is acknowledged. The sender may receive acknowledgments for sequence numbers k, where $na \leq k < ns$, in any possible order; yet, only when a block acknowledgment for the contiguous sequence numbers (na,n), where $n < ns$, has been received is the value of `na` slid forward to $n + 1$. If a timeout action occurs before message `na` is acknowledged, then it is resent.

The receiver maintains the following pointers. The variable `nd` points to the lowest sequence number that has yet to be delivered to the application layer. The variable `lr` points the highest sequence number that has yet to be received with the constraint that $lr \leq nd + rw$. The receiver accepts messages for sequence numbers k, where $lr \leq k < nd+rw$, in any order, and ignores messages out of this range. When the receiver has received the contiguous block of sequence numbers (nd,n) the pointer `nd` is slid forward to $n+1$ and the corresponding messages are delivered to the application layer. The variable `la` points to the last acknowledged sequence number, i.e., messages with a sequence number below `la` have all been acknowledged. Note that messages with a sequence number n, where $la \leq n \leq nd - 1$, have been received and delivered, but not yet acknowledged. Periodically, GDP sends the block acknowledgment for sequence numbers $(la, n - 1)$ and `la` is reset to `nd`.

4.5 Application Layer

The sender and receiver processes at the application layer are each composed of two state machines. At the sender, one machine maintains a pointer to the next message in `to-GDP` to be sent, copies that message to `App-to-GDP`, and increments the pointer. The other machine behaves similarly by copying messages from `to-WDP` to `App-to-WDP`. The receiver processes move messages from `GDP-to-App` to `from-GDP` and from `WDP-to-App` to `from-WDP`.

4.6   Composing Models

For each one of the WDP and GDP protocols, we will assume that we have two processes: a sender process and a receiver process. The WDP sender and receiver processes are called WDPSender? and WDPReceiver?, respectively. Similarly, the GDP sender and receiver processes are called GDPSender? and GDPReceiver?, respectively. These processes behave in a non-deterministic way. Hence, each one of them is defined as a relation between the current state and one of the possible next states. For instance, GDPSender?, which relates the current state of the GDP sender process and a possible next state, is defined as either a GDPSenderNext transition, a LinkNext transition, or a EtherNext transition, where the fields that are not modified by the transitions remain unchanged. The transitions are a function from the current state and an action to perform to the next state. In order to model the non-deterministic selection of actions, we use existential quantifiers to generate actions for each transition. The relation GDPSender? is formally expressed as follows:

GDPSender?$(s, n :$ GDPSender$) =$
  $(\exists\, a :$ GDPSenderAction. $n =$ GPDSenderNext$(s, a))$
$\bigvee$
  $(\exists\, a :$ LinkAction. $n_l =$ LinkNext(s_l, a)
    $\wedge\, n$'App_to_GDP $= s$'App_to_GDP $\wedge\, s$'winsender $= n$'winsender $)$
$\bigvee$
  $(\exists\, a :$ EtherAction. $n_e =$ EtherNext(s_e, a)
    $\wedge\, n$'link $= s$'link $\wedge\, n$'App_to_GDP $= s$'App_to_GDP
    $\wedge\, s$'winsender $= n$'winsender $),$

where s and n stand for the current and next GDPSender state, respectively, and the back-quote symbol is the field access operator. We denote by sub-indices l and e the projections of states s, n into Link and Ether states, respectively. The GDP receiver and WDP processes have a similar model.

5   Protocol Verification

In this paper, we focus on the functional correctness of WDP and GDP. The functional correctness of a system is usually expressed by *invariant safety and liveness properties*, i.e., predicates that hold in every reachable state of the system. For the purpose of this verification, we consider a system of two distributed nodes, one of which is the sender and the other is the receiver. The two nodes interact only trough the ether.

There are many relationships that are local to either the sender or the receiver. For instance, the property that states that the index of the next message to be sent is greater than or equal to the index of the next message waiting to be acknowledged, i.e., $na \leq ns$, only concerns the sender, and the property that states that the index of the next message to be delivered to the application layer is greater than or equal to the index of the last message to be acknowledged, i.e., $\mathtt{la} \le \mathtt{nd}$, only concerns the receiver. As these properties can be described solely in terms of the states of the GDP sender or the GDP receiver processes, they can be easily encoded using the PVS's subtype and dependent type system. These generate type correctness conditions, which most of the time can be automatically proved by the PVS type checker. The remainder of this section will focus on properties that relate the sender and receiver processes and consequently require more complex reasoning.

Let us consider the case of a system of two nodes *exclusively* running the WDP protocol. The state of this system, represented by the type WDPSystem, is a n-tuple composed of the union of the fields in WDPSender and WDPReceiver such that the input and output channels of the ether interface in the sender are connected, respectively, to the output and input channels of the ether interface in the receiver. The invariant predicate that expresses the correctness property of WDP is defined as follows:

$$\mathtt{wdp\_sound}(s : \mathtt{WDPSystem}) \equiv \mathtt{from\text{-}WDP}_s \subseteq \mathtt{to\text{-}WDP}_s,$$

where s refers to a reachable state. Henceforth, we will sub-indicate variables with the state to which they belong, e.g., $\mathtt{from\text{-}WDP}_s$ refers to state of the sequence from-WDP in state s and $\mathtt{to\text{-}WDP}_s$ refers to the state of the to-WDP sequence in s. This invariant states that all WDP messages that the receiver node delivers to the application layer were indeed sent by the sender's application layer.

In the case of a system of two nodes *exclusively* running the GDP protocol, the state, represented by the type GDPSystem, is a n-tuple composed of the union of the fields in GDPSender and GDPReceiver. The ether in the sender and receiver sides are connected in a similar way as in the WDP. The invariant predicate that expresses the correctness property of GDP is defined as follows:

$$\mathtt{gdp\_sound}(s : \mathtt{GDPSystem}) \equiv \mathtt{from\text{-}GDP}_s \preceq \mathtt{to\text{-}GDP}_s,$$

where $\preceq$ is the prefix relation between sequences. This invariant states that GDP messages are delivered by the receiver to the application layer in the same order as they were sent by the sender's application layer.

For GDP, we consider a traditional fairness property [16], which states that all messages in the to-GDPqueue are eventually sent. That is, for every message in to-GDP, it is eventually the case that a state is recorded where each message has been sent. Since it is an invariant that $\mathtt{ns}$ always points to the next item to be sent, we can state the fairness property as saying that given any run of the protocol, for every sequence number m the run records a state where $\mathtt{ns} > m$. This is stated formally as follows:

$$\mathrm{fair}[(run)] = \lambda(r : (run)) : \ \forall(m : \mathrm{Nat}) : \ \exists(n : \mathrm{Nat}) : r_n\mathrm{'ns} > m.$$

The predicate live states that all data is eventually delivered. Formally, this is expressed as a predicate on the runs of the protocol as follows:

$$\text{live}[(\text{run})] = \lambda(r : (run)) : \forall(m : \text{Nat}) : \exists(n : \text{Nat}) : r_n \text{'nd} > m.$$

The liveness property is then given as:

$$\text{liveness}[(\text{run})] = \lambda(r : (run)) : \text{fair}(r) \Rightarrow \text{live}(r).$$

Our primary verification objective is to formally prove that the predicates, wdp_sound, gdp_sound, and liveness are indeed invariants when both WDP *and* GDP run simultaneously in each node. Technically, this system is the *asynchronous composition* of WDP and GDP and we will denote it by WDP ∥ GDP. To verify wdp_sound, gdp_sound, and liveness in the composed system, we propose a compositional approach where each invariant is independently proved for its respective system, i.e., wdp_sound is an invariant of WDP and gdp_sound is an invariant of GDP, and then we provide a general framework that enables us to lift an invariant on one system, e.g., gdp_sound on GDP, to an invariant on a composition of systems, e.g., gdp_sound on WDP ∥ GDP.

5.1 Proving Invariants on WDP and GDP, Independently

Proving invariants on transition systems, such as WDP or GDP, are routine in the theorem proving community. It usually entails the transformation of the initial invariant to a weaker form that can be proved by induction. In our case, we use a simple set of theories developed by Rusu [16] for proving invariants on discrete transition systems by natural induction on the length of the system traces. The nontrivial task of finding auxiliary invariants that enable the inductive proof of the original invariant is subject to the ingenuity of the human prover.

For WDP and GDP the problem is made harder by the fact that we have to consider the full protocol stack and all possible interleavings between the sender and receiver processes. We have seen in Section 4.6 that the sender and receiver components of each protocol are formed from the disjunction of a number of relations representing the layers of the stack. This means that that an invariant must be shown to hold under each transition in each layer. Consequently, each proof requires the discharge of a large number of cases. For each one of these cases we have to prove that if an invariant is satisfied at step n, it is also satisfied at step $n + 1$. This is a considerable amount of work even though many of the cases can be easily discharged by using general properties of bags, queues, and buffers.

To automate the verification task, we have defined a set of proof strategies that are applied to discrete transition systems defined in PVS using Rusu's theories. The use of such strategies form the basis of a methodology that we believe will allow Rusu's techniques to scale to industrial-size problems. The strategies basically unfold the transition relations and discharge the easy cases of inductive proofs. For instance, to prove an invariant on GDP, we invoke the strategy unroll-gdp that, in turn, invokes strategies unroll-gdp-sender and `unroll-gdp-receiver` as well as strategies to unroll the application layer sender and receiver processes. The `unroll-gdp-sender` strategy, for example, expands the relational definitions, instantiating and skolemizing quantifiers as needed, until it finally expands the definitions of the state machines. In the case of the state machine `GDPSenderNext`, the strategy "lifts" the conditionals so as to expose the guarded cases, which, in turn, are discharged using PVS's assert decision procedure. Additional support strategies are employed that apply properties of structures such as bags, FIFO queues, and bounded buffers to simplify expressions to the point where basic decision procedures can be applied to complete the proof. Even in the cases where the strategies do not succeed, they generate enough information to assist a developer in finding weaker invariants.

To perform the proof of `wdp_sound`, the first command is our strategy `discharge-inv`, which automatically proves all but two inductive cases. The first case is discharged by simply unfolding a definition. The second unproven case suggests the need for an invariant saying that all frames in `WDP-to-App` are in `to-WDP`:

$$\texttt{WDP-to-App}_s \subseteq \texttt{to-WDP}_s.$$

To prove this we need an additional auxiliary invariant that states that WDP frames in the link layer and in the ether belong to `to-WDP`. Once this invariant is added as a lemma to the theory, the proof is finished by using our strategy `use-inv`. To prove the auxiliary invariant, we use the same approach, which suggests the new invariant:

$$\texttt{App-to-WDP}_s \subseteq \texttt{to-WDP}_s.$$

This new invariant is automatically discharged by `discharge-inv`.

The proof of `gdp_sound` is considerably more complicated, but the general method is the same. We use our strategy `discharge-inv` to eliminate the easy cases and we add new invariants to discharge the unproven cases via `use-inv`. We iterate this approach on the new invariants. In total we have added 6 auxiliary invariants to the GDP theory, including the following relations between the sender's and receiver's windows:

- The counter of received messages is less than or equal to the counter of sent messages: $\texttt{lr}_s \leq \texttt{ns}_s$
- The counter of delivered messages is less than or equal to the counter of sent messages: $\texttt{nd}_s \leq \texttt{ns}_s$
- The largest sequence number for which an acknowledgment has been received is less than or equal to the counter of the sent acknowledgments

$$\texttt{na}_s + \texttt{last\_true}(\texttt{ackd}_s) \leq \texttt{la}_s,$$

where the function `last_true` returns the difference between $\texttt{na}_s$ and the largest sequence number for which an acknowledgment has been received.

The stack structure considerably affects the size of the proofs as we need to ensure that an invariant is not violated at different layers. Although most of the manual tasks are routine, scale becomes a prohibitive factor that will get worse in larger models. If heavy-weight formal methods are to be used in industrial practice, they must accommodate an iterative design process. Manually proving the GDP process after even a simple design change can take much of a day and the prospect of repeatedly doing so for each design iteration is not practical. Our strategies are written in a lisp-like PVS scripting language and are composed of 937 lines of code. To maintain a high degree of automation, changes to the model are reflected in the strategy code, which is an integral part of our iterative design methodology. All the strategies and proofs can be found at the aforementioned web site.

5.2 Proving Invariants on the Asynchronous Composition of WDP and GDP

We have seen that `wdp_sound` is an invariant of WDP and that `gdp_sound` is an invariant of GDP. However, our verification objective is to show that both of them are also invariants of WDP ∥ GDP. This goal could be trivially achieved if WDP and GDP were completely independent. They are not. The GDP and WDP sender and receiver processes share the same link layer and ether interfaces. We could prove `wdp_sound` and `gdp_sound` are invariants of WDP ∥ GDP using the method explained in the previous section. However, in that case we do not profit from the invariants we have already proven for WDP and GDP independently, and we are obliged to reprove these invariants for all possible interleavings of WDP and GDP.

We propose a different approach. Instead of reproving all the invariants, we develop, in PVS, a general theory of asynchronous composition of transition systems where invariants on one system can be *lifted* to the composed system. To this end, we consider that the state of a transition system consists of a private state and a shared state. The state of the composed system has a copy of the private states of each transition system but only one shared state common to both of them. When the composed system performs a transition of one system, the private state of the other system remains unchanged.

We define a transition system as follows. Let V be a finite set of typed variables and Θ an initial condition defined on the variables. Define state S_V as a type-consistent valuation of the variables. A transition is a relation $\rightarrow$ in $S_V \times S_V$. A transition system is defined as the tuple $T = (S_V, \Theta, \rightarrow)$. Given two transition systems $T_1 = (S_{V_1}, \Theta_1, \rightarrow_{T_1})$ and $T_2 = (S_{V_2}, \Theta_2, \rightarrow_{T_2})$, we define $T_1 \parallel T_2 = (S_{V_1 \cup V_2}, \Theta_{T_1 \parallel T_2}, \rightarrow_{T_1 \parallel T_2})$ as follows: the state space $S_{V_1 \cup V_2}$ is a valuation of the variables in V_1 and V_2. Let $s \in S_{V_1 \cup V_2}$, we then define the restriction operators $s{\downarrow}_{T_i}$ and $s{\downarrow}_{[T_i]}$, for $i = \{1, 2\}$. The first operator projects the composed state to the state of T_i, which only includes the private and shared state of T_i. The second operator only projects the private part of T_i.

The composed initial state is defined as

$$\Theta_{T_1 \parallel T_2} = \{ s : S_{V_1 \cup V_2} \mid s{\downarrow}_{T_1} \in \Theta_{T_1} \wedge s{\downarrow}_{T_2} \in \Theta_{T_2} \},$$

and the composed transition relation is defined as

$$s \rightarrow_{T_1 \| T_2} s' \ = \ \{(s, s') : S_{V_1 \cup V_2} \times S_{V_1 \cup V_2} \mid s{\downarrow}_{T_1} \rightarrow_{T_1} s'{\downarrow}_{T_1} \wedge s{\downarrow}_{[T_2]} = s'{\downarrow}_{[T_2]}$$
$$\vee \ s{\downarrow}_{T_2} \rightarrow_{T_2} s'{\downarrow}_{T_2} \wedge s{\downarrow}_{[T_1]} = s'{\downarrow}_{[T_1]}\}.$$

We define a simulation relation that we call an *abstraction* α of a transition system T as a function that maps states into states such that

1. if s_0 is an initial state in T, then $\alpha(s_0)$ is also an initial state of T, and
2. if $s_n \rightarrow_T s_{n+1}$ then $\alpha(s_n) \rightarrow_T \alpha(s_{n+1})$.

The following theorem tells us when an invariant on the left-hand side of the parallel operator is an invariant of the composed system.

Theorem 1 (Invariant Left-Lifting). *Let P be an invariant of a transition system T_1. The predicate $P_{T_1 \| T_2}$, where $P_{T_1 \| T_2}(s : S_{V_1 \cup V_2}) \equiv P(s{\downarrow}_{T_1})$, is an invariant of the transition system $T_1 \| T_2$ if there is an abstraction α of T_1 such that the following conditions are met:*

1. *α is fixed under P, i.e., $P(\alpha(s{\downarrow}_{T_1}))$ implies $P(s{\downarrow}_{T_1})$, and*
2. *under the abstraction α, T_2 does not interfere with T_1, i.e., given s_n, s_{n+1} : $S_{V_1 \cup V_2}$, if $s_n{\downarrow}_{T_2} \rightarrow_{T_2} s_{n+1}{\downarrow}_{T_2}$ then $\alpha(s_n{\downarrow}_{T_1}) \rightarrow_{T_1} \alpha(s_{n+1}{\downarrow}_{T_1})$.*

Proof (Sketch of PVS Proof). Consider an arbitrary trace $s_0, \ldots, s_n$ in $T_1 \| T_2$. We will show that P holds in s_n. First, we show that $\alpha(s_0{\downarrow}_{T_1}), \ldots, \alpha(s_n{\downarrow}_{T_1})$ is a trace in T_1. There are two cases:

1. The transition (s_i, s_{i+1}) is transition in T_1. In this case, $\alpha(s_i{\downarrow}_{T_1}) \rightarrow_{T_1} \alpha(s_{i+1}{\downarrow}_{T_1})$ since α is an abstraction of T_1.
2. The transition (s_i, s_{i+1}) is a transition in T_2. In this case, $\alpha(s_i{\downarrow}_{T_1}) \rightarrow_{T_1} \alpha(s_{i+1}{\downarrow}_{T_1})$ since T_2 does not interfere with T_1.

Therefore, $\alpha(s_0{\downarrow}_{T_1}), \ldots, \alpha(s_n{\downarrow}_{T_1})$ is a trace in T_1. Since P is an invariant on T_1, P holds in $\alpha(s_i{\downarrow}_{T_1})$, for $i \leq n$. Since α is fixed under P, P holds in $s_i{\downarrow}_{T_1}$ as well. The result then follows from the fact that $P_{T_1 \| T_2}(s_i)$ is defined as $P(s_i{\downarrow}_{T_1})$. $\square$

A symmetric theorem for the right transition system can be proved in a similar way. Both theorems have been mechanically proven in PVS and both the formalization and proof can be found online.

For the case of the distributed system WDP $\|$ GDP, the queues App-to-WDP and WDP-to-App are private to WDP. Although the sequences to-WDP and from-WDP reside in the application layer, for analytical purposes we can view them as belonging to WDP since they are not shared in any way with the GDP processes. The queues App-to-GDP and GDP-to-App as well as the fields winsender and winreceiver are private to GDP. All the other fields. i.e., the link and the ether interfaces, are shared. It should be noted that although these structures are shared, it is not like classical shared variable concurrency in the sense that the WDP and GDP processes do not share variables to which they both read and write. Instead, the shared structures provide a service to the WDP and GDP layers, but by design, the frames written by one higher-layer protocol will never be transformed into frames from a different layer protocol and frames written by a higher-layer protocol will never be delivered to a different higher-layer protocol.

We now show that wdp_sound is an invariant of WDP ∥ GDP via an application of Invariant Lifting.

Theorem 2 (WDP Soundness). *WDP_sound is an invariant on WDP ∥ GDP.*

For the proof of WDP, the abstractions that we need are filters that remove, respectively, GDP packets from the link layer and the ether interface.

Proof (Sketch of PVS Proof). We consider an abstraction $\alpha_w(s : \text{WDP})$ such that $\alpha_w(s) = s$ in all fields but:

$$\alpha_w(s`\text{link`GDP\_to\_Link}) = \text{empty},$$
$$\alpha_w(s`\text{link`Link\_to\_GDP}) = \text{empty},$$
$$\alpha_w(s`\text{ether`input}) = \text{remove\_gdp}(s`\text{ether`input}),$$
$$\alpha_w(s`\text{ether`output}) = \text{remove\_gdp}(s`\text{ether`output}),$$

where empty is the empty queue and remove_gdp removes all GDP frames from a multiset. Then, we prove that α_w is indeed an abstraction of WDP, that WDP_sound is fixed to α_w, and that, under α_w, GDP does not interfere with WDP. Therefore, by the fact that the invariant WDP_sound holds on WDP and theorem 1, WDP_sound is an invariant on WDP ∥ GDP.   □

The hypotheses to the theorem are automatically discharged by strategies that we have developed to prove that a given function is an abstraction, that an abstraction is fixed to an invariant, and that the noninterference condition holds. The statement and proof that gdp_sound is an invariant of WDP ∥ GDP is similar.

6   Related Work and Conclusion

Numerous variations of the basic sliding window protocol have been subjected to hand verification techniques. Stenning [18] is likely to have been the first to discuss the correctness of such protocols. Snepscheut [6] and Hoogerwoord [10] are representative of this work. Process algebras have also been used to manually verify one-bit sliding window protocols [20,3]. Like our own work [1] considers a protocol with arbitrary, but finite window size while others assume an unbounded window size. Model checking has been applied to verifying a number of sliding window protocols e.g. [9,12,17], but to prevent state explosion the window size has to be kept to a relatively small size.

Others have applied automated theorem provers to verify sliding window protocols. Cardell-Oliver used HOL to verify safety properties [4]. A timed model was given in [5] and a safety property is verified using PVS. Rusu [16] proved safety and liveness of a protocol with unbounded window size in PVS.

Concurrently executing programs are complex artifacts making it difficult to reason about their correctness. For parallel programs with shared variables, the classical theory of Owicki and Gries [14] was the first breakthrough for reasoning about the correctness of parallel programs having shared variables, but the theory is not compositional. Assume-Guarantee methods modify the theory to be compositional [11,21]. Nieto [13] formalized rely-guarantee in Isabelle. Our approach is not as general as these techniques, but was targeted toward the system under analysis, yet is largely mechanizable as we have shown here.

We have presented the verification of a small communication protocol stack intended to be used by remotely operated vehicles. We have formulated and proved the soundness and liveness properties of the GDP and WDP stack components.

All the mathematical development presented here, including the framework to compose transition systems, was formally carried out in the PVS verification system and is publicly available. In order to facilitate an iterative design process, we developed novel proof strategies to automate tedious and complex tasks in the verification process, such as finding inductive invariants and proving safety properties of composed systems. As an added feature, the strategies are robust to changes in the protocol specification. Therefore, protocol modifications usually require only minor changes in the soundness proofs rather than having to redo all the proofs by hand. We believe that this complements the techniques in [16] by allowing them to be applied to larger systems where the designs evolve over time.

Finally, since the protocol is specified in the declarative specification language of PVS, it is amenable to rapid prototyping. Indeed, using recently added PVS features, we were able to automatically generate Java code that implements the functional and deterministic aspects of the protocol, although we recognize that an actual implementation will likely be structured somewhat differently for efficiency. However, we expect the semantics to be preserved allowing our prototype to serve as a semantic benchmark for the implementation.

Acknowledgements

The author would like to thank the AirSTAR team and in particular David Cox for their technical support, and Eric Cooper, Paul Miner and the anonymous referees for their comments that help to improve the presentation of this work.

References

1. Badban, B., Fokkink, W., Groote, J., Pang, J., van de Pol, J.: Verification of a sliding window protocol in μCRL and PVS. Formal Aspects of Computing 17, 342–388 (2005)
2. Bailey, R., Hostetler, R., Barnes, K., Belcastro, C., Belcastro, C.: Experimental validation subscale aircraft ground facilities and integrated test capability. In: Proceedings of the AIAA Guidance Navigation, and Control Conference and Exhibit 2005, San Francisco, California (2005)

 3. Brunekreff, J.: Sliding window protocols. In: Algebraic Specification of Protocols. Cambridge Tracts in Theoretical Computer Science, vol. 36, pp. 71–112 (1993)
 4. Cardell-Oliver, R.M.: The Formal Verification of Hard Real-Time Systems, PhD thesis. University of Cambridge, Cambridge (1992)
 5. Chkliaev, D., Hooman, J., de Vink, E.: Verification and improvement of the sliding windonw protocol. In: Garavel, H., Hatcliff, J. (eds.) TACAS 2003. LNCS, vol. 2619, pp. 113–127. Springer, Heidelberg (2003)
 6. Van de Snepscheut, J.L.A.: The sliding-window protocol revisited. Formal Aspects of Computing 7, 3–17 (1995)
 7. Gouda, M.: Elements of Network Protocols. Wiley-Interscience, Hoboken (1998)
 8. Gouda, M., Multari, N.: Stabilizing communication protocols. IEEE Transactions on Computers 40(4), 448–458 (1991)
 9. Holzmann, G.: The model checker Spin. IEEE Transactionsactions of Software Engineerng 23(4), 279–295 (1997)
10. Hoogerwoord, R.: A formal derviation of a sliding window protocol. Technical University of Eindhoven (2006)
11. Jones, C.: Tentative steps toward a method for interfering programs. ACM Transactions of Programming Languages and Systems (TOPLAS) 5(4), 596–619 (1983)
12. Kaivola, R.: Using compositional preorders in the verification of a sliding window protocol. In: Grumberg, O. (ed.) CAV 1997. LNCS, vol. 1254, pp. 48–59. Springer, Heidelberg (1997)
13. Nieto, L.: The rely-guarantee method in Isabelle/HOL. In: Degano, P. (ed.) ESOP 2003. LNCS, vol. 2618, pp. 348–362. Springer, Heidelberg (2003)
14. Owicki, S., Gries, D.: An axiomatic proof technique for parallel programs. Acta Informatica 6, 319–340 (1976)
15. Owre, S., Rushby, J., Shankar, N.: PVS: A prototype verification system. In: Kapur, D. (ed.) CADE 1992. LNCS, vol. 607, pp. 748–752. Springer, Heidelberg (1992)
16. Rusu, V.: Verifying a Sliding-Window Using PVS. In: Formal Techniques for Networked and Distributed Systems (FORTE 2001), pp. 251–266. Kluwer Academic, Dordrecht (2001)
17. Stahl, K., Baukus, K., Lakhnech, K., Steffen, Y.: Divide, abstract, and model check. In: Dams, D.R., Gerth, R., Leue, S., Massink, M. (eds.) SPIN 1999. LNCS, vol. 1680, pp. 57–76. Springer, Heidelberg (1999)
18. Stenning, N.: A data transfer protocol. Computer Networks 1(2), 99–110 (1976)
19. Tannenbaum, A.: Computer Networks, 3rd edn. Prentice Hall, Englewood Cliffs (1996)
20. Vaandrager, F.: Verification of two communication protocol by means of process algebra. Technical report, CWI (1986)
21. Xu, Q., de Roever, W., He, J.: The rely-guarantee method for verifying shared variable concurrent programs. Formal Aspects of Computing 9(2), 149–174 (1997)

Modeling Concurrent Systems
with Shared Resources

Ángel Herranz[1], Julio Mariño[1], Manuel Carro[1], and Juan José Moreno Navarro[2]

[1] Universidad Politécnica de Madrid
[2] Spanish Ministry of Science and Innovation

Abstract. Testing is the more widely used approach to (partial) system validation in industry. The introduction of concurrency makes exhaustive testing extremely costly or just impossible, requiring shifting to formal verification techniques. We propose a methodology to design and verify a concurrent system that
splits the verification problem in two independent tasks: internal verification of
shared resources, where some concurrency aspects like mutual exclusion and conditional synchronisation are isolated, and external verification of processes, where
synchronisation mechanisms are not relevant. Our method is language independent, non-intrusive for the development process, and improves the portability of
the resulting system. We demonstrate it by actually checking several properties
of an example application using the TLC model checker.

Keywords: Validation, Verification, Shared resource, Concurrency.

1 Introduction

Concurrency is a key aspect in many software systems and often a reason for their
failure as well, as programming concurrent systems is notoriously more difficult and
error-prone than programming sequential systems. Almost every aspect the programming gets worse when several processes have to be considered at once: language constructs, library availability (and multi-thread safeness), debugging, runtime exceptions
and their semantics, specification and verification, etc.

Although it is common for industrial software to restrict features that can be a potential source of hazards (e.g. by enforcing adherence to certain coding rule sets), many
applications show some degree of implicit concurrency that cannot be ignored, or which
brings about advantages which make them highly interesting. A recent example is the
trend towards multi-task web browsers where every web page, or even every component in a web page, is handed out to a different thread in order to improve security and
stability by sandboxing these threads.

Unfortunately, there is still much room for improvement in terms of methods, tools
and language support for the development of concurrent software in industrial environments. To make things worse, software developers are in general insufficiently trained.
The following paragraphs outline what we think are some of the most salient issues.

Good Language Support. While some languages deploy good support for concurrency, with some of them providing developers with platform-independent constructs

M. Alpuente, B. Cook, and C. Joubert (Eds.): FMICS 2009, LNCS 5825, pp. 102–116, 2009.

(e.g. Ada, Java, C#...), there are still application niches where the use of languages less suited for concurrency, like C or C++, is mandatory. In these cases, concurrency is only possible through the use of certain mechanisms with not so clear semantics and, sometimes, subject to change. Even when support is good, clear design guidelines / patterns are not in widespread use.

Methodology. There are no standard notations or tools to model concurrent systems which at the same time help developers in clearly documenting this aspect of software in isolation from other requirements — the concurrency equivalent for UML/OCL is not yet here. As a result, concurrency is often poorly documented and the chances that some concurrency requirements are lost are considerable.

Validation and verification. The inherent nondeterminism introduced by concurrency and the execution conditions often specific to the application itself (specially in an industrial environment) make standard testing techniques unreliable, more expensive, or directly inapplicable. This is one of the reasons to emphasise the use of formal techniques for the verification of this kind of software. Unfortunately, support for concurrency is still scarce in existing verification tools, which only deal with language subsets which do not include synchronisation and communication primitives. An ongoing European COST action on verification of O.O. software [2] places concurrency among one of the three major challenges of verification technology for O.O. languages, along with genericity and components.

Portability. Given the dependability often associated with industrial software, the risks (and costs) associated with making an upgrade or porting a running system are huge. Very often, systems of this kind become legacy code fossils that nobody dares to touch. The risk, then, is that any seemingly innocent change in the execution environment (hardware, operating system, running conditions...) may affect its behaviour in unpredictable ways.[1]

There probably no single solution for these problems. But it seems that promoting the separation of concerns when designing, providing developers with (graphical) notations that address concurrency at the same level as other aspects, isolating the code which depends on synchronisation and communication primitives from the rest, and giving hints for the practical verification of concurrent software are steps in the right direction.

Here, we are proposing an approach to the development of concurrent systems based on a sharp distinction between *active* (processes, clients) and *passive* (interactions, resources) entities. This admittedly simplistic view of concurrency will help us, however, in achieving some of the aforementioned goals. For example, synchronisation and communication primitives (often language-dependent) will appear only inside the implementation of the shared resources, not in the process code. This separation will make possible to work on the verification of the processes on relatively standard grounds. On the other hand, the implementation of the shared resources will be ensured to be correct *by construction*, using template-based code generation schemes both for shared

---

[1] And, in fact, it is the case that whole lines of hardware and tools (e.g., compilers) have been maintained for the sole purpose of keeping this kind of systems running untouched.

memory and message-passing schemes [1], rather than verified *a posteriori*. This enormously simplifies portability. Also, the method is supported by a graphical notation intended to be reminiscent of UML class and collaboration diagrams.

The rest of the paper is organised as follows: Section 2 gives an informal overview of the method and the notation by means of an example. Section 3 presents a translation of shared resources into TLA. This serves two purposes: on one hand, it provides an *interlingua* semantics, and, secondly, the translation is used as the basis for a practical method to check properties of a concurrent system using the TLC model checker (Section 4). Section 5 summarises our results, discusses related approaches, and points out to future improvements.

2   Specifying Shared Resources by Example

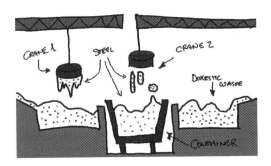

Fig. 1. Recycling plant

In this section we will introduce an example which will be used throughout the rest of the paper and we will use this example to present our resource-oriented notation [1]. We will present the intended semantics of the specification language without formal apparatus but, hopefully, with clarity enough to justify its translation into TLA+ and to grasp the more relevant points of our notation.

2.1   The Recycling Plant Example

In a recycling plant (Fig. 1), steel is recovered from unsorted domestic waste with automatically controlled cranes equipped with electromagnets: cranes collect steel and deposit it in a container until the container is (nearly) full. The crane controller is accessed using a library with a public API, part of which appears next.

```
package Cranes is
   MAX_CRANES : constant Positive := 5;
   subtype Crane_Id is Positive range 1 .. MAX_CRANES;
   MIN_W_CRANE : constant Positive := 1000;
   MAX_W_CRANE : constant Positive := 1500;
   subtype Weight is Positive range MIN_W_CRANE .. MAX_W_CRANE;
   -- Grab the steel and report its weight
   procedure Collect (N : in Crane_Id; W : out Weight);
   -- Move the crane to a dropping point and
   -- deactivate the electromagnet.
   procedure Drop (I : Crane_Id);
end Cranes;
```

The container is also electronically controlled, and its relevant API is:

```
package Container is
    MAX_W_CONTAINER : constant Natural := 20000;
    -- Replace the current container with an empty one
    procedure Replace;
end Container;
```

Our aim is to specify and verify a concurrent system which controls the cranes and the container so that the cranes simultaneously collect steel and fill in the container without exceeding its maximum capacity, and replace full containers with empty ones, making sure that cranes do not try to deposit debris when containers are being replaced. We assume space enough for several cranes to deposit steel in the container without interacting with each other.

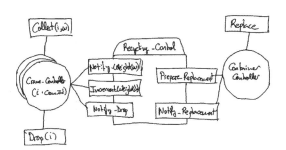

Fig. 2. System Design

We assume that the system can be expressed as a collection of processes interacting through a shared resource (see Fig. 2), an instance of what we term a **CADT** (**C**oncurrent **A**bstract **D**ata **T**ype). Using a generalization of data abstractions as the base for concurrency puts the emphasis on the interaction with the environment instead of on internal organization and algorithms, and also separates the functionality and implementation (i.e., message passing vs. shared memory).

Unlike other proposals, our specification language does not capture process behavior, which is instead written directly in a very simple programming language (Section 2.3). In what follows we will give a brief account of the main characteristics of the specification language using the crane example.

2.2 Design of a Resource-Based Solution

We are not aiming at describing the design process itself here, as to some extent, this relies on experience and common sense.[2] We will instead present a finished design and describe how it is assumed to work.

A process is assigned to every crane and to the container. A shared resource will be used as central point for synchronization. The state of the shared resource is rich enough to to determine when a container change is needed and when it has been changed. In particular, it contains the *replacement state*, which can take the following values: *ready* (there is room for more waste), *to_replace* (a crane carries more steel than what the container can hold, and the crane has decided to order an empty container), and *replacing* (the container is being replaced). Even if the *to_replace* state is entered, a crane carrying an amount of steel which still fits into the container can unload it as long as the *replacing* state has not been entered yet.

---

[2] Although there are, of course, guidelines which help in removing from an early stage many clearly wrong designs or which help in moving towards arguably better designs.

This approach does not maximize the container load, as the replacement process can start when some crane still carries a load which fits in the container. The alternative solution of storing the weight on every crane in the resource and making a central decision on which crane leaves its load was not chosen since it reduces concurrency.

Updates to the state need to be performed atomically. We define the resource as providing this atomicity for every operation, as well as more complex, data-dependent synchronization operations (Section 2.4).

2.3 Processes

Our starting point is to express the behavior of the system in terms of processes and then decide how they have to synchronize. As this is done exclusively by means of the shared resource, processes drive the design of the shared resource. As an less desirable but unavoidable side effect, this can result in resources with little reusability. We will see later how to detect the lack of certain reusability properties.

A crane process controller follow. Variable `Recycling_C` represents the shared resource and variable `I` (with `I` different for every process) identifies the crane managed by that process. The shared resource is represented by the object `Recycling` and all operations prefixed by it belong to the resource.

```
loop   -- Controller for the I-th crane
   Cranes.Collect (I, W);
   Recycling.Notify_Weight (Recycling_C, W);
   Recycling.Increment_Weight (Recycling_C, W);
   Cranes.Drop (I);
   Recycling.Notify_Drop (Recycling_C);
end loop;
```

`Notify_Weight` decides if the container has to be replaced. `Increment_Weight` suspends if the load cannot be unloaded because there is no space in the container or it is being replaced. Otherwise, it increments the container weight before actually dropping the steel. A counter of the cranes which have committed to unload but have not done it yet is kept to avoid the container to be replaced when some cranes are not yet through.

The container controller **waits** for the container to be replaceable, changes its state to *replacing*, replaces the container, and, atomically, changes the state to *ready* again.

```
loop   -- Container controller main loop
   Recycling.Prepare_Replacement (Recycling_C);
   Container.Replace;
   Recycling.Notify_Replacement (Recycling_C);
end loop;
```

2.4 Anatomy of a Specification

Our specification language is based on first-order logic, which is sufficiently known not to need but a quick brush-up in most cases. Its core ideas are inspired on a simplification of well-known formal methods (notably VDM [5]) with additional constructions to address concurrency. Following [11], our specifications are state-based, with the state accessible only through a set of public operations. Fig. 3 shows a partial specification of the resource at hand, which we will explain in this section.

CADT Recycling_Control
  OPERATIONS
  ACTION Prepare_Replacement: *Recycling_Control [io]*
  ACTION Notify_Replacement: *Recycling_Control [io]*
  ACTION Notify_Weight: *Recycling_Control [io] × Weight[i]*
  ACTION Increment_Weight: *Recycling_Control [io] × Weight[i]*
  ACTION Notify_Drop: *Recycling_Control [io]*

SEMANTICS
  DOMAIN:
  TYPE: *Recycling_Control = (weight:* $\mathbb{N}$× *state: State_Ty × accessing:* $\mathbb{N}$)
        State_Ty = ready | to_replace | replacing
        Weight = MIN_W_CRANE .. MAX_W_CRANE

  INVARIANT: $\forall r \in Recycling\_Control\bullet\ r.weight \leq MAX\_W\_CONTAINER \wedge$
        $r.accessing \leq MAX\_CRANES$

  CPRE: $r = (\_, to\_replace, 0)$
    Prepare_Replacement(r)
  POST: $r^{\mathrm{out}} = (r^{\mathrm{in}}.weight, replacing, 0)$

  PRE: $w \leq MAX\_W\_CRANE$
  CPRE: $r.weight + w \leq MAX\_W \wedge r.state \neq replacing$
    Increment_Weight(r, w)
  POST: $r^{\mathrm{in}} = (cw, e, a) \wedge r^{\mathrm{out}} = (cw + w, e, a + 1)$

Fig. 3. Partial CADT for the central crane controller

Public Interface: Actions and Their Signatures. The **OPERATIONS** section defines the names and signatures of the public operations and (optionally) tags arguments as input and/or output. The state of the resource itself is currently not directly available to the body of the specification; it must instead be a formal parameter (by convention, the first one) of every operation.[3]

Domain: Types. The *Domain* section contains type definitions for the resource and, optionally, an *invariant* which restricts the values of the resource state to those which are admissible in the problem.

In this example, the resource state contains the weight in the container, its replacement state (of enumerated type *State_Ty*), and how many cranes remain to deposit their load. `Weight` represents valid crane loads.

Basic types include Booleans, naturals, integers, and reals, and complex types are built on them by means of algebraic types (free types). A series of predefined non-basic types, such as we also provide sequences (indexable flexible-length arrays), sets, and finite mappings, with a complete set of operations on them, are also provided.

---

[3] This is not a strong requirement and is kept for compatibility with procedural languages.

Domain: Invariants. The invariant is a formula which constrains the range of values in the resource (maybe relating different state components). This allows restricting the admissible states to those which are legal, and, therefore, it also specifies which states the resource must **not** evolve into. It is defined on the *current* state and has no direct means to refer to past or future states. It is the responsibility of the resource specification to ensure that forbidden states are not reached. In our case, the container cannot carry more weight than the maximum allowed, and the number of cranes waiting to unload cannot exceed the total number of cranes.

Specifying the Effect of Operations. Preconditions and postconditions describe when operations can proceed (i.e., they express synchronization) and how these operations change the resource state. Both are first-order formulas which involve the resource and the arguments of the operation.

Synchronization. The resource semantics assumes mutual exclusion between operations, and ensuring this is left to the final implementation. More involved operation synchronization is taken care of by means of concurrency preconditions (CPRE), which are evaluated against the resource state, and which are aimed at expressing *safety* conditions. A call whose CPRE is evaluated to *false* will block until a change in the resource (done by some other process) makes it *true*. Only one operation among those whose CPRE evaluates to true is allowed to proceed. We do not assume any fixed selection procedure — not even fairness.

Sequential preconditions (PRE) can be added to the operations to express conditions which have to hold for the operations to be safely executed. While a CPRE states synchronization, a PRE deals mainly with data structure coherence.

Updating Resources and Arguments. Changes in the resource and in the operation arguments are specified using a postcondition (POST) for every operation which relates the state of the resource and of the parameters before and after the call. The PRE and CPRE of the operation and the invariant have to hold after a POSTs is *executed*, assuming they held before. Values before and after the operation are decorated with the superscripts "in" and "out", respectively.

In our case study, preparing the replacement keeps the number of cranes accessing the container (to zero, as was necessary to make the CPRE true) and the *weight* in the container, and sets the container state to *replacing*.

3   Translating Shared Resources into TLA

In this section we present an interlingua-based semantics for our notation. The interlingua is the specification language TLA+ [7,9], a combination of a linear-time temporal logic (The Temporal Logic of Actions [8]) and Zermelo-Fränkel set theory. We will present the semantics in an informal way, introducing some general information about the translation process and using the system specified in Section 2 to illustrate it.

3.1 Anatomy of a Translation

Roughly speaking, a TLA+ specification is a formula S written as a conjunction of a TLA predicate I that states the initial value of TLA variables x, y, ... representing the state of the system and a next-state relation N (TLA action) that specifies valid value changes of the variables: $S \triangleq I \wedge \Box[N]_{\langle x, y, ...\rangle}$.

Resource state. Each component of the domain of the specification in our notation will be translated into a TLA variable.

Example: TLA variables that represent the resource domain:

VARIABLES $weight$, $state$, $accessing$

Types and predicates. Types are translated into sets and predicates (initial state predicate, invariant, preconditions, and concurrency preconditions) into TLA predicates.

Example: TLA set that represents type $Weight$:

$Weight \triangleq (MIN\_W\_CRANE \mathrel{..} MAX\_W\_CRANE)$

Example: TLA predicate that represents the initial state:

$Init \triangleq \wedge weight = 0 \wedge state = $ "ready" $\wedge accessing = 0$

Postconditions are translated into TLA *actions* (a TLA action is a predicate which relates input and output states). The value of a variable before an action is represented using the variable name, and its value after the action is represented with the same name primed; so we replace x^{in} by x and x^{out} by x'.

Example: Type information, PRE, CPRE, POST of $Increment\_Weight$ in TLA:

$TYPE\_Increment\_Weight(w) \triangleq w \in Weight$

$PRE\_Increment\_Weight(w) \triangleq w \le MAX\_W\_CRANE$

$CPRE\_Increment\_Weight(w) \triangleq$
$\wedge weight + w \le MAX_W_CONTAINER \wedge state \ne $ "replacing"

$POST\_Increment\_Weight(w) \triangleq$
$weight' = weight + w \wedge$ UNCHANGED $state \wedge accessing' = accessing + 1$

We will not present in detail the translation of types, predicates and expressions, as it is a non difficult compilation exercise made easier by the richness and expressiveness of the mathematical toolkit of TLA+.

Operations. Every operation is translated into a TLA action which is the conjunction of the predicates collecting type information, precondition, concurrency precondition, and postcondition of the operation. This action will represent an atomic, valid transition of the system.

Example: TLA action that represents operation $Increment\_Weight$:

$Increment\_Weight(w) \triangleq$
$\wedge TYPE\_Increment\_Weight(w) \wedge PRE\_Increment\_Weight(w)$
$\wedge CPRE\_Increment\_Weight(w) \wedge POST\_Increment\_Weight(w)$

Putting It All Together . The TLA formula that gives semantics to the resource specification as a dynamic system is given by the definition of the *next-step* relation as the
disjunction of all actions resulting from the translation of operations. Informally, every
transition (step) the resource may experience is triggered by the execution of some of
its operations. We are deliberately ignoring the restrictions that the processes impose
on the possible operation interleavings.

Example: A TLA action that represent the execution of any operation:

$Next \stackrel{\Delta}{=}$
$\quad Prepare\_Replacement \lor Notify\_Replacement$
$\quad \lor \exists w \in Weight : Notify\_Weight(w) \lor \exists w \in Weight : Increment\_Weight(w)$
$\quad \lor Notify\_Drop$

The formula *Spec* which specifies that the system starts in a valid state and every transition it takes is one of these defined by the *Next* formula, maybe leaving variables
weight, *state*, or *accessing* unchanged, is then

$Spec \stackrel{\Delta}{=} Init \land \Box[Next]_{\langle weight, state, accessing \rangle}$

3.2 Translation Explained

Let us summarise some of the most relevant points in the previous translation:

- The TLA specification syntactically reflects most of the components of our notation.
- Type information has been explicitly introduced in (the untyped) TLA by representing types as sets. Variable typing is therefore translated into set membership and
  type declarations have been translated as guarded TLA formulae — for example,
  Weight, which is used in the definition of predicate $TYPE\_Increment\_Weight$,
  itself part of the action $Increment\_Weight$, and the in the bounded existential
  quantification in the definition of *Next*.
- The invariant will be also eventually translated into the TLA resulting specification.
  It will be used during the checking stage (Section 4).
- Output parameters of operations which are private to processes are represented by
  new TLA variables visible by all operations but, conceptually not part of the resource. They are however necessary to faithfully represent the operation behaviour
  and, since all operations are continuously available, the interleavings this specification can represent are a superset of the ones the processes can perform.

4 Verifying System Properties Using TLC

In this section we will see how some execution properties of our example can be studied
thanks to the translation of shared resources into TLA and, eventually, the use of the
TLC model checker. Being able to use such a tool does not guarantee, in general, the
correctness of the system, but it helps to find possible inconsistencies or holes in the
specifications.

Some of the properties to check are generic (i.e., the invariant always holds) and
some of them depend on the system at hand. We will use in fact two variants of the

specification. The first one is what we described in Section 3.1, which leaves complete freedom to the interleaving of the operations, and is adequate to verify safety properties which are connected with resource reuse. The second one includes the necessary machinery to enact interleaving constraints which model the behaviour of the process.

4.1   Checking the Resource Integrity

With no information about the context in which the specified resource will be used, only the integrity of the invariant and type information of variables can be checked.

Example: Checking the invariant

The invariant has been translated into the following TLA specification:

$$Types \stackrel{\Delta}{=} weight \in Nat \wedge state \in State\_Ty \wedge accessing \in Nat$$

$$Invariant \stackrel{\Delta}{=}$$
$$\wedge\ weight \leq MAX\_W\_CONTAINER \wedge accessing \leq MAX\_CRANES$$

The input to the model checker TLC (Fig. 4) consists of the TLA specification plus the definition of values for constants and the properties (invariants in this case) to be checked. The model checker found two violations of the invariant. The first one is a type error:

```
Error: Invariant Types is violated. The behavior up to this point is:
STATE 1: <Initial predicate>
/\ state = "ready" /\ weight = 0 /\ accessing = 0
STATE 2: <Action Notify_Drop>
/\ state = "ready" /\ weight = 0 /\ accessing = -1
```

```
CONSTANTS
  MAX_CRANES = 5
  MIN_W_CRANE = 1000
  MAX_W_CRANE = 1010
  MAX_W_CONTAINER = 20000
  SPECIFICATION Spec
  INVARIANT Types
  INVARIANT Invariant
```

Fig. 4. TLC definition of the system to check

The second one is the violation of the property $weight \leq MAX\_W\_CONTAINER$. We have modified the specification by introducing a **CPRE** in the operations *Increment_Weight* and *Notify_Drop* ($accessing < MAX\_W\_CRANE$ and $accessing > 0$, respectively). After this, it seems that our resource specification has reached a better degree of integrity. The model checker did not find more errors during the checking of the specified resource invariant. Note that, since we did not impose any restriction to the interleavings of the operations due to the way processes are defined, the properties we are checking here will be valid in any context of the resource, guaranteeing the reusability of the shared resource.

4.2   *Cooking* the Processes

Studying properties which take wholly into account how processes and resources are defined as needs some additional *cooking* in order to encode their behaviour in TLA. We have followed this systematic method:

1. Introducing per-process program counters and local variables to represent the internal state of every process.

2. Establishing relevant program points for every type of process.
3. Introducing next-step relations in the specification for every process.
4. Mixing next-step relations of processes with next-step relations of the resource.
5. Writing the whole system specification with the initial state, the disjunction of all *cooked* TLA actions, and weak fairness conditions on every TLA action.

Example: *Cooking* `Crane_Controllers`

1. Variables $Crane\_Controller\_PC$ and $Crane\_Controller\_w$ represent the internal state of the every crane controller:

   VARIABLES $Crane\_Controller\_PC$, $Crane\_Controller\_w$

2. `Crane_Controller` program points:

   $Crane\_Controller\_Points \stackrel{\Delta}{=}$
   {"toNotify_Weight", "toIncrement_Weight", "dropping", "toNotify_Drop"}
   The following fragment captures the type of program counters, local variables and initial state of the processes:

   $Processes\_Types \stackrel{\Delta}{=}$
   $\quad \wedge Crane\_Controller\_PC \in [Crane\_Id \rightarrow Crane\_Controller\_Points]$
   $\quad \wedge Crane\_Controller\_w \in [Crane\_Id \rightarrow Weight]$

   $Processes\_Init \stackrel{\Delta}{=}$
   $\quad \wedge Crane\_Controller\_PC = [i \in Crane\_Id \mapsto \text{"toNotify\_Weight"}]$
   $\quad \wedge Crane\_Controller\_w = [i \in Crane\_Id \mapsto \text{CHOOSE } w \in Weight : \text{TRUE}]$

3. The next-step relations for the process `Crane_Controller` are the invocation of shared resource operation and the invocation of the `Cranes` API. Actually, just one new next-step relation is relevant: the transition from the invocation of `Increment_Weight` to the invocation of `Cranes.Drop`:

   $Dropping \stackrel{\Delta}{=}$
   $\quad \exists i \in Crane\_Id :$
   $\quad\quad \wedge Crane\_Controller\_PC[i] = \text{"dropping"}$
   $\quad\quad \wedge Crane\_Controller\_PC' =$
   $\quad\quad\quad [Crane\_Controller\_PC \text{ EXCEPT } ![i] = \text{"toNotify\_Drop"}]$
   $\quad\quad \wedge \text{UNCHANGED } Container\_Controller\_PC$
   $\quad\quad \wedge \text{UNCHANGED } Crane\_Controller\_w$
   $\quad\quad \wedge \text{UNCHANGED } weight \wedge \text{UNCHANGED } state \wedge \text{UNCHANGED } accessing$

4. We extend the next-step relations of the resource with the valid state changes in the processes:

   $Cooked\_Notify\_Weight(w) \stackrel{\Delta}{=}$
   $\quad \exists i \in Crane\_Id :$
   $\quad\quad \wedge Crane\_Controller\_PC[i] = \text{"toNotify\_Weight"}$
   $\quad\quad \wedge Crane\_Controller\_w[i] = w$
   $\quad\quad \wedge Notify\_Weight(w)$
   $\quad\quad \wedge Crane\_Controller\_PC' =$
   $\quad\quad\quad [Crane\_Controller\_PC \text{ EXCEPT } ![i] = \text{"toIncrement\_Weight"}]$
   $\quad\quad \wedge \text{UNCHANGED } Container\_Controller\_PC$
   $\quad\quad \wedge \text{UNCHANGED } Crane\_Controller\_w$

$Cooked\_Increment\_Weight(w) \stackrel{\Delta}{=}$
    $\exists\, i \in Crane\_Id :$
        $\wedge\ Crane\_Controller\_PC[i] =$ "toIncrement_Weight"
        $\wedge\ Crane\_Controller\_w[i] = w$
        $\wedge\ Increment\_Weight(w)$
        $\wedge\ Crane\_Controller\_PC' =$
            $[\,Crane\_Controller\_PC$ EXCEPT $![i] =$ "dropping"$]$
        $\wedge$ UNCHANGED $Container\_Controller\_PC$
        $\wedge$ UNCHANGED $Crane\_Controller\_w$

$Cooked\_Notify\_Drop \stackrel{\Delta}{=}$
    $\exists\, i \in Crane\_Id : \exists\, w \in Weight :$
        $\wedge\ Crane\_Controller\_PC[i] =$ "toNotify_Drop"
        $\wedge\ Notify\_Drop$
        $\wedge\ Crane\_Controller\_PC' =$
            $[\,Crane\_Controller\_PC$ EXCEPT $![i] =$ "toNotify_Weight"$]$
        $\wedge$ UNCHANGED $Container\_Controller\_PC$
        $\wedge\ Crane\_Controller\_w' = [\,Crane\_Controller\_w$ EXCEPT $![i] = w\,]$

5. Putting it all together:

$Cooked\_Next \stackrel{\Delta}{=}$
    $\vee\ Cooked\_Prepare\_Replacement \vee Cooked\_Notify\_Replacement$
    $\vee\ \exists\, w \in Weight : Cooked\_Notify\_Weight(w)$
    $\vee\ \exists\, w \in Weight : Cooked\_Increment\_Weight(w)$
    $\vee\ Cooked\_Notify\_Drop$
    $\vee\ Dropping \vee Replacing$

$Cooked\_Spec \stackrel{\Delta}{=}\ Cooked\_Init \wedge \square[\,Cooked\_Next\,]_{Cooked\_State}$

4.3   Checking System Properties

With this *cooked* specification we can check the following system properties:

1. Absence of deadlock (this is automatically provided by TLC).
2. That no cranes drop any material while the container is being replaced:

    $No\_Dropping\_While\_Replacing \stackrel{\Delta}{=}$
        $\square(\neg(\ \wedge \exists\, i \in Crane\_Id : Crane\_Controller\_PC[i] =$ "dropping"
            $\wedge\ Container\_Controller\_PC =$ "replacing"$))$

3. Component *state* in the resource has a cyclic behaviour (*ready* $\rightarrow$ *to_replace* $\rightarrow$ *replacing* $\rightarrow$ *ready* ...):

    $State\_Is\_Cyclic \stackrel{\Delta}{=}$
        $\square[\ \vee\ state =$ "ready" $\wedge\ state' =$ "to_replace"
            $\vee\ state =$ "to_replace" $\wedge\ state' =$ "replacing"
            $\vee\ state =$ "replacing" $\wedge\ state =$ "ready"$]_{state}$

TLC then detects the violation of one of the properties:

```
Error: Action property State_Is_Cyclic is violated. The behavior up to this point is:
...
STATE 76: <Action Notify_Weight>
/\ state = "to_replace" /\ weight = 19000 /\ accessing = 1
/\ Crane_Controller_PC = <<"toNotify_Weight", "toIncrement_Weight", "dropping">>
/\ Crane_Controller_w = <<1000, 1001, 1000>>
/\ Container_Controller_PC = "toPrepare_Replacement"
STATE 77: <Action Notify_Weight>
/\ state = "ready" /\ weight = 19000 /\ accessing = 1
/\ Crane_Controller_PC = <<"toIncrement_Weight", "toIncrement_Weight", "dropping">>
/\ Crane_Controller_w = <<1000, 1001, 1000>>
/\ Container_Controller_PC = "toPrepare_Replacement"
273320 states generated, 77163 distinct states found, 3008 states left on queue.
The depth of the complete state graph search is 77.
```

4.4 Analysis of the Error Detected

During the design process, the specifier decided to write the following specification for
Notify_ Weight (already translated into TLA):

$Notify\_Weight(w) \overset{\Delta}{=}$

> $CPRE$
> $\wedge\ state \neq$ "replacing"
> $POST$
> $\wedge$ UNCHANGED *weight* $\wedge$ UNCHANGED *accessing*
> $\wedge\ weight + w > MAX\_W\_CONTAINER \Rightarrow state' =$ "to_replace"
> $\wedge\ weight + w \leq MAX\_W\_CONTAINER \Rightarrow state' =$ "ready"

The motivation to write such specification is that just because one crane asks for a
replacement ($state' = to\_replace$ if the weight of its load exceeds the limit) no other
crane with a valid load weight should wait to drop (resulting in changing the value of
state to *ready* and avoiding the container to be replaced).

Is the formalised system a right system? Is $State\_Is\_Cyclic$ a desirable property of
the system to be built? At least, the violation of the property revealed a liveness issue
in the formalisation: if a crane controller i asks for a replacement ($state' = to\_replace$)
and another crane controller j invalidates that request ($state' = ready$), then the crane
i will have to wait (conditional synchronisation of operation $Increment\_Weight$) until
another crane k (probably j) reactivates a new request.

5 Conclusion

We have presented a method for structuring and analysing concurrent software that
allows developers to focus on concurrency in isolation from other aspects. Although
conceptually simple, it enables the use of formal methods in order to verify nontrivial
properties of realistic systems.

We sketched a semantics for our shared resource specifications based on a translation of CADTs into Temporal Logic of Actions. This translation has two practical
advantages that can be relevant for a wider industrial adoption of similar approaches.
On one hand, we think that a CADT is much easier to write and understand than the

corresponding TLA specification; although it forces a more rigid architecture, in many cases it is arguably more advantageous to have a series of tools / mechanisms which are easy to apply to different scenarios instead of a generic, more complex, one. Our CADT is an example of such a perhaps more specific approach.

On the other hand, the availability of tools such as TLC gives system designers the ability to pinpoint mistakes / misconceptions at an early stage. The automatic translation from a more "focused" formalism to a general, powerful tool helps their adoption. Additionally, from a formal standpoint, providing an interlingua semantics can be easier to follow than introducing a new calculus, specially considering a formalism in evolution.

The process structure presented here is a very simple one. More sophisticated schemes have been proposed in the literature, all of them with the common goals of providing language and platform independence when designing and reasoning about concurrent applications. Models such as *Creol* [4], that proposes a formal model of distributed concurrent objects based on asynchronous message passing, or *CoBoxes* [10] which unifies active objects with structured heaps, are relatively recent proposals that elaborate on previous ones such as the *actors* model.

In the service-oriented computing paradigm, which is attracting much attention in the last years and which is inherently concurrent, languages like BPEL [6] have been used to implement business processes. While BPEL is very powerful and can express complex service networks, their full verification is challenging, partly because of its complex semantics.

Although it can be argued that these alternatives allow to express more complex process structures, the absence of a clear separation between active and passive entities does not favour a simple analysis of the behaviour of systems. On the other hand, it is usually a requirement of many industrial software system to avoid complexity as much as possible. In other words, some models can be *far more expressive* than needed or wanted in practise.

Several relatives to our resources can also be found in the literature. It is worth mentioning the concurrency features in VDM++ [3], similar in spirit, although our CADT's relax some of their restrictions as can be seen in [1]. Moreover, the CADT formalism permits some extensions for improving the expressiveness of CPREs that still allow semi-automatic code generation. We have not used these extensions in this paper for the sake of simplicity.

One of the shortcomings of our method, in its current state, is that system properties, unlike shared resources, must be specified directly in TLA. One possible way to overcome this would be to enrich CADTs with trace-dependent conditions which could, in turn, simplify the way in which liveness properties are specified.

Our original CADT notation included a construct similar to the *history counters* in VDM [3]: number of times each operation has been requested, activated and completed with information about process identifiers and actual parameters. Formulae on history counters can be very expressive (path expressions or UML protocol state machines can be easily encoded with them) and protocol order between operations or certain liveness conditions can be formalised.

As some programming languages come equipped with constructs that allow to check the lock state of processes at run time, automatic code generation from these specifications seems feasible. These extensions, and a more formal specification of the translation into TLA, are subject of future work.

References

1. Carro, M., Mariño, J., Herranz, Á., Moreno-Navarro, J.J.: Teaching how to derive correct concurrent programs (from state-based specifications and code patterns). In: Dean, C.N., Boute, R.T. (eds.) TFM 2004. LNCS, vol. 3294, pp. 85–106. Springer, Heidelberg (2004)
2. COST Action IC 0701 on Verification of Object Oriented Software, http://www.cost-ic0701.org
3. Fitzgerald, J., Larsen, P.G., Mukherjee, P., Plat, N., Verhoef, M.: Validated Designs for Object-oriented Systems. Springer, Heidelberg (2004)
4. Johnsen, E.B., Owe, O., Yu, I.C.: Creol: A type-safe object-oriented model for distributed concurrent systems. In: Theoretical Computer Science (2006)
5. Jones, C.B.: Systematic Software Development Using VDM. Prentice-Hall, Upper Saddle River (1995)
6. Jordan, D., Evdemon, J., Alves, A., Arkin, A., Askary, S., Barreto, C., Bloch, B., Curbera, F., Ford, M., Goland, Y., Guízar, A., Kartha, N., Liu, C.K., Khalaf, R., König, D., Marin, M., Mehta, V., Thatte, S., van der Rijn, D., Yendluri, P., Yiu, A.: Web Services Business Process Execution Language Version 2.0. Technical report, IBM, Microsoft, BEA, Intalio, Individual, Adobe Systems, Systinet, Active Endpoints, JBoss, Sterling Commerce, SAP, Deloitte, TIBCO Software, webMethods Oracle (2007)
7. Leslie Lamport. The TLA home page, http://www.research.microsoft.com/users/lamport/tla/tla.html
8. Lamport, L.: The temporal logic of actions. ACM Trans. Program. Lang. Syst. 16(3), 872–923 (1994)
9. Lamport, L.: Specifying Systems: The TLA+ Language and Tools for Hardware and Software Engineers. Pearson Education, Inc., London (2002)
10. Schäfer, J., Poetzsch-Heffter, A.: Coboxes: Unifying active objects and structured heaps. In: Barthe, G., de Boer, F.S. (eds.) FMOODS 2008. LNCS, vol. 5051, pp. 201–219. Springer, Heidelberg (2008)
11. van Lamsweerde, A.: Formal Specification: a Roadmap. In: Finkelstein, A. (ed.) The Future of Software Engineering, pp. 147–159. ACM Press, New York (2000)

Platform-Specific Restrictions on Concurrency in Model Checking of Java Programs

Pavel Parizek and Tomas Kalibera

Distributed Systems Research Group, Department of Software Engineering,
Faculty of Mathematics and Physics, Charles University in Prague
Malostranske namesti 25, 118 00 Prague 1, Czech Republic
{parizek,kalibera}@dsrg.mff.cuni.cz

Abstract. The main limitation of software model checking is that, due to state explosion, it does not scale to real-world multi-threaded programs. One of the reasons is that current software model checkers adhere to full semantics of programming languages, which are based on very permissive models of concurrency. Current runtime platforms for programs, however, restrict concurrency in various ways — it is visible especially in the case of critical embedded systems, which typically involve only a single processor and use a threading model based on limited preemption.

In this paper, we present a technique for addressing state explosion in model checking of Java programs for embedded systems, which exploits restrictions on concurrency common to current Java platforms for such systems. We have implemented the technique in Java PathFinder and performed a number of experiments on Purdue Collision Detector, which is a non-trivial multi-threaded Java program. Results of experiments show that use of the restrictions on concurrency in model checking with Java PathFinder reduces the state space size by an order of magnitude and also reduces the time needed to discover errors in Java programs.

Keywords: model checking, Java programs, embedded systems, state explosion, restrictions of concurrency.

1 Introduction

Software for mission- and safety-critical systems is typically based on multi-threaded programs, since such systems must be able to process concurrent inputs from their environment in a timely manner. This is the case, for example, of software in control systems in vehicles (cars, aircrafts) and software running on high-availability server systems. A significant part of the development process of programs for critical systems is devoted to testing and verification, since runtime errors in such programs are very costly. The errors particularly relevant for multi-threaded software used in critical systems are violations of temporal safety and liveness properties and also concurrency errors (e.g., deadlocks and race conditions). The verification technique most suitable for detection of such errors is model checking. A model checker systematically traverses the whole state

M. Alpuente, B. Cook, and C. Joubert (Eds.): FMICS 2009, LNCS 5825, pp. 117–132, 2009.

space of a given program with the goal of detecting property violations and errors.

The main limitation of model checking is that it does not scale to complex multi-threaded programs, which are often used in critical systems, due to the well-known problem of *state explosion*. The state space of a program, which a model checker has to explore, captures all possible sequences of thread scheduling choices and all possible threads interleavings that can occur during program's execution — the size of the state space depends roughly exponentially on the number of threads. Although many techniques for addressing state explosion have been designed and implemented in various model checkers over the years [17], state explosion still occurs in model checking of large and complex multi-threaded programs written in mainstream programming languages. One of the reasons is that semantics of mainstream programming languages (e.g., Java, C and C#) are based on very permissive models of concurrency. For example, semantics of such languages allow preemption to happen at any program point and impose no restrictions on thread scheduling algorithms (e.g., any runnable thread can be scheduled when another thread is suspended). Model checkers for programs in such languages [24,7,2] then have to adhere to the full semantics of the languages for the sake of generality — in particular, the model checkers have to systematically check the behavior of programs under all possible thread scheduling sequences allowed by the semantics of the programming languages, including those thread scheduling sequences that cannot happen in practice due to concurrency-related characteristics of runtime platforms for programs. We propose to address state explosion in model checking by exploiting restrictions on concurrency that are based on characteristics and behavior of runtime platforms formed by hardware, operating systems and, in case of languages like Java and C#, also by virtual machines. The goal is to reduce the state space size of multi-threaded programs such that the chance of traversing the whole state space of such programs in limited memory and reasonable time, and thus the chance of discovering more errors, is much greater.

To be more specific, the main contributions of this paper are:

- a technique for efficient model checking of multi-threaded Java programs, which is based on platform-specific restrictions of concurrency,
- an implementation of the technique as an extension to the Java PathFinder model checker (JPF) [24], and
- evaluation of the technique on Purdue Collision Detector, which is a non-trivial multi-threaded Java program.

We focus on model checking of Java programs, since Java is used for implementation of software for many critical server-side systems and is also becoming a language of choice for implementation of multi-threaded software for critical embedded systems.

2   Current Platforms for Java Programs

In this section, we provide an overview of concurrency-related characteristics and behavior of current runtime platforms for Java programs from the perspective of model checking with JPF and we also define terminology that is used throughout the rest of the paper.

We consider a runtime platform for Java programs, further denoted as a *Java platform*, to be a specific combination of a hardware configuration, an operating system (OS), and a Java virtual machine (JVM). The key concurrency-related characteristics of Java platforms are:

- the maximal number of Java threads that can run in parallel,
- a threading and scheduling model that determines the level, at which threads in Java programs (Java threads) are implemented and scheduled, and
- a set of program points (Java bytecode instructions), at which a running thread may be suspended (preempted) by a platform — such program points are further referred to as *thread yield points*.

The maximal number of threads that can possibly run in parallel is bounded by the number of processors in a particular hardware configuration, and can be further limited by JVM — some processors can be dedicated to garbage collection or non-Java tasks, or the JVM can explicitly support only a single processor. In this text, we use the term *processor* to denote a logical processing unit of any kind, including a single processor (CPU) in a multi-processor machine or a single core in a multi-core CPU. Threading and scheduling models are typically implemented by the operating system and/or the JVM. The scheduling models implemented in most of the current Java platforms are based on preemption. The platforms differ in the set of thread yield points, i.e. in the set of program points where a running thread can be suspended, and also in the kind of preemption that they use — some use *time preemption*, in which case a thread can be suspended at any program point (i.e., all program points are considered as thread yield points in that case), while other platforms use limited preemption, in which case only specific Java bytecode instructions and calls of specific methods are considered as thread yield points.

The specifications of the Java language [9] and JVM [15] define a very permissive model of concurrency with respect to the characteristics listed above. In particular, (i) they do not put any restrictions on the maximal number of Java threads running in parallel, (ii) they do not specify any particular threading and scheduling model that should be used, and (iii) they allow threads to be preempted at any bytecode instruction and at call of any method, i.e. they allow the set of thread yield points to be defined as an arbitrary subset of the set of all program points. On the other hand, the current Java platforms restrict the concurrency in Java programs in various ways. The platforms can be divided into the following two groups depending on the way they restrict concurrency: (1) Java platforms for embedded systems and (2) Java platforms for server and desktop systems.

2.1   Java Platforms for Embedded Systems

Typically, Java platforms for embedded systems use the *green threading* model, hardware configurations in such platforms are based on a single processor, and the set of thread yield points contains only a subset of all program points. The key idea behind green threading is that Java threads are managed and scheduled by a JVM (at the level of JVM), out of control of the underlying operating system. All Java threads in a program are mapped to a single native (OS-level) process in which the JVM runs (Fig. 1a), and therefore only a single thread can run at a time — the threads in a program are effectively interleaved. The green threading model is supported, for example, by Purdue OVM [3], which is a research JVM aiming at embedded and real-time systems, and also by the CLDC HotSpot Implementation [5], which is an industrial JVM for embedded devices compliant with the Java ME CLCD profile (e.g., mobile phones). Java platforms in this group also do not use scheduling based on time preemption. The platforms typically consider as thread yield points only those program points that correspond to one of the following actions: acquiring and releasing of locks (monitors), calls of blocking native methods (I/O), calls of selected methods of the Thread class (e.g., sleep, start, and yield), calls of the wait and notify methods, and, in case of more complex JVMs, also method invocations (method prologues), returns from methods (method epilogues), and back-branches (back-jumps to the beginning of a loop). For example, Purdue OVM considers back-branches as thread yield points, while the CLDC Hotspot Implementation does not. Selection of program points to be used as thread yield points is motivated mainly by performance and implementation reasons — the goal is to ensure that all threads get a fair share of processor time and also to allow easier implementation of JVM.

Although most embedded systems use only a single processor, there are also some embedded systems that employ multiple processors and therefore can run multiple threads in parallel. In case of such systems, either native threading model (explained in Sect. 2.2) or *quasi-preemptive* threading model can be used. The quasi-preemptive threading model is a generalization of green threading to multiple processors, which supports mapping of Java threads to N native (OS-level) processes such that $N \geq 2$ — the native processes may run truly in parallel and therefore also Java threads mapped to them may run truly in parallel. Still, Java threads are suspended and scheduled only at specific program points enumerated above (at the same program points as in the green threading model). A specific variant of the quasi-preemptive threading model is implemented in the Jikes Research Virtual Machine (RVM) [14].

An important subclass of embedded systems is formed by real-time systems, which must satisfy temporal constraints (e.g., meeting all deadlines). The key characteristic of real-time systems is that thread schedulers strictly enforce thread priorities. In case of non-real-time systems, thread priorities are not strictly enforced; however, threads with higher priorities should be in general scheduled more likely compared to threads with lower priorities.

To summarize, the key restrictions of concurrency in Java platforms for embedded systems are: (i) a bound on the number of threads that can run in

a)

b)

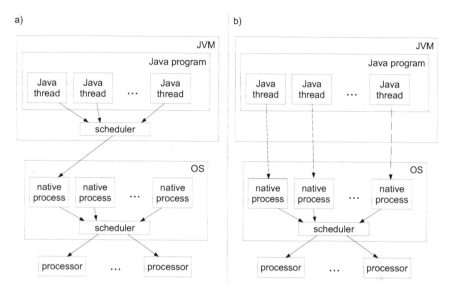

Fig. 1. Threading models in Java platforms: a) green threads; b) native threads

parallel, which is determined by the number of processors, (ii) use of green threading model such that only specific bytecode instructions and calls of specific methods are considered as thread yield points, and, in case of real-time systems, (iii) strict enforcement of thread priorities.

2.2   Java Platforms for Server and Desktop Systems

Java platforms for server and desktop systems use *native threading* model, and the hardware configurations in such platforms are typically based on multiple processors. In the case of a native threading model, Java threads are directly mapped to native (OS-level) threads that are scheduled by the OS-level scheduler (Fig. 1b); therefore, Java threads can run truly in parallel if multiple processors are available in a Java platform. Moreover, since schedulers in current operating systems use time preemption, the Java threads can be suspended at any program point (i.e., all program points have to be considered as potential thread yield points). It follows that the only important restriction of concurrency used in Java platforms for server and desktop systems is the bound on the number of threads that can possibly run in parallel.

Note that most industrial JVMs use native threading and time preemption-based scheduling — in particular, this applies to Sun Java Hotspot [23] and IBM J9 [12], which are both state-of-the-art industrial JVMs for desktop and server-side Java applications.

3   Running Example

The concepts and ideas presented in the paper will be illustrated on the Java program shown in Fig. 2, which is an instance of the producer-consumer design

```
1  class Consumer extends Thread {
2    private Object[] buffer;
3
4    public void run() {
5      int pos = 0;
6      while (true) {
7        synchronized (buffer) {
8          while (buffer[pos] == null) buffer.wait();
9        }
10
11         Object msg = buffer[pos];
12         buffer[pos] = null;
13         pos++;
14         synchronized (buffer) {
15           buffer.notify();
16         }
17       }
18     }
19 }
20
21 class Producer extends Thread {
22   private Object[] buffer;
23
24   public void run() {
25     int pos = 0;
26     while (true) {
27       synchronized (buffer) {
28         while (buffer[pos] != null) buffer.wait();
29       }
30
31       // code that creates a message is omitted
32       buffer[pos] = msg;
33       pos++;
34       synchronized (buffer) {
35         buffer.notify();
36       }
37     }
38   }
39 }
40
41 public static void main(String[] args) {
42   Object[] buffer = new Object[10];
43   Consumer cons = new Consumer(buffer);
44   Producer prod = new Producer(buffer);
45   cons.start();
46   prod.start();
47 }
```

Fig. 2. Example Java program: producer-consumer pattern

pattern. We selected the producer-consumer design pattern, since it forms the basis of many multi-threaded programs for critical systems (both embedded and server-side), including Purdue Collision Detector (PCD) that we use for evaluation of the proposed technique (details in Sect. 6).

4   Java PathFinder

Java PathFinder (JPF) [24] is an explicit state model checker for Java bytecode programs, which is based on a special Java virtual machine (JPF VM) that supports backtracking and state matching. It is highly extensible and configurable, and supports common optimizations of state space traversal like partial order reduction and thread/heap symmetry reduction.

The key features of JPF in the context of this paper are that (i) it implements the concurrency model of Java with no restrictions (i.e., it adheres to the full semantics of Java) and (ii) it does not model real time. To be more specific, JPF checks the behavior of a given Java program under the following assumptions:

- an unlimited number of processors is available,
- time preemption-based scheduling with an arbitrary (and dynamically changing) size of time slots is used, and
- all program points are considered as potential thread yield points.

The contention of multiple threads for shared data (variables) under such a model of concurrency is captured in JPF by systematic exploration of all interleavings of concurrent accesses to shared variables that are performed by individual threads. Technically, JPF suspends threads also at Java bytecode instructions corresponding to accesses to shared variables in addition to thread yield points, and selects the thread to be scheduled from the set of all runnable threads (including the one that was just suspended, if it is not blocked) at each thread scheduling choice point — this means that when a thread performs an access to a shared variable and is then suspended, any runnable thread may execute the next access to a shared variable. This is sufficient to capture the contention for shared variables both in case of threads running concurrently on a single processor, which are effectively interleaved, and also in case of threads running truly in parallel (on multiple processors), since parallel accesses to shared memory are actually serialized in the hardware (a particular interleaving of the parallel accesses is non-deterministically selected by hardware).

The actual state space of a given Java program is constructed by JPF on-the-fly in a way that reflects the concurrency model described above and the supported optimizations of state space traversal. A transition is a sequence of bytecode instructions performed by a single thread, which is terminated either by a scheduling-relevant instruction (thread yield point or an access to a shared variable) or by an instruction corresponding to non-deterministic data choice (e.g., use of a random generator). A state in the state space of a Java program is a snapshot of the current state of the JPF VM at the end of a transition, including complete heap and stacks of all threads.

Given the Java program on Fig. 2, JPF may terminate a transition at any instruction corresponding to the following program points:

- accesses to the `buffer` variable in all threads (source code lines 8, 11, 12, 28, and 32),
- attempts to acquire a monitor, i.e. attempts to enter a `synchronized` block (lines 7, 14, 27, and 34),
- calls of the `wait` and `notify` methods (lines 8, 15, 28, 35), and
- start of a new thread (lines 45 and 46).

JPF provides a powerful API that allows to extend it in various ways. With respect to the technique proposed in this paper, the key parts of JPF's API are: (i) configurable scheduling model and (ii) choice generators. Configurability of thread scheduling allows to use a domain-specific scheduling algorithm (e.g., one based on thread priorities) and, in particular, to restrict concurrency in various ways. The mechanism of choice generators unifies all possible causes for a branch in the state space of a Java program, including thread scheduling and non-deterministic data value choice. A specific instance of a choice generator is associated with each state — it maintains the list of enabled and unexplored transitions leading from the state. The choice generator API also provides means for altering the set of enabled and unexplored transitions; for example, it is possible to select specific transitions that should be explored.

5   Restrictions of Concurrency in Model Checking Java Programs with Java PathFinder

The key idea behind our approach is that it is not necessary to check the behavior of a Java program under all possible sequences of thread scheduling choices that are allowed by the concurrency model and semantics of Java, when Java platforms restrict concurrency in such a way that some of the sequences of thread scheduling choices cannot occur during execution of a Java program.

It follows from the overview of current Java platforms (Sect. 2) and JPF (Sect. 4) that no significant restriction of concurrency in model checking with JPF is possible in case of Java platforms for server and desktop systems, which typically involve multiple processors and use native threading with time preemption-based scheduling. Therefore we focus only on Java platforms for embedded systems, where significant restrictions of concurrency are possible. Such platforms typically involve only a single processor, in which case the green threading model is used, or a very low number of multiple processors, in which case the quasi-preemptive threading can be used. In both cases, time preemption-based scheduling is not used and thus only specific program points are considered as thread yield points. As indicated in Sect. 2.1, there are also Java platforms for real-time embedded systems that strictly enforce thread priorities and perform priority-based thread scheduling. However, in this paper we focus only on Java platforms for non-real-time embedded systems that involve JVMs like CLDC [5] — we assume (i) that all threads in a Java program have the same priority during the whole lifetime of a program and (ii) that bytecode instructions corresponding to back-branches, method prologues and method epilogues are not used as thread yield points by the JVM. We leave support for thread priorities and priority-based scheduling to our future work (see the end of Sect. 7 for details).

We propose to use two platform-specific restrictions of concurrency for the purpose of addressing state explosion in model checking of Java programs for such platforms with JPF — specifically, we propose (i) to bound the maximal number of threads that can run in parallel, and (ii) to consider only specific bytecode instructions and calls of specific methods as thread yield points.

Maximal number of parallel threads. The rationale behind this restriction is that if there are N processors in a Java platform and M threads running in parallel, such that $M > N$, only at most N threads can compete for a particular shared variable at a specific moment in time (exactly N threads can compete only if there are N active threads at the moment). Therefore, if this restriction is applied, JPF has to explore only those thread interleavings that correspond to parallel execution of some N threads at most at each point in the program's running time. In particular, it is not necessary to explore those interleavings that involve suspending of a thread T_i, $1 \leq i \leq N$, and scheduling of another thread T_j, $N + 1 \leq j \leq M$, when an access to a shared variable occurs in T_i.

Thread yield points. Since we focus only on Java platforms for non-real-time embedded systems that involve JVMs like CLDC, for the purpose of model checking of Java programs with JPF it is sufficient to consider as thread yield points only those bytecode instructions and method calls, whose effects are visible to other threads and may therefore influence their behavior. Effects visible to other threads are, most notably, changes of shared variables' values and changes of threads' status (including synchronization). Therefore, the set of program points considered as thread yield points by JPF has to include (i) bytecode instructions that correspond to acquiring and releasing of monitors (locks) and (ii) calls of methods that change status of a thread (specific methods of the `Thread` class, and the `wait` and `notify` methods). If the platform involves multiple processors, JPF has to consider as thread yield points also bytecode instructions corresponding to accesses to shared variables — this is necessary in order to properly capture the contention for the shared variables among multiple threads running concurrently or truly in parallel.

Consequences on model checking with JPF. A consequence of application of both restrictions of concurrency in model checking with JPF is that the number of thread scheduling choices on any execution path in a checked Java program is greatly reduced, which implies that the number of paths (branches) in the state space of the Java program is greatly reduced. Therefore, the whole reachable state space of a multi-threaded Java program is much smaller and thus model checking of such a program with JPF is less prone to state explosion. Note, however, that if there is a thread yield point (e.g., acquire of a monitor or call of `wait`) between each pair of accesses to shared variables in the program code, then the proposed restrictions would not help very much (even if the number of processors is set to 1) — the state space size would be the same as in the case of default JPF with no restriction.

Given the Java program on Fig. 2, JPF with both restrictions and the number of processors set to 1 may terminate transitions (i.e. suspend and schedule threads) only at program points corresponding to bytecode instructions for: entry to a `synchronized` block (source code lines 7, 14, 27 and 34), call of the `wait` method (lines 8 and 28), call of the `notify` method (lines 15 and 35), and start of a thread (lines 45 and 46). This means, for example, that the code at lines 11 and 12 will be executed atomically (in a single transition) by JPF. If the number of processors is set to 2, JPF may terminate transitions also at program points (bytecode instructions) corresponding to accesses to shared variables — this includes, in particular, accesses to the `buffer` variable (source code lines 8, 11, 12, 28 and 32).

JPF extension. We have implemented the proposed restrictions of concurrency in a JPF extension. The extension has two components: a custom choice generator, which maintains the mapping of threads to processors, and a custom scheduler, which creates an instance of the choice generator at each scheduling-relevant instruction (corresponding to a thread yield point or an access to a shared variable). An instance of the choice generator, which is associated with a particular state, determines the correct set of threads that can be scheduled at that state with respect to the JPF extension's configuration. The configuration consists of the number of processors in a Java platform (unlimited by default) and of a boolean flag that determines whether thread yield points should be attached only to selected program points (for green or quasi-preemptive threading) or to all program points (for time preemption).

6   Experiments

We have performed a number of experiments with our JPF extension in order to find how much the proposed platform-specific restrictions of concurrency help in addressing state explosion in model checking of multi-threaded Java programs with JPF. To be more specific, we performed two sets of experiments — the goal of the first set of experiments was to show how much the restrictions of concurrency reduce the size of the whole state space, and the goal of the second set of experiments was to show how much the restrictions reduce the time and memory needed to find concurrency errors.

All the experiments were performed on the Purdue Java Collision Detector (PCD), which is a plain-Java version of the Purdue Real-Time Collision Detector [18,1] developed at the Purdue university as a benchmark for Java virtual machines. PCD is a non-trivial model (12Kloc in Java) of a multi-threaded Java application that could be run on Java platforms for embedded systems. The architecture of PCD is an instance of the classic producer-consumer pattern that involves three threads running in parallel — the main thread that starts other threads and waits till they finish (via `Thread.join`), simulator thread (producer), and detector thread (consumer). The simulator thread computes actual positions of physical objects (aircrafts) with respect to time and generates messages with information about positions of the objects, which it sends to the detector thread via a shared buffer. The detector thread performs the actual detection of collisions on the basis of information received from the simulator thread. The aspect of PCD's code that has the greatest influence on the size of its state space is the number of messages generated by the simulator thread and sent to the detector thread — the number of messages to be exchanged between the threads in a particular run of PCD can be specified via one of the PCD's configuration variables.

Configuration of each experiment consists of (i) the number of messages exchanged between the simulator and detector threads and (ii) the list of restrictions of concurrency that are applied. If the restriction of the maximal number of threads that can run in parallel is used, then also the number of processors in a platform has to be provided. We selected two relatively low numbers of messages in PCD — 5 and 10 — in order to make checking with JPF finish in reasonable time. As for JPF, we have used three different configurations:

- native threading with time preemption and no bound on the number of threads running in parallel (default in JPF),
- quasi-preemptive threading with two processors, and
- green threading with a single processor.

Note that both the restriction of the set of thread yield points and the bound on the number of threads running in parallel are applied in the latter two configurations. The difference is in the number of processors, which determines the bound on the number of threads running in parallel. For the purpose of experiments in the first set, we turned off the search for errors of any kind in JPF in order to let JPF traverse the whole state space of PCD and we also put a limit on the maximal running time of JPF and on the available memory — the limits were set to 5 days (432000 seconds) and 3 GB, respectively.

Table 1. Results of experiments on PCD: traversal of the whole state space

Restrictions	Time (s)	Mem (MB)	States
5 messages			
default JPF (no restriction)	> 432000	1967	19992569
quasi-preemptive threading + two processors	2317	1535	102482
green threading + single processor	127	740	5217
10 messages			
default JPF (no restriction)	> 432000	1725	19986412
quasi-preemptive threading + two processors	41803	2249	2016072
green threading + single processor	3369	1336	162093

Table 2. Results of experiments on PCD: search for concurrency errors

Restrictions	Time (s)	Mem (MB)	States
5 messages			
default JPF (no restriction)	38	487	1260
quasi-preemptive threading + two processors	16	396	236
green threading + single processor	17	401	236
10 messages			
default JPF (no restriction)	42	496	1420
quasi-preemptive threading + two processors	21	416	391
green threading + single processor	20	411	391

The results of experiments are listed in Tables 1 and 2. We measured the following characteristics of JPF runs: time in seconds, memory in MB and total number of states. If checking with JPF exceeded the time limit in case of experiments in the first set, then the value of the 'Time' column is set to "> 432000" (number of seconds in 5 days) and the value of the 'Memory' column shows the peak in memory usage up to the point of limit's exceeding. Similarly, if checking with JPF run out of available memory, then the value of the 'Memory' column is set to "> 3 GB" and the value of the 'Time' column shows the time of running out of memory. The 'States' column shows the number of states traversed up to the moment of exceeding the limit in both cases. The concurrency errors discovered by experiments in the second set were race conditions in accesses to the shared buffer that were already present in the code of PCD.

7   Evaluation and Related Work

The results of experiments on PCD (Sect. 6) show that the proposed platform-specific restrictions of concurrency help quite significantly in addressing state explosion in model checking of multi-threaded Java programs for embedded systems with JPF. Specifically, the restrictions reduce the size of the state space of such Java programs by an order of magnitude and they also reduce the time needed to discover concurrency errors in the code. In case of really complex multi-threaded Java programs, for which model checking with JPF may still not be realistic due to state explosion, the proposed restrictions at least make it possible for JPF to explore a larger part of the programs' state space and thus also to discover more errors in the code. This is very important in particular for programs used in critical systems, where the costs of errors (and fixing of errors in already deployed systems) are typically very high.

An inherent drawback of the proposed restrictions is that results of model checking with JPF are specific to a particular platform. A given Java program has to be verified separately for each Java platform on which it will be deployed, since a run of JPF will discover only those errors that may occur on a particular Java platform characterized by the specific configuration of the restrictions. Nevertheless, this is not a big issue in the domain of embedded systems, since both the hardware and software configurations of an embedded platform are typically specified in advance — this is the case especially for critical embedded systems.

Also, the restrictions of concurrency are not specific to Java programs and neither to model checking with JPF — the same or similar platform-specific restrictions could be applicable to programs in any mainstream programming language that supports multi-threading (e.g., C# and C), and they could be implemented in any model checker for such languages with the goal of improving performance and scalability of verification.

Related work. Many techniques for addressing state explosion in model checking were proposed and implemented over the years — an extensive overview of the techniques can be found in [17]. Focusing on model checking of multi-threaded programs, the techniques most closely related to our approach can be divided into two groups:

1. techniques for reduction of the number of states and paths in the state space that have to be explored in order to check the behavior of a given program under all possible sequences of thread scheduling choices, and
2. techniques for efficient discovery of some errors only that are based on traversal of a part of the state space.

The first group of techniques includes, for example, partial order reduction [8] and thread symmetry reduction [13], while the second group includes heuristics for state space traversal [10] (directed model checking) and techniques based on bounding of the number of thread context switches [19,20,16]. All these techniques are complementary to our approach — they can be applied in combination with the platform-specific restrictions of concurrency in order to mitigate state explosion even further.

We are, however, not aware of any approach or technique that attempts to exploit concurrency-related characteristics and properties of a specific platform (runtime environment) for programs with the goal of addressing state explosion. The only approach in a similar direction that we are aware of is memory model-sensitive model checking [11,6], which aims to improve the completeness of model checking with respect to behavior of state-of-the-art compilers for modern programming languages (Java, C#). The key idea is to also take into account possible reorderings of operations that are allowed by the memory model and/or concurrency model of a language — typically, reorderings of writes to variables are performed by compilers for the purpose of performance optimization.

Future directions. Although the proposed restrictions of concurrency help quite significantly in addressing state explosion in model checking of multi-threaded Java programs with JPF, still there is much space for further optimization. We have identified several additional platform-specific restrictions of concurrency that could reduce the state space size of multi-threaded Java programs even further, thus making model checking with JPF even more scalable. The additional restrictions can be divided into two groups: (i) restrictions imposed by the Real-Time Specification for Java (RTSJ) [4] and (ii) more realistic modeling of time preemption.

Ad (i) The key aspect of concurrency imposed by RTSJ is strict enforcement of thread priorities, which means that a runnable thread with the highest priority always has to be scheduled at each thread scheduling choice point. The number of thread scheduling sequences can be significantly reduced in this way. On the other hand, it is necessary to capture asynchronous unblocking of threads with high priorities (e.g., when a higher priority thread was blocked in an attempt to read data from a file and the data become available) and dynamic changes of priorities during a program run (e.g., via the `setPriority` method of the `Thread` class). Moreover, bytecode instructions corresponding to back-branches, and probably also bytecode instructions corresponding to method prologues and epilogues, would have to be considered as thread yield points by JPF in order to faithfully capture the concurrency-related behavior and characteristics of Java platforms for real-time systems (e.g., such that involve Purdue OVM [3]). Another option related to real-time programs is to consider only those sequences of thread scheduling choices that are determined as valid with respect to temporal constraints (e.g., real-time deadlines) by WCET analysis [25]. Technically, the restriction to valid sequences of thread scheduling choices can be implemented by a specific choice generator and the WCET analysis can be performed by an external tool.

Ad (ii) A possible approach to more realistic modeling of time preemption in JPF is to suspend a thread at a Java bytecode instruction with visible effects on shared variables only when the thread has run out of its time slot. This way it could be possible to model-check complex server-side business applications in Java (i.e. such as those that typically run on Java platforms for server and desktop systems), which are characteristic by a great number of accesses to shared variables. Nevertheless, a prerequisite for this optimization is support for modeling of real time and execution cost of bytecode instructions in JPF.

Restrictions of concurrency of some form could also be applied for the purpose of efficient model checking of programs that use actor concurrency and huge numbers of lightweight threads (JVM-level threads). This is, for example, the case of programs written in the Scala language [21], which are compiled to Java bytecode and run on JVMs, or Java programs using the Kilim library [22].

8   Conclusion

In this paper, we proposed a technique for addressing state explosion in model checking of multi-threaded Java programs for embedded systems, which is based on restrictions of concurrency and thread scheduling that are common in current Java platforms for embedded systems. The technique is complementary to existing approaches for addressing state explosion — it aims to reduce the size of the whole state space of a given program, while most of the existing techniques aim to reduce the number of states and paths in the state space that have to be explored by a model checker to check all behaviors of a program. We have implemented the technique as an extension to Java PathFinder and performed several experiments on Purdue Collision Detector, which is a non-trivial multi-threaded

Java program, in order to show the benefits of the technique. The results of our experiments show that the proposed restrictions (i) reduce the state space size of Java programs by an order of magnitude and (ii) reduce the time needed to discover concurrency errors.

While the proposed technique helps in addressing state explosion quite significantly, there is a number of additional platform-specific restrictions of concurrency and optimizations that could be used to mitigate state explosion even further. We plan to focus especially on restrictions and optimizations related to Real-Time Specification for Java (RTSJ), since software for critical embedded systems often has real-time characteristics.

Acknowledgments. This work was partially supported by the Czech Academy of Sciences project 1ET400300504 and by the Grant Agency of the Czech Republic project 201/08/0266.

References

1. Andreae, C., Coady, Y., Gibbs, C., Noble, J., Vitek, J., Zhao, T.: Scoped Types and Aspects for Real-Time Java. In: Thomas, D. (ed.) ECOOP 2006. LNCS, vol. 4067, pp. 124–147. Springer, Heidelberg (2006)
2. Andrews, T., Qadeer, S., Rajamani, S.K., Rehof, J., Xie, Y.: Zing: A Model Checker for Concurrent Software. In: Alur, R., Peled, D.A. (eds.) CAV 2004. LNCS, vol. 3114, pp. 484–487. Springer, Heidelberg (2004)
3. Armbuster, A., Baker, J., Cunei, A., Flack, C., Holmes, D., Pizlo, F., Pla, E., Prochazka, M., Vitek, J.: A Real-Time Java Virtual Machine for Avionics. ACM Transactions on Embedded Computing Systems 7(1) (2007)
4. Bollella, G., Gosling, J., Brosgol, B., Dibble, P., Furr, S., Turnbull, M.: The Real-Time Specification for Java. Java Series. Addison-Wesley, Reading (2000)
5. CLDC HotSpot Implementation Virtual Machine, White Paper, Sun Microsystems, http://java.sun.com/products/cldc/wp/CLDC_HI_WhitePaper.pdf (accessed in March 2009)
6. De, A., Roychoudhury, A., D'Souza, D.: Java Memory Model aware Software Validation. In: Proceedings of the 8th ACM Workshop on Program Analysis for Software Tools and Engineering (PASTE 2008). ACM Press, New York (2008)
7. Dwyer, M.B., Hatcliff, J., Hoosier, M., Robby: Building Your Own Software Model Checker Using The Bogor Extensible Model Checking Framework. In: Etessami, K., Rajamani, S.K. (eds.) CAV 2005. LNCS, vol. 3576, pp. 148–152. Springer, Heidelberg (2005)
8. Godefroid, P.: Partial-Order Methods for the Verification of Concurrent Systems. LNCS, vol. 1032. Springer, Heidelberg (1996)
9. Gosling, J., Joy, B., Steele, G., Bracha, G.: The Java Language Specification, 3rd edn. Addison-Wesley, Reading (2005)
10. Groce, A., Visser, W.: Heuristics for Model Checking Java Programs. International Journal on Software Tools for Technology Transfer 6(4) (2004)
11. Huynh, T.Q., Roychoudhury, A.: A Memory Model Sensitive Checker for C#. In: Misra, J., Nipkow, T., Sekerinski, E. (eds.) FM 2006. LNCS, vol. 4085, pp. 476–491. Springer, Heidelberg (2006)

12. IBM J9 Java Virtual Machine, http://wiki.eclipse.org/index.php/J9 (accessed March 2009)
13. Iosif, R.: Symmetry Reductions for Model Checking of Concurrent Dynamic Software. International Journal on Software Tools for Technology Transfer (STTT) 6(4) (2004)
14. Jikes RVM (Research Virtual Machine), http://jikesrvm.org (accessed in March 2009)
15. Lindholm, T., Yellin, F.: The Java Virtual Machine Specification, 2nd edn. Prentice Hall, Englewood Cliffs (1999)
16. Musuvathi, M., Qadeer, S.: Iterative Context Bounding for Systematic Testing of Multithreaded Programs. In: Proceedings of the ACM SIGPLAN Conference on Programming Language Design and Implementation (PLDI 2007). ACM Press, New York (2007)
17. Pelanek, R.: Fighting State Space Explosion: Review and Evaluation. In: Cofer, D., Fantechi, A. (eds.) FMICS 2008. LNCS, vol. 5596, pp. 37–52. Springer, Heidelberg (2009)
18. Pizlo, F., Fox, J., Holmes, D., Vitek, J.: Real-time Java Scoped Memory: Design patterns and Semantics. In: Proceedings of the 7th IEEE International Symposium on Object-Oriented Real-Time Distributed Computing (ISORC 2004). IEEE CS, Los Alamitos (2004)
19. Qadeer, S., Rehof, J.: Context-Bounded Model Checking of Concurrent Software. In: Halbwachs, N., Zuck, L.D. (eds.) TACAS 2005. LNCS, vol. 3440, pp. 93–107. Springer, Heidelberg (2005)
20. Rabinovitz, I., Grumberg, O.: Bounded Model Checking of Concurrent Programs. In: Etessami, K., Rajamani, S.K. (eds.) CAV 2005. LNCS, vol. 3576, pp. 82–97. Springer, Heidelberg (2005)
21. The Scala Programming Language, http://www.scala-lang.org/ (accessed in March 2009)
22. Srinivasan, S., Mycroft, A.: Kilim: Isolation-Typed Actors for Java. In: Vitek, J. (ed.) ECOOP 2008. LNCS, vol. 5142, pp. 104–128. Springer, Heidelberg (2008)
23. Sun Java SE HotSpot, Sun Microsystems, http://java.sun.com/javase/technologies/hotspot/ (accessed in March 2009)
24. Visser, W., Havelund, K., Brat, G., Park, S., Lerda, F.: Model Checking Programs. Automated Software Engineering Journal 10(2) (2003)
25. Wilhelm, R., Engblom, J., Ermedahl, A., Holsti, N., Thesing, S., Whalley, D.B., Bernat, G., Ferdinand, C., Heckmann, R., Mitra, T., Mueller, F., Puaut, I., Puschner, P.P., Staschulat, J., Stenstrom, P.: The Worst-Case Execution-Time Problem - Overview of Methods and Survey of Tools. ACM Transactions on Embedded Computing Systems 7(3) (2008)

Formal Analysis of Non-determinism in Verilog Cell Library Simulation Models

Matthias Raffelsieper[1], MohammadReza Mousavi[1], Jan-Willem Roorda[2], Chris Strolenberg[2], and Hans Zantema[1,3]

[1] Department of Computer Science, TU Eindhoven,
P.O. Box 513, Eindhoven, The Netherlands
{M.Raffelsieper,M.R.Mousavi,H.Zantema}@tue.nl
[2] Fenix Design Automation,
P.O. Box 920, Eindhoven, The Netherlands
{janwillem,chris}@fenix-da.com
[3] Institute for Computing and Information Sciences, Radboud University
P.O. Box 9010, Nijmegen, The Netherlands

Abstract. Cell libraries often contain a simulation model in a system design language, such as Verilog. These languages usually involve non-determinism, which in turn, poses a challenge to their validation. Simulators often resolve such problems by using certain rules to make the specification deterministic. This however is not justified by the behavior of the hardware that is to be modeled. Hence, simulation might not be able to detect certain errors. In this paper we develop a technique to prove whether non-determinism does not affect the behavior of the simulation model, or whether there exists a situation in which the simulation model might produce different results. To make our technique efficient, we show that the global property of equal behavior for all possible evaluations is equivalent to checking only a certain local property.

1   Introduction

System description languages such as (System)Verilog and SystemC provide several abstraction layers for specifying designs. At higher levels of abstraction, such languages allow for designs with non-deterministic behavior. Although this facility is desirable for high-level designs, it poses a serious challenge for their validation. The common practice in hardware design is to use dynamic validation using simulation kernels, which in turn usually fix a scheduler (i.e., fix several, otherwise arbitrary, parameters) in order to obtain an execution trace of the system. As a result, many plausible runs of the system may be hidden during the validation phase but only show up in the subsequent lower layers and thus, jeopardize the correctness of the final outcome.

An exhaustive search of all possible non-deterministic behavior, using symbolic model-checking techniques, can theoretically solve this challenge. However, in most practical cases, taking all combinations of non-deterministic behavior of components leads to an intractable (symbolic) state space. To alleviate this problem, two main techniques are used: language-based techniques, which make use

M. Alpuente, B. Cook, and C. Joubert (Eds.): FMICS 2009, LNCS 5825, pp. 133–148, 2009.

of language (e.g., Verilog) constructs to rule out irrelevant/impossible combinations at design time and reduction techniques, which propose efficient algorithms to explore only a fraction of the state space while providing sound verification results. The aim of the present paper is to tackle this challenge by combining the above-mentioned techniques in the verification of Verilog cell libraries.

The main motivation for this paper comes from our ongoing cooperation with Fenix Design Automation on the verification of cell libraries. In our earlier publication [8], we report on a formal semantics for the subset of Verilog used in cell libraries. There we observed that the IEEE Standard for Verilog [1], allows for non-deterministic behavior, due to the unspecified order of processing input changes (in case of simultaneous changes in the inputs). Tackling this hugely non-deterministic structure naively (by using a brute-force search) is bound for failure according to our past experience.

In this paper, we propose exhaustive analysis techniques for Verilog cell libraries while addressing their non-deterministic behavior. Our approach is inspired by confluence-checking and confluence reduction techniques from term rewriting and makes use of Verilog timing checks (taking into account constructs such as $hold and $recovery). Although we develop and apply our techniques to the verification of cell libraries in Verilog, the general problem addressed in this paper is ubiquitous in system design and thus, the techniques can be adapted to and adopted for other domains and input languages. To aid this, we abstract from the exact implementation of evaluating user defined primitives in Verilog and fix only the structure of the computation and two intuitive properties.

Related work. In [5], an application of dynamic partial-order reduction techniques is used to efficiently explore all possible execution runs of a test-suite for parallel SystemC processes. To this end, the code of parallel SystemC processes is analyzed and non-commutative transitions are detected. Subsequently, all possible permutations of non-commutative actions are considered in order to generate all schedules that may possibly lead to different final states. The technique reported in [5] is comparable to our confluence-detection and -reduction technique (used in [5] for the purpose of testing instead of exhaustive model-checking). The input language considered in [5] is very rich and hence to cater for the dynamic communication structure of parallel processes some manual code instrumentation is required there, which may be a restrictive factor in industrial cases. In [6], the approach of [5] is enhanced with slicing techniques and combined with static partial order reduction techniques.

Neither of the approaches reported in [5,6] claim the minimality of the generated schedules. Our approach, however, guarantees that for each two generated schedules, they do produce different output from some initial state and thus, there is a formal justification for including both.

In [4], the technique of [5] is extended to test the vulnerability of a system against changes in the timing specification. To this end, they consider the deviation in timing specification as an ordinary set of inputs for the test process, and thus, check whether a certain choice of deviation for timing specification can result in a new schedule (order of execution), which was not possible before. Conceptually, this might be considered as dual to our approach, where we make sure that extra, possibly erroneous, execution traces are ruled out by an appropriate timing specification.

Structure of the paper. In Section 2, we recall some preliminary concepts. In Section 3, we introduce our basic analysis techniques, namely, commuting diamond analysis and timing checks. In Section 4, we show how to combine these techniques and use model-checking in order to generate concrete counter-examples witnessing all sources of non-determinism in a Verilog cell library. In Section 5, we report on the result of experiments with open source and propri-etary cell libraries. Section 6 concludes the paper.

2 Preliminaries

2.1 Basic Concepts

Permutations and Lists. We let Π_n denote the set of all *permutations* on the set $\{1, \ldots, n\}$, that is, all bijective functions from $\{1, \ldots, n\}$ to $\{1, \ldots, n\}$. Composi-tion of permutations is denoted by juxtaposition, where $(\pi_1 \, \pi_2)\,(x) = \pi_1(\pi_2(x))$. The identity permutation is denoted by id. It is well known that every permu-tation can be expressed as the composition of *adjacent transpositions*. A trans-position is a permutation denoted $(a\,b)$ and defined as $(a\,b)(a) = b$, $(a\,b)(b) = a$, and $(a\,b)(i) = i$ for all $1 \leq i \leq n$, $i \notin \{a, b\}$. $(a\,b)$ is called *adjacent* if $b = a + 1$.

The set $\overline{\Pi}_n$ denotes the set of all *lists* of numbers from 1 to n which do not contain duplicates. A list $\ell \in \overline{\Pi}_n$ is denoted $\ell = j_1 : \ldots : j_k :$ nil, with the constructor : associating to the right. This list ℓ is interpreted as the start of a permutation π_ℓ, i.e., an injective function from $\{1, \ldots, k\}$ to $\{1, \ldots n\}$, for which we have $\pi_\ell(m) = j_m$ for all $1 \leq m \leq k$. The length of a list is denoted $|\ell|$ and is defined as $|j : \ell'| = 1 + |\ell'|$ and $|\text{nil}| = 0$. Therefore, we have that ℓ is a permutation if $|\ell| = n$. We identify every permutation $\pi \in \Pi_n$ with the list $\pi(1) : \ldots : \pi(n) :$ nil. A list $\ell = j_1 : \ldots : j_k :$ nil $\in \overline{\Pi}_n$ can be constructed by *concatenating* two lists $\ell_1, \ell_2 \in \overline{\Pi}_n$, denoted $\ell_1 + \!\!+ \ell_2 = \ell$, if $\ell_1 = j_1 : \ldots : j_m :$ nil and $\ell_2 = j_{m+1} : \ldots : j_k :$ nil for some $1 \leq m \leq k$.

User defined primitives (UDPs). UDPs are the main building blocks in the Ver-ilog specification of cell libraries. They specify the behavior of basic IP blocks in the form of tables defining an output value corresponding to a set of input values (or changes therein). UDPs can be *combinational* or *sequential*, where in the latter the current value of output is not only dependent on inputs but also on the previous value of outputs. Verilog provides different notation for com-binational and sequential circuits, with which we deal in our implementation; however, for the sake of uniformity, we only consider sequential UDPs. (Combi-national UDPs are of little relevance for our study of non-determinism anyway.) In this setting, combinational UDPs can be considered as sequential UDPs, in which the row corresponding to the previous value of output is arbitrary (de-noted by ?). Henceforth, we drop the word sequential and simply write UDP for sequential UDP.

UDPs work on the *ternary values* $\mathbb{T}$, defined as $\{0, 1, \mathsf{X}\}$. Here, the values 0 and 1 correspond to the Boolean values false and true, respectively. The third value X can be thought of as representing an unknown value, however this is not enforced for UDPs. A *UDP* with n inputs is a set of rows of the shape $i_1 \ldots i_n : o^p : o$, where $o^p, o \in \mathbb{T}$, there exists at most one j, with $1 \leq j \leq n$, such that $i_j \in \mathbb{T} \times \mathbb{T}$, and for all $1 \leq k \leq n$ with $k \neq j$, $i_k \in \mathbb{T}$. The input specification for i_j is called an *edge*, the other specifications are called *levels*. Note that at most one edge specification is allowed in a row; hence, multiple changes in the inputs should be handled one by one and by matching against different rows. Furthermore, for each two rows $r_1 = i_1 \ldots i_n : o^p : o_1$ and $r_2 = i_1 \ldots i_n : o^p : o_2$ in a UDP it holds that $o_1 = o_2$, i.e., two rows specifying the same input and previous output should also produce the same output.

The set of UDPs with n inputs is denoted by UDPs_n. Note that in Verilog, row definitions often contain syntactic sugar that allows to combine multiple row specification in a single row. For example, the symbol ? represents all levels (i.e., all of the three values $0, 1, \mathsf{X}$), whereas the symbol $*$ represents all edges (i.e., all specifications $(v\,w)$ with $v, w \in \mathbb{T}$ and $v \neq w$). Furthermore, the symbol $-$ can be used in the last column of the row, which indicates the current output value for this row. This symbol stands for no change in the output, i.e., if the value in the previous column, indicating the previous output value, is a value from $\mathbb{T}$, then it can be placed here. A row is called *level-sensitive* if all of its specifications are levels, otherwise, if it contains an edge, it is called *edge-sensitive*. A UDP can be instantiated in a *module* specification.

An example of a sequential UDP, a D Flip-Flop with an enable input, together with a module that instantiates it, is given in Figure 1. A sequential UDP can be distinguished by the keyword **reg**, which declares that the output holds its value between assignments. We use this UDP as our running example throughout the paper. In particular, we check whether prim_ff_en uniquely determines an output function regardless of the order of evaluating its inputs. In other words, we would like to check whether this UDP is *order-independent*.

2.2 Semantics of UDPs

We defined the formal semantics of UDPs in [8]. In this section, we briefly recall this semantics and define some notations (for the computation of intermediate states). Furthermore, we state some semantic properties, which are of relevance for the technical developments in the remainder of the paper.

For a UDP *udp* with n inputs, we define the set of all *input vectors* for this UDP to be $I_{udp} = (\mathbb{T} \times \mathbb{T})^n$. We drop the subscript *udp* whenever the considered UDP is clear from the context. Given a UDP and an input vector $\vec{i} = ((i_1^p, i_1), \ldots, (i_n^p, i_n)) \in I$ for it, we define *projections* on it: For $1 \leq k \leq n$, the projections $\rho_k^p, \rho_k : I \to \mathbb{T}$ are defined as $\rho_k^p(\vec{i}) = i_k^p$ and $\rho_k(\vec{i}) = i_k$. The set of all projections for a given UDP *udp* is denoted Proj_{udp}. We drop the subscript when the *udp* is understood from the context. Furthermore, a *substitution* for such a vector is denoted by $\sigma = [a_1^p := v_1, \ldots, a_r^p := v_r, b_1 := w_1, \ldots, b_s := w_s]$ where $a_1, \ldots, a_r, b_1, \ldots, b_s \in \{1, \ldots, n\}, v_1, \ldots, v_r, w_1, \ldots, w_s \in \mathbb{T}$, and for every

```
primitive prim_ff_en (q, d, ck, en);
    output q; reg q;
    input d, ck, en;

    table
    //  d   ck   en  :  q  :  q+
        0  (01)  1   :  ?  :  0;
        1  (01)  1   :  ?  :  1;
        ?  (10)  ?   :  ?  :  -;
        *   ?    ?   :  ?  :  -;
        ?   ?    0   :  ?  :  -;
        ?   ?    *   :  ?  :  -;
    endtable
endprimitive



module ff_en (q, d, ck, en);
    output q;
    input d, ck, en;

    prim_ff_en (q, d, ck, en);
endmodule
```

Fig. 1. D Flip-Flop with Enable

$1 \leq i, j \leq r$ with $i \neq j$ we have $a_i \neq a_j$ and also for every $1 \leq i, j \leq s$ with $i \neq j$ we have $b_i \neq b_j$. The application of a substitution σ to a vector $\vec{i}$ is denoted $\vec{i}\sigma$ and is defined for all $1 \leq k \leq n$ as $\rho_k^p(\vec{i}\sigma) = v$ if $k^p := v \in \sigma$, $\rho_k(\vec{i}\sigma) = w$ if $k := w \in \sigma$, and $\rho_k^p(\vec{i}\sigma) = \rho_k^p(\vec{i})$, $\rho_k(\vec{i}\sigma) = \rho_k(\vec{i})$ in the respective other cases.

We formally defined the semantics of UDP evaluation previously in [8]. This semantics works by considering one input at a time as changed and computing the corresponding next output, which is then used as previous output during the next computation. Intuitively, the next output is computed as follows: First, it is checked whether the considered input has changed. If not, then also the output remains unchanged. Otherwise, the output is determined by looking up a matching row (taking into account that, according to the IEEE standard [1], level-sensitive rows have precedence over edge-sensitive rows) and using its output value. If no such row exists, but the considered input has changed, the next output is set to the default value X.

In this paper, we do not need the full formal definition of the functions, denoted $\Phi_j : I \times \mathbb{T} \rightarrow \mathbb{T}$, that are used repeatedly to compute the output when considering the j-th input as changed. Instead, we abstract from the concrete implementation in Verilog and only require two properties of these functions.

The first requirement is that when the input considered by such a function is unchanged, then also the output remains unchanged. This clearly holds for Verilog, as can already be seen from the above informal description.

Property 1. Let $1 \leq j \leq n$ and let $\vec{i} \in I$ such that $\rho_j^p(\vec{i}) = \rho_j(\vec{i})$. Then for all $o^p \in \mathbb{T}$, $\Phi_j(\vec{i}, o^p) = o^p$.

The second requirement states that the computation of a next output value only depends on the previous values of the inputs, except for the currently considered one. Therefore, one may change a non-considered input of a UDP and will still get the same next output value.

Property 2. Let $1 \leq j \leq n$, let $1 \leq k \leq n$ with $k \neq j$, let $\vec{i} \in I$, and let $v, o^p \in \mathbb{T}$. Then $\Phi_j(\vec{i}, o^p) = \Phi_j(\vec{i}[k := v], o^p)$.

Also this property holds for the concrete functions Φ_j used in Verilog. Intuitively, this is the case since a change on a different position has either already taken place, or it will only take place shortly after the current change.

The semantics of UDP evaluation repeatedly updates the output value, using the above output functions Φ_j in some specified order. It is defined by the function $[\![\cdot]\!] : \mathrm{UDPs}_n \times I \times \mathbb{T} \times \overline{\Pi}_n \rightarrow \mathbb{T}$, which differs slightly from the definition in [8] since in this paper we are also interested in output values after considering only certain inputs, instead of full permutations. Hence, we use a list, instead of a permutation and an index, to identify the input to be considered next. For a $udp \in \mathrm{UDPs}_n$, a vector $\vec{i} \in I$ of previous and current input values, a previous output value $o^p \in \mathbb{T}$, and a list $j : \ell \in \overline{\Pi}_n$ the evaluation is defined recursively:

$$[\![udp, \vec{i}, o^p, \text{ nil }]\!] = o^p$$
$$[\![udp, \vec{i}, o^p, j : \ell]\!] = [\![udp, \vec{i}[j^p := \rho_j(\vec{i})], \Phi_j(\vec{i}, o^p), \ell]\!]$$

We will drop the argument udp from the above function if the evaluated UDP is clear from the context. Hence, instead of $[\![udp, \vec{i}, o^p, \ell]\!]$ we write $[\![\vec{i}, o^p, \ell]\!]$.

Order Independence. A sequential UDP udp with n inputs is called *order-independent*, if for all previous and current inputs $\vec{i}$, all previous outputs o^p, and all permutations $\pi, \pi' \in \Pi_n$ considered as lists, as defined above, we have $[\![\vec{i}, o^p, \pi]\!] = [\![\vec{i}, o^p, \pi']\!]$. Otherwise, it is called *order-dependent*.

In the example of Figure 1, we have that the order of the inputs d and ck matters for the output of the UDP: For example, if both inputs change from 0 to 1 and the flip-flop is enabled by setting input en to 1, then the value of the output q depends on whether the previous or the current value of input d is used, since in the former case the first row is applicable and sets the output of the UDP to 0, whereas in the latter case the second row is applicable and sets the output to 1. Formally, we have for the UDP prim_ff_en that $[\![((0, 1), (0, 1), (1, 1)), o^p, 2 : 1 : 3 : \text{nil}]\!] = 0 \neq 1 = [\![((0, 1), (0, 1), (1, 1)), o^p, 1 : 2 : 3 : \text{nil}]\!]$ for all previous output values $o^p \in \mathbb{T}$.

3   Order Dependency Analysis

3.1   Commuting Diamond Analysis

As stated in the preliminaries, a UDP is called order-dependent if two different orders of evaluation lead to different output values. This description leads to

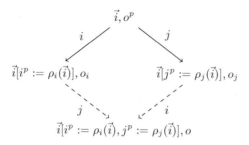

Fig. 2. Commuting Diamond Property

a very simple test for order independence, namely to enumerate all pairs of permutations and testing whether the output is the same for all pairs. This naive approach can be slightly improved, by observing that one of the orders can be fixed, for example to the identity permutation.

Lemma 3. *A UDP $udp \in \mathrm{UDPs}_n$ is order-independent iff $[\![\vec{i}, o^p, \pi]\!] = [\![\vec{i}, o^p, \mathrm{id}]\!]$ for all $\vec{i} \in I$, $o^p \in \mathbb{T}$, $\pi \in \Pi_n$.*

Proof. The "only if"-direction is trivial from the definition given in the preliminaries. The "if"-part follows from the transitivity of equality.   □

This reduces the number of comparisons from $O((n!)^2)$ to $O(n!)$. As we show in the remainder of this section, a quadratic number of comparisons is sufficient to prove order-independence. To this end, we consider pairs of inputs and check whether they satisfy the *commuting diamond property*. Informally, this property expresses that the order of two inputs does not influence the output.

Definition 4. *Let $udp \in \mathrm{UDPs}_n$.*
We say that inputs $1 \leq i, j \leq n$, $i \neq j$ have the commuting diamond property, *denoted $i \diamond_{udp} j$, iff for all $\vec{i} \in I$, $o^p \in \mathbb{T}$:*

$$[\![udp, \vec{i}, o^p, i : j : \mathrm{nil}]\!] = [\![udp, \vec{i}, o^p, j : i : \mathrm{nil}]\!]$$

The commuting diamond property is a well-known property from term rewriting, e.g., given in [2, Section 2.7.1]. The idea is that each two one-step rewrites (evaluations) can be joined again by executing the respective other step. Graphically, this is depicted in Figure 2, where only the inputs and the output value are denoted. The solid lines are universally quantified, whereas the dashed lines are existentially quantified.

Considering one-step evaluation as a rewrite step, the commuting diamond property implies confluence in the induced term-rewrite system, i.e., the final state (and hence especially the output) is unique regardless of the order of considering inputs. In the sequel we prove a stronger result, namely, that the commuting diamond property and confluence *coincide* in the case of UDP evaluation. This relies on the semantics of UDPs and does not hold in the general setting of term rewriting. For sake of completeness, we will also include the proof of sufficiency of the commuting diamond property (for the purpose of confluence).

The formal definition of the commuting diamond property amounts to checking that in case of two simultaneous changes in the input, both orders of considering them leads to the same output. To put such evaluations into longer evaluations, where more elements exist in the list of input numbers to be considered, the following lemma shows that this does not change the behavior.

Lemma 5. *For a udp* $\in \mathrm{UDPs}_n$, $\vec{i} \in I$, $o^p \in \mathbb{T}$, *and a list* $\ell_1 {+}{+} \ell_2 \in \overline{\Pi}_n$ *with* $\ell_1 = k_1 : \ldots : k_{|\ell_1|} : \mathrm{nil}:$

$$[\![\vec{i}, o^p, \ell_1 {+}{+} \ell_2]\!] = [\![\vec{i}[k_r^p := \rho_{k_r}(\vec{i}) \mid 1 \le r \le |\ell_1|], [\![\vec{i}, o^p, \ell_1]\!], \ell_2]\!]$$

Proof. Induction is performed on $|\ell_1|$.

If $|\ell_1| = 0$, then $\ell_1 = \mathrm{nil}$, $[\![\vec{i}, o^p, \ell_1]\!] = o^p$, and $\vec{i}[k_r^p := \rho_{k_r}(\vec{i}) \mid 1 \le r \le |\ell_1|] = \vec{i}$. Hence, $[\![\vec{i}, o^p, \ell_1 {+}{+} \ell_2]\!] = [\![\vec{i}, o^p, \ell_2]\!] = [\![\vec{i}, [\![\vec{i}, o^p, \ell_1]\!], \ell_2]\!]$.

Otherwise, let $|\ell_1| > 0$ and $\ell_1 = k_1 : \ell$ with $\ell = k_2 : \ldots : k_{|\ell_1|} : \mathrm{nil}$. Then $[\![\vec{i}, o^p, \ell_1]\!] = [\![\vec{i}, o^p, k_1 : \ell]\!] = [\![\vec{i}[k_1^p := \rho_{k_1}(\vec{i})], o', \ell]\!]$ for $o' = \Phi_{k_1}(\vec{i}, o^p)$. Furthermore, $[\![\vec{i}, o^p, \ell_1 {+}{+} \ell_2]\!] = [\![\vec{i}, o^p, k_1 : \ell {+}{+} \ell_2]\!] = [\![\vec{i}[k_1^p := \rho_{k_1}(\vec{i})], o', \ell {+}{+} \ell_2]\!]$. The induction hypothesis is applicable to ℓ, which proves the theorem:

$$
\begin{aligned}
&[\![\vec{i}, o^p, \ell_1 {+}{+} \ell_2]\!] \\
={}& [\![\vec{i}[k_1^p := \rho_{k_1}(\vec{i})], o', \ell {+}{+} \ell_2]\!] \\
\overset{\mathrm{IH}}{=}{}& [\![\vec{i}[k_1^p := \rho_{k_1}(\vec{i})][k_r^p := \rho_{k_r}(\vec{i}) \mid 2 \le r \le |\ell_1|], [\![\vec{i}[k_1^p := \rho_{k_1}(\vec{i})], o', \ell]\!], \ell_2]\!] \\
={}& [\![\vec{i}[k_r^p := \rho_{k_r}(\vec{i}) \mid 1 \le r \le |\ell_1|], [\![\vec{i}[k_1^p := \rho_{k_1}(\vec{i})], o', \ell]\!], \ell_2]\!] \\
={}& [\![\vec{i}[k_r^p := \rho_{k_r}(\vec{i}) \mid 1 \le r \le |\ell_1|], [\![\vec{i}, o^p, \ell_1]\!], \ell_2]\!]
\end{aligned}
$$

$\square$

Using the commuting diamond property, we can now show our main lemma. This lemma states that the commuting diamond property is a necessary and sufficient condition to be able to swap the order of two inputs.

Lemma 6. *Let* $udp \in \mathrm{UDPs}_n$ *and let* $i : j : \ell \in \overline{\Pi}_n$.
We have $i \diamond_{udp} j$, *iff for all* $\vec{i} \in I$ *and* $o^p \in \mathbb{T}$, $[\![\vec{i}, o^p, i : j : \ell]\!] = [\![\vec{i}, o^p, j : i : \ell]\!]$.

Proof. In the "only if"-direction, we have the following two computations:

$$
\begin{aligned}
[\![\vec{i}, o^p, i : j : \ell]\!] &= [\![\vec{i}[i^p := \rho_i(\vec{i}), j^p := \rho_j(\vec{i})], o\,, \ell]\!] \\
[\![\vec{i}, o^p, j : i : \ell]\!] &= [\![\vec{i}[i^p := \rho_i(\vec{i}), j^p := \rho_j(\vec{i})], o', \ell]\!]
\end{aligned}
$$

Lemma 5 tells us that we can split these computations, and because $i \diamond j$ holds by assumption, we have $o = [\![\vec{i}, o^p, i : j : \mathrm{nil}]\!] = [\![\vec{i}, o^p, j : i : \mathrm{nil}]\!] = o'$. Since the remaining computation is the same, we have shown this direction.

To show the "if"-direction, let $i \not\diamond j$. Then $\vec{i} \in I$ and $o^p, o, o' \in \mathbb{T}$ exist such that:

$$o = [\![\vec{i}, o^p, i : j : \mathrm{nil}]\!] \ne [\![\vec{i}, o^p, j : i : \mathrm{nil}]\!] = o'$$

Define $\vec{i}' = \vec{i}[k := \rho_k^p(\vec{i}) \mid 1 \le k \le n, k \notin \{i, j\}]$, i.e., set all current values to their previous values except for those on positions i and j. Due to Property 2 we still have $o = [\![\vec{i'}, o^p, i : j : \text{nil}]\!]$ and $o' = [\![\vec{i'}, o^p, j : i : \text{nil}]\!]$. Because of Lemma 5 we have the following two evaluations:

$$[\![\vec{i'}, o^p, i : j : \ell]\!] = [\![\vec{i'}[i^p := \rho_i(\vec{i}), j^p := \rho_j(\vec{i})], o, \ell]\!]$$
$$[\![\vec{i'}, o^p, j : i : \ell]\!] = [\![\vec{i'}[i^p := \rho_i(\vec{i}), j^p := \rho_j(\vec{i})], o', \ell]\!]$$

By the requirements on lists in $\overline{\Pi}_n$, all remaining elements in ℓ are neither i nor j. Formally, let $\ell = k_1 : \ldots : k_{|\ell|} : \text{nil}$, then $k_r \notin \{i, j\}$ for all $1 \leq r \leq |\ell|$. Hence, we have $\rho_{k_r}^p(\vec{i'}) = \rho_{k_r}(\vec{i'})$ by construction of $\vec{i'}$ for all $1 \leq r \leq |\ell|$. This allows to repeatedly apply Property 1 to prove this lemma:

$$
\begin{aligned}
[\![\vec{i'}, o^p, i : j : \ell]\!] &= [\![\vec{i'}[i^p := \rho_i(\vec{i}), j^p := \rho_j(\vec{i})], o, \ell]\!] \\
&= o \\
&\neq o' \\
&= [\![\vec{i'}[i^p := \rho_i(\vec{i}), j^p := \rho_j(\vec{i})], o', \ell]\!] \\
&= [\![\vec{i'}, o^p, j : i : \ell]\!]
\end{aligned}
$$

$\square$

Using the above lemma, we can now prove our desired theorem stating that order-independence is equivalent to all pairs of inputs having the commuting diamond property.

Theorem 7. *A UDP $udp \in \text{UDPs}_n$ with n inputs is order-independent, iff for all pairs $1 \leq i < j \leq n$ we have $i \diamond_{udp} j$.*

Proof. To show the "only if"-direction, let $i \not\diamond j$. Define list $\ell = 1 : \ldots : i - 1 : i+1 : \ldots : j-1 : j+1 : \ldots : n : \text{nil}$. Then by construction both $\pi = i : j : \ell \in \Pi_n$ and $\pi' = j : i : \ell \in \Pi_n$. Lemma 6 tells us that $\vec{i} \in I$ and $o^p \in \mathbb{T}$ exist such that $[\![\vec{i}, o^p, i : j : \ell]\!] \neq [\![\vec{i}, o^p, j : i : \ell]\!]$, which proves that udp is order-dependent.

To show the "if"-direction, we assume that $i \diamond j$ for all $1 \leq i < j \leq n$. Let $\pi \in \Pi_n$ with $\pi = (a_1\ a_1+1) \cdots (a_k\ a_k+1)$. Induction on k is performed to prove the property of Lemma 3.

If $k = 0$, then $\pi = \text{id}$ and hence trivially $[\![\vec{i}, o^p, \pi]\!] = [\![\vec{i}, o^p, \text{id}]\!]$.

Otherwise, let $\pi' = (a_1\ a_1+1) \cdots (a_{k-1}\ a_{k-1}+1)$. Then for $\vec{i'} = \vec{i}[\pi(r)^p := \rho_{\pi(r)}(\vec{i}) \mid 1 \leq r < a_k]$, $o = [\![\vec{i}, o^p, \pi(1) : \ldots : \pi(a_k-1) : \text{nil}]\!]$, and $\ell = \pi(a_k+2) : \ldots : \pi(n) : \text{nil}$ we get the following due to Lemmas 5 and 6, since $\pi'(a_k) \diamond \pi'(a_k+1)$ by assumption:

$$
\begin{aligned}
[\![\vec{i}, o^p, \pi]\!] &= [\![\vec{i}, o^p, \pi'\ (a_k\ a_k+1)]\!] \\
&= [\![\vec{i'}, o, \pi'(a_k+1) : \pi'(a_k) : \ell]\!] \\
&= [\![\vec{i'}, o, \pi'(a_k) : \pi'(a_k+1) : \ell]\!]
\end{aligned}
$$

Furthermore, for all $1 \leq m \leq n$ with $m \notin \{a_k, a_k + 1\}$ we have that $\pi(m) = \pi'(m)$. Therefore, by Lemma 5, $[\![\vec{i'}, o, \pi'(a_k) : \pi'(a_k+1) : \ell]\!] = [\![\vec{i}, o^p, \pi']\!]$, to which we can apply the induction hypothesis $[\![\vec{i}, o^p, \pi']\!] = [\![\vec{i}, o^p, \text{id}]\!]$ which shows the theorem. $\square$

Coming back to the problem stated at the beginning of this section, we have now a method to check order-independence of UDPs in just $O(n^2)$ function comparisons. To do this, we construct for every pair $1 \leq i < j \leq n$ of inputs the BDDs of the two functions $[\![udp, \vec{i}, o^p, i : j : \mathsf{nil}]\!]$ and $[\![udp, \vec{i}, o^p, j : i : \mathsf{nil}]\!]$, which are then compared for equality. If we have equality of every such pair of functions, then we can conclude order-independence of the UDP, due to the above theorem. If however we find two functions that compute different outputs, then their XOR describes the counterexample states and we have found that the UDP is order-dependent. Furthermore, the construction in the proof of Lemma 6 allows us to conclude that there is a previous output value and an input vector in which only the currently considered inputs are changed that leads to two different outputs depending on the order of the two considered inputs.

When applying this method to the UDP prim_ff_en of Figure 1, then we find, among others, also the example for the input pair d and ck where both inputs change from 0 to 1, which we already described previously.

For the pair d and en however, no order-dependence exists. This is intuitively true because both changes in d and en will simply keep the current output value, since the output of a Flip-Flop is only changed on a positive edge of the clock.

3.2 Verilog Timing Checks

Verilog provides a number of language constructs to specify that critical events (do not) happen within a specified time interval. These constructs are widely used, among others, by the designers of cell libraries for timing specifications that may influence the functional correctness of the designed circuits. The most popular constructs used for this purpose are: $setup, $hold, $recovery, and $removal. The syntax of these constructs is given below:

```
$setup/$hold( reference_event, data_event, timing_check_limit
                                            [, notifier] );
```

The reference_event is usually an edge of the clock signal (positive, negative or arbitrary, prefixed by posedge, negedge, or no prefix, respectively). The argument data_event is a change in any data signal, and timing_check_limit specifies the length of a timing interval in a specified unit of time, e.g., in nanoseconds. Optionally, a notifier can be supplied, which is a variable that changes its value whenever the timing check was violated.

The syntax of the $recovery and $removal timing checks is identical to above, but reference_event for these statements denotes an edge of (an asynchronous) control signal. To unclutter the presentation, we only mention $setup and $hold in the remainder of this paper but the same techniques are applied to $recovery and $removal constructs.

The semantics of the $setup statement enforces that no data_event may happen in the (left- and right-) open interval starting timing_check_limit before the occurrence of reference_event and ending by the occurrence of reference_event. The $hold statement is dual to $setup; it ensures that the data_event cannot occur in the left-closed right-open interval starting from the occurrence of reference_event and ending timing_check_limit time units later. Thus, a pair of $setup and $hold constructs guarantee a safe margin around any change in the reference_event during which the data_event cannot occur. In particular, the $hold statement prevents the reference_event and the data_event from happening simultaneously. (Note that the $setup statement does not exclude this possibility.)

Constraints Imposed by Timing Checks.   As stated above, timing checks are added to assert a certain behavior of the system. Otherwise, if this behavior is not encountered, an error is triggered. Hence, for our purposes we can regard the timing checks as describing illegal behavior. Since we are only interested in whether two inputs might change simultaneously, we do not regard the actual time limits nor the notifier variable. We only make use of the restriction that the events of a $hold timing check may not occur simultaneously in any execution that is considered legal.

Such constraints can reduce the number of counterexample states for which an order-dependence is found. However, for this to work we have to infer information about the inputs of UDPs from these constraints. The constraints are usually defined on the inputs of the cell which are not necessarily the inputs of the UDP.

If the output of another UDP is used as input to the UDP that is currently checked for order-independence, then we handle this case by making this internal signal a new input of the module. This input might therefore exhibit behavior that is not possible in the implementation, i.e., we might find an order-dependence that does not occur in the implementation.

For the combinational logic driving the inputs of the currently considered UDP, we require that it does not contain loops and we assume that it computes its value instantaneously. Under these assumptions, we can create functions in the external inputs and the outputs of other UDPs (which are now also assumed to be external inputs) and use these as inputs when checking the commuting diamond property. Thereby, we exclude behavior that cannot occur due to functional dependencies of the UDP inputs, and furthermore we get counterexample states that are expressed using these external inputs and the output value of the current UDP.

From these counterexample states we then remove all those states that violate one of the constraints imposed by the $hold timing checks. This way, certain input signals of the UDP might become order-independent in all of the allowed executions of the module. Note however, that this order-independence does not solely depend on the UDP anymore, but also especially on the combinational logic and the timing checks present in the module that instantiates the UDP.

To illustrate this, we again consider the UDP prim_ff_en of Figure 1 which admits an order-dependent counterexample for the pair d and ck of inputs, as discussed above. However, this situation is usually considered to be illegal for a D Flip-Flop, hence a designer is likely to add the following timing checks:

```
$hold(posedge ck, negedge d, t1);
$hold(posedge ck, posedge d, t2);
```

These timing checks rule out the behavior leading to the order-dependent counterexample that was described earlier, since the second timing check expresses that it is illegal for the inputs ck and d to change both from 0 to 1 simultaneously.

Similarly, all other possible counterexample states involving inputs ck and d are ruled out by these timing constraints, therefore the UDP prim_ff_en has no order-dependency for these two inputs anymore under these constraints.

4   Verifying Counterexamples

In the previous sections, we presented how to check order-independence of a UDP and how to restrict this check to only those cases which are not ruled out by the timing specification in the form of $hold and $recovery timing checks. However, when we report a counterexample this might still be a spurious one. This is due to our overapproximation of UDP outputs and the fact that Verilog has a predetermined initial state, in which all signals have the value X. From this initial state not all counterexample states have to be reachable. Therefore, the idea is to do a reachability analysis, to determine whether a found counterexample is spurious or not.

4.1   Required Permutations for Reachability Analysis

Whether a counterexample is spurious or not depends on whether from the initial state one of the counterexample states can be reached or not. However, in contrast to our earlier approach [8], we want to consider all possible execution traces, instead of just those that correspond to the order chosen by the simulator. Our approach is to consider every evaluation of a UDP as independent, i.e., for every evaluation of a UDP the order might be a different one than the order used in another evaluation. This models the behavior of uncontrollable external influences that might determine the order.

Since we want to keep the amount of non-determinism in the generated model as small as possible, we do not generate all orders, but only as many orders as needed for the UDP to exhibit all different behaviors. For this purpose, we use the commuting diamond property presented in Section 3.1 to reduce the number of permutations we have to consider. To this end, we create the set of equivalence classes with respect to the transitive closure of swapping neighboring inputs that have this property. For example, if we have $2 \diamond 3$, then the permutations $2 : 3 : 1 : nil$ and $3 : 2 : 1 : nil$ are in the same equivalence class and we only have to consider one of them.

Definition 8. *For a UDP $udp \in UDPs_n$ we define a relation $\leftrightarrow_{udp}$ on Π_n, where $\pi \leftrightarrow_{udp} \pi'$ iff a $1 \leq k < n$ exists such that $\pi = \pi' (k \; k+1)$ and $\pi'(k) \diamond_{udp} \pi'(k+1)$. Using this relation we define the equivalence relation $\equiv_{udp}$ on Π_n as the reflexive transitive closure of $\leftrightarrow_{udp}$.*

This equivalence relation can then be used to partition the set of all permutations into equivalence classes. These equivalence classes still capture all required permutations.

Lemma 9. *Let $udp \in UDPs_n$. For all $\vec{i} \in I$, $o^p \in \mathbb{T}$, and all permutations $\pi \equiv_{udp} \pi' \in \Pi_n$ we have that $[\![\vec{i}, o^p, \pi]\!] = [\![\vec{i}, o^p, \pi']\!]$.*

Proof. Let $\pi \equiv \pi'$. Then $\pi = \pi'\,(a_1\ a_1{+}1)\cdots(a_k\ a_k{+}1)$ for some $a_1,\ldots,a_k \in \{1,\ldots,n-1\}$ with $\pi_{l-1}(a_l) \diamond \pi_{l-1}(a_l+1)$ for all $1 \le l \le k$, where for every $0 \le l < k$ we define $\pi_l = \pi'\,(a_1\ a_1{+}1)\cdots(a_l\ a_l{+}1)$. Induction on k is performed.

If $k = 0$, then $\pi = \pi'$, which directly shows the desired property.

Otherwise, $\pi = \pi_{k-1}\,(a_k\ a_k{+}1)$. Because of $\pi_{k-1}(a_k) \diamond \pi_{k-1}(a_k{+}1)$ we can apply Lemmas 5 and 6, which give us for $\vec{i'} = \vec{i}[\pi(r)^p := \rho_{\pi(r)}(\vec{i}) \mid 1 \le r < a_k]$, $o = [\![\vec{i}, o^p, \pi(1) : \ldots : \pi(a_k{-}1) : \text{nil}]\!]$, and $\ell = \pi_{k-1}(a_k{+}2) : \ldots : \pi_{k-1}(n) : \text{nil}$:

$$[\![\vec{i}, o^p, \pi]\!] = [\![\vec{i}, o^p, \pi_{k-1}\,(a_k\ a_k{+}1)]\!]$$
$$= [\![\vec{i'}, o, \pi_{k-1}(a_k{+}1) : \pi_{k-1}(a_k) : \ell]\!]$$
$$= [\![\vec{i'}, o, \pi_{k-1}(a_k) : \pi_{k-1}(a_k{+}1) : \ell]\!]$$

Furthermore, since $\pi(m) = \pi_{k-1}(m)$ for all $1 \le m < a_k$, we have that $[\![\vec{i'}, o,$ $\pi_{k-1}(a_k) : \pi_{k-1}(a_k{+}1) : \ell]\!] = [\![\vec{i}, o^p, \pi_{k-1}]\!]$ because of Lemma 5. Hence, we can apply the induction hypothesis which gives us $[\![\vec{i}, o^p, \pi_{k-1}]\!] = [\![\vec{i}, o^p, \pi']\!]$. □

Note that above we only use the commuting diamond property and not the $\$hold$ timing checks. To integrate the latter, we extend the commuting diamond property to a property $\diamond_{udp}^{module}$ by removing counterexample states that were ruled out, as described in the previous section. The resulting equivalence relation is denoted $\equiv_{udp}^{module}$. Also for this relation the above lemma holds, when restricting to only those inputs that do not conflict with the combinational logic and that are not ruled out by a timing check.

These equivalence classes are used in the next section to implement the non-deterministic reachability check. This is done by using only one permutation from each equivalence class, the above lemma tells us that we thereby have considered all possible behaviors of that UDP.

4.2 Non-deterministic Reachability Analysis

In order to check reachability, we follow the approach of [8] and encode the problem as a Boolean Transition System (BTS), which is a transition system with vectors of Booleans as states. However, in contrast to [8], we consider all possible behaviors of the UDPs. For this purpose, we use the required permutations as presented in the previous section and encode the problem in a (non-deterministic) transition relation. This transition relation is defined as the conjunction of the following formulas for each UDP in the cell:

$$\bigvee_{\pi \in \Pi_n / {\equiv_{udp}^{module}}} next(o) \leftrightarrow [\![udp, \vec{i}, o, \pi]\!]_{\mathbb{B} \times \mathbb{B}}$$

To make these formulas work on Booleans, we also use a dual-rail encoding of the ternary values, where we define $0 = (\text{true}, \text{false})$, $1 = (\text{false}, \text{true})$, and $\mathsf{X} = (\text{true}, \text{true})$. Furthermore, $(v_L, v_H) \leftrightarrow (w_L, w_H) = (v_L \leftrightarrow w_L) \wedge (w_L \leftrightarrow w_H)$. The dual-rail encoding $[\![\cdot]\!]_{\mathbb{B} \times \mathbb{B}}$ of UDPs is a straight-forward modification of the

```
primitive prim_ff_en_rst (q, d, ck, en, rst);
  output q; reg q;
  input d, ck, en, rst;

table
// d  ck  en  rst  :  q  :  q+
   0 (01)  1    ?   :  ?  :  0;
   1 (01)  1    0   :  ?  :  1;
   ? (10)  ?    0   :  ?  :  -;
   *   ?   ?    0   :  ?  :  -;
   ?   ?   0    0   :  ?  :  -;
   ?   ?   *    0   :  ?  :  -;
   ?   ?   ?    1   :  ?  :  0;
   ?   ?   ?    *   :  0  :  0;
endtable
endprimitive
```

Fig. 3. D Flip-Flop with Enable and Reset

dual-rail encoding given in [8], where instead of modeling the order used by simulators we use the order given as extra argument.

Using such a non-deterministic BTS, we can now express the reachability problem in the input language of the SMV model checker. The property we want to verify is the negation of the counterexample states that we want to reach. This way, we get a trace leading to a counterexample state in case an order-dependent UDP can exhibit this behavior in an execution. Note however that we have to restrict the considered traces to the legal traces, as specified by the $hold timing checks. This is implemented by adding a state variable *hold_constraints* that is true if all states of the currently considered trace have not violated any timing check.

The LTL formula to be checked for a pair i and j of order-dependent inputs is the following, where, by slight abuse of notation, we let $i \phi_{udp}^{module} j$ denote the set of all counterexample states for this pair:

$$\mathsf{G} \neg \left(hold\_constraints \wedge \bigvee_{s \in i \phi_{udp}^{module} j} s \right)$$

As an example, we extend the UDP given in Figure 1 with an asynchronous reset signal as shown in Figure 3. Furthermore, we consider the same $hold timing checks for the ck and d inputs that were discussed in Section 3.2.

For this UDP our method finds a counterexample for the inputs d and rst. However, this counterexample depends on the previous output value being 1 or X and the input rst having the previous value 1. Such a configuration is not reachable, since setting the input rst to 1 in some previous state always results in the value 0 for the output. This is verified by the SMV model checker, reporting that none of the reachable states is a counterexample state.

No order-dependency between the inputs d and ck is found by our method due to the $hold timing checks, as discussed in Section 3.2, and therefore no orders have to be considered which differ in these two inputs.

For the inputs ck and en however, a set of counterexample states is found. When applying the encoding and checking reachability, a trace to a counterexample state is produced, where the previous output is 1, inputs d and rst are 0, and both inputs ck and en change from 0 to 1. This indeed may lead to two different outputs of the UDP, since either the output remains unchanged if the enable signal en is still 0 while the change in the clock ck is processed, or the output takes on the value 0 from the input d if the enable signal is first set to 1 and then the rising edge of ck is considered.

5   Experimental Results

To check the applicability of our method, we used it on the Nangate Open Cell Library [7]. It contains 10 different cells that instantiate a sequential UDP and that are in the subset of Verilog studied in this paper.

Using the SMV encoding of the previous section and the NuSMV model checker [3], we found a reachable order-dependent state for all of the cells. However, these counterexamples were due to the value X being allowed as an input of the cell, something that is not possible in a hardware implementation. Hence, we restricted the external inputs to be binary, i.e., to be either 0 or 1. With this restriction, only for 6 cells states exist that can cause an order-dependency. For 4 of these cells none of the counterexample states can be reached, hence the UDPs used in these cells with binary inputs are order-independent.

For the last 2 cells, which are the cells DFFRS and SDFFRS implementing a Flip-Flop (with scan logic) that can be set and reset, a counterexample state can still be reached. The inputs that cause this behavior are in both cases the set and reset inputs. When switching both from active to inactive, the order of this deactivation determines the output of the cell. When deactivating the set signal first, then the reset is still active, forcing the output to be 0. Otherwise, when first deactivating the reset signal, the activated set signal will set the output to be 1. Looking at the Verilog implementation, it seems that for this combination of inputs a $hold check was forgotten, since a $setup check has been specified. This demonstrates that formal verification of these timing checks is needed and that our method is able to indicate what timing checks might be missing.

We measured the time it took NuSMV to model check reachability of possible counterexample states for both the presented method based on the commuting diamond property and the naive approach based on Lemma 3. It showed that the approach based on the diamond property was consistently faster. Particularly for the largest cell SDFFRS the model checking time could be reduced from more than 40 minutes to less than 40 seconds. Also NuSMV's memory consumption was reduced, in the case of the cell SDFFRS from more than 880 MB to ca. 110 MB.

Moreover, we have verified a proprietary cell library provided by a client to Fenix Design Automation and found a reachable order dependency there. The reported counterexample is more complex in nature and cannot be traced back to (and possibly even solved by the addition of) missing $hold checks. We are investigating other timing specifications / analyses that can generically solve such order dependencies.

6   Conclusions

In this paper, we presented formal analysis techniques for detecting nondeterminism in Verilog cell libraries. The source of non-determinism in cell libraries is the arbitrary order of handling multiple changes in inputs. We showed that instead of checking all possible ordering, which is exponential in the number of inputs, it suffices to check the two possible evaluations for each pair of inputs. This approach not only efficiently detects possible sources of non-determinism, but is also complete in that any detected source of non-determinism can lead to two different outputs from some initial state. Our approach is complemented with the language-based control of non-determinism using setup and hold constructs in Verilog. We combined these two approaches and implemented them in a model-checking tool. Open source as well as proprietary cell libraries were analyzed using our implementation and in both cases a number of counterexamples (reachable nondeterministic behavior) were reported using our implementation.

References

1. IEEE Std 1364-2005: IEEE Standard for Verilog Hardware Description Language. IEEE Computer Society Press, Los Alamitos (2006)
2. Baader, F., Nipkow, T.: Term Rewriting and All That. Cambridge University Press, Cambridge (1998)
3. Cimatti, A., et al.: NuSMV Version 2: An OpenSource Tool for Symbolic Model Checking. In: Brinksma, E., Larsen, K.G. (eds.) CAV 2002. LNCS, vol. 2404, pp. 359–364. Springer, Heidelberg (2002), http://nusmv.irst.itc.it
4. Helmstetter, C., Maraninchi, F., Maillet-Contoz, L.: Test coverage for loose timing annotations. In: Brim, L., Haverkort, B.R., Leucker, M., van de Pol, J. (eds.) FMICS 2006 and PDMC 2006. LNCS, vol. 4346, pp. 100–115. Springer, Heidelberg (2007)
5. Helmstetter, C., Maraninchi, F., Maillet-Contoz, L., Moy, M.: Automatic generation of schedulings for improving the test coverage of Systems-on-a-Chip. In: Proceedings of FMCAD 2006, pp. 171–178. IEEE Computer Society Press, Los Alamitos (2006)
6. Kundu, S., Ganai, M.K., Gupta, R.: Partial order reduction for scalable testing of SystemC TLM designs. In: Proc. of DAC 2008, pp. 936–941. ACM Press, New York (2008)
7. Nangate Inc. Open Cell Library v2008_05 (2008), http://www.nangate.com/openlibrary/
8. Raffelsieper, M., Roorda, J.-W., Mousavi, M.R.: Model Checking Verilog Descriptions of Cell Libraries. In: Proceedings of ACSD 2009, pp. 128–137. IEEE Computer Society Press, Los Alamitos (2009)

Preemption Abstraction
A Lightweight Approach to Modelling Concurrency

Erik Schierboom[3], Alejandro Tamalet[1,*], Hendrik Tews[1,**],
Marko van Eekelen[1,2], and Sjaak Smetsers[3]

[1] Digital Security Group, Radboud Universiteit Nijmegen
[2] Faculty of Computer Science, Open University
[3] BliXem Internet Services
{eschierb,tamalet,tews,marko,s.smetsers}@cs.ru.nl

Abstract. This paper presents the *preemption abstraction*, an abstraction technique for lightweight verification of one sequential component of a concurrent system. Thereby, different components of the system are permitted to interfere with each other. The preemption abstraction yields a sequential abstract system that can easily be described in the higher-order logic of a theorem prover. One can therefore avoid the cumbersome and costly reasoning about all possible interleavings of state changes of each system component. The preemption abstraction is best suited for components that use preemption points, that is, where the concurrently running environment can only interfere at a limited number of points.

The preemption abstraction has been used to model the IPC subsystem of the Fiasco microkernel. We proved two practically relevant properties of the model. On the attempt to prove a third property, namely that the assertions in the code are always valid, we discovered a bug that could potentially crash the whole system.

1 Introduction

In this paper we focus on the verification of the following kind of systems: a component C is running in a concurrent environment $\mathcal{E}$, where $\mathcal{E}$ interferes asynchronously with the component C by, for instance, changing some state variables of C. The goal is to prove some specified property about the component, regardless of how the environment behaves.

This kind of problem appears for instance in operating-system verification. Every recent operating system permits several threads of execution running in quasi parallel, even on a system with only one processor core. Typically each such thread might invoke any operating-system call. Nevertheless, the effects the different threads might have on each other are relatively limited. For the verification of the operating system, it is therefore often sufficient to consider only

---

* Sponsored by the Netherlands Organization for Scientific Research grant 612.063.511.
** Supported by the European Union through PASR grant 104600.

M. Alpuente, B. Cook, and C. Joubert (Eds.): FMICS 2009, LNCS 5825, pp. 149–164, 2009.

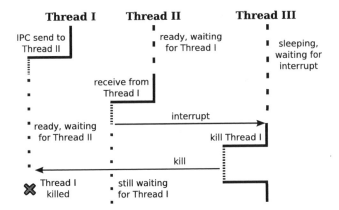

Fig. 1. Environment (thread II + III) asynchronously interfering with thread I. The zigzags in the lines represent system calls: the threads are executing user code in the solid lines and operating-system code in the dotted lines. Dashed lines and separated dots indicate that the thread is not scheduled.

one thread of execution, and to model all the threads that can asynchronously affect the given thread as some kind of environment.

As an example, Figure 1 shows three threads. Initially, thread I and thread II want to exchange a message via inter-process communication (IPC), while thread III is sleeping. Thread II and thread III can be considered as the environment of thread I, that is, they can asynchronously affect thread I. When thread I performs a system call in order to send a message to thread II, the environment could react in several ways (where only the last one is displayed in Figure 1):

– The environment could do nothing, corresponding to a situation where thread II never performs the system call necessary to receive from thread I.
– The environment could engage in IPC with thread I, corresponding to a situation where thread II successfully receives the message from thread I.
– The environment kills thread I, as displayed in Figure 1. Here thread II starts the system call to receive from thread I, but then an external interrupt wakes up thread III. Thread III immediately gets scheduled (for instance because it has a higher priority) and kills thread I.

It is important to notice here that the number of different effects that the environment can have on thread I, is rather limited. Although every thread runs arbitrary user code, there is only a limited number of system calls and only few of them can have an effect on thread I.

Only few operating-system kernels are fully interruptible, meaning that rescheduling of a different thread can occur at every point in every kernel procedure. Maintaining consistency of kernel data structures for a fully interruptible kernel is difficult, therefore many kernels disable rescheduling or even interrupts over large portions of the kernel. When real-time properties are a concern, a kernel design with *preemption points* is sometimes used. In this design, interrupts (and therefore rescheduling) are generally disabled, except at well-defined points —the preemption points. Pending interrupts are then delivered only at these points. Kernel data structures are synchronized before any preemption point so that rescheduling a different thread (which might engage in different kernel activities) can be done without danger of corruption.

In this article we describe and use the *preemption abstraction,* an abstraction technique tailored for this kind of systems. The technique has been developed for creating and verifying models in the higher-order logic of an interactive theorem prover. The preemption abstraction is equally well applicable in a model-checking environment, although its benefits there will not be as remarkable as in interactive theorem proving. We used the abstraction technique in the modeling and verification of the inter-process communication (IPC) facilities of the microkernel Fiasco [HH01, Hoh98, HP01]. Our verification attempt identified one programming error, although the part of the IPC subsystem that was modelled was thoroughly tested and in daily use. The bug could only be triggered when a specific interrupt occurred precisely in a very short time frame during the execution of the IPC system call. It was therefore so unlikely to trigger the bug that it could have stayed unidentified for decades.

This paper is organized as follows. The next section describes the preemption abstraction while Section 3 describes Fiasco, in particular its IPC subsystem. In Section 4 the PVS model is discused, with emphasis on the application of the preemption abstraction. Section 5 comments on the properties that were verified and on the programming error that was found. In Section 6 we evaluate the case study and give pointers to future work. Finally, Section 8 draws conclusions.

2   The Preemption Abstraction

Consider a parallel system S, as exemplified in the introduction, with the following properties. S consists of an arbitrary number of threads and each thread consists of a sequence of atomic blocks. Between each two atomic blocks there is a preemption point, in which no computations and state changes are performed (in practice a preemption point consist of one or two NOP instructions). For each atomic block, each thread acquires a global lock, which is released during the preemption points. Thus, a computation of the whole system consists of one sequential interleaving of all the atomic blocks. Apart from the sequential interleaving, the threads may interfere in arbitrary ways, for instance, a thread t_1 may change the state of another thread t_2. Because of the sequential interleaving, t_2 is of course waiting in a preemption point when t_1 changes its state.

The preemption abstraction focuses on one selected thread t. All other threads are considered as the environment of t. When t is waiting for the global lock in a preemption point, any thread from the environment can change the state of t. All such potential changes are collected in the set of side effects SE. For real systems this set would typically have a small finite cardinality, but the correctness of the abstraction does not depend on that. In this work we assume that the events in SE are independent, however, the abstraction could still be applied if such dependencies are made explicit on the model.

In the following we consider (finite) lists of side effects taken from SE. Note that one particular side effect can occur multiple times in such a list.

The preemption abstraction $\mathcal{A}$ of the system $\mathcal{S}$ consists *only* of the thread t with the following changes:

- The *preemption-point function* is substituted for all preemption points in t. The preemption-point function nondeterministically chooses an arbitrary list of side effects and executes it.
- The global lock, its acquisition and release are abstracted away.

In the preemption abstraction all the other threads of $\mathcal{S}$ that form the environment of t are condensed into the preemption-point function.

The preemption abstraction $\mathcal{A}$ is a sequential model of $\mathcal{S}$ that faithfully models the behavior of the thread t. Under the assumption that there are no dependencies between the threads the abstraction suffices to prove arbitrary (functional) properties of t that can be proved in $\mathcal{S}$. Since it takes the point of view of a single thread, the abstraction cannot be used to prove properties about cooperating threads. The abstraction is sound in the sense that every property proved for t in $\mathcal{A}$ also holds in $\mathcal{S}$. The soundness crucially depends on the completeness of the set of side effects SE.

The main advantage of the preemption abstraction $\mathcal{A}$ is that it is a sequential model, consisting of only one thread. For a description of its behavior one does not have to consider different interleavings of atomic blocks. The abstraction $\mathcal{A}$ can therefore be conveniently described as a functional model in the higher-order logic of an interactive theorem prover. In contrast, modelling the behavior of $\mathcal{S}$ with all possible interleavings of its threads in higher-order logic would be a major hassle. The preemption abstraction is therefore absolutely necessary in order to verify nontrivial systems $\mathcal{S}$ in an interactive theorem prover.

The preemption abstraction can also be applied in a model-checking context. Because model checkers have built-in support for parallel systems the sequentiality of the preemption abstraction is not an advantage per se. However, the reduction of the system $\mathcal{S}$ with its arbitrarily many threads to just one thread should make the state space much smaller. Using the preemption abstraction for model checking remains future work.

3   Interprocess Communication in Fiasco

The Fiasco microkernel belongs to the L4 microkernel family. It has been developed since 1998 at TU Dresden, Germany. It is mainly written in C++ with some inline assembly and assembly short-cuts for the most performance critical system calls. In a microkernel based system many operating-system services are implemented as separate modules, which are running as normal application programs. Therefore inter-process communication (IPC) is often the bottleneck of microkernel based systems. With very stringent optimizations, the L4 microkernel interface and some of its implementations remedied this problem, achieving

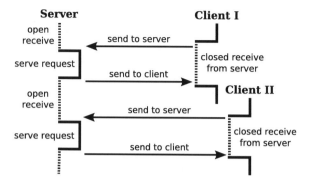

Fig. 2. Typical communication pattern for applications running on an L4 microkernel. As before solid lines indicate user code and dotted lines indicate operating-system code.

performance within 5% of traditionally designed systems [HHW98]. The L4 family (and other microkernels) is therefore sometimes referred to as a microkernel of the second generation.

The Fiasco microkernel implements processes, threads, address spaces, interprocess communication and delegation of memory resources. The only device that the kernel controls itself is the interrupt controller. Drivers for all other devices, such as hard disks, graphic cards and keyboards run outside of the kernel as normal application programs.

IPC will play an important role for this paper, so let us elaborate a little bit on it. IPC in the L4 interface is optimized for the common case of client-server communication. There is just one system call for IPC, whose precise behavior can be modified via certain parameters. IPC in Fiasco is always synchronous, that is, sender and receiver must perform a rendezvous. If either the sender or the receiver is not ready, the other party blocks. In general the IPC system call always performs a send operation followed by a receive. Both the send and the receive operation are optional and can be disabled via parameters to obtain a send-only or receive-only IPC system call. If the send operation is enabled it always sends to a specified destination thread. The receive operation can be either *open* or *closed*. In an open receive any IPC partner is accepted, while in a closed receive only messages from one specified thread are accepted. Both the send and the receive operation always transfer two registers plus, optionally, some memory contents. If some memory is copied it is called *long IPC*, otherwise *short IPC*. Typically short IPC prevails and shared memory is used for bulk data transfer. The time the IPC system call blocks in either the send or the receive operation can be controlled via timeout parameters. As special cases the timeout can be zero (abort IPC if the partner is not ready) or infinite (no timeout).

Figure 2 shows how the IPC operation is exploited in client-server communication. At the beginning the server blocks with infinite timeout in an open receive until client I starts a complete IPC call. This call consists of a send operation and a closed receive, both with the server as IPC partner. When the send operation from client I to the server is complete, the server finishes its IPC system call and starts working on the client request. Meanwhile, client I blocks in a closed receive (typically with infinite timeout) until the server answers.

When the server finishes working on the request, it starts a new complete IPC system call. In the send operation it sends its answer back to client I. Client I thereby finishes its IPC system call and continues normal computation. After sending the answer, the server blocks in an open receive waiting for the next client. The server can thus be programmed in a loop with one IPC system call as last statement of the loop. At server boot time, just before entering its main loop, the server does an open receive without send operation.

In Fiasco IPC is implemented such that the sender is the active part. That is, the sending IPC partner performs the necessary locking and copies the message. The receiving IPC partner simply waits until some sender finished its job.[1]

In Fiasco, thread ID's are 64-bit numbers. They are used to denote potential senders and receivers. There are two special thread ID's: the invalid thread ID, sometimes referred to as null-thread ID, and the nil-thread ID. The nil-thread ID can for instance be used in a closed receive with some timeout. As effect the thread will sleep until the timeout elapses.

4   The Model

This section describes our model of Fiasco's inter-process communication with special emphasis on the abstraction described in Section 2.

For the formalization we chose the theorem proving approach and, in particular, we used the PVS theorem prover [OSRS01]. Section 7 describes other works that used the model checking approach to model the same subsystem.

PVS consists of a specification language based on higher-order logic with dependent types and predicate subtyping, and tools to create and manipulate proofs. Its intuitive syntax is reminiscent of functional languages like Haskell.

The code that had to be modelled was written in a small subset of C++: mainly assignments, conditionals and method calls. We reduced it even more by abstracting most loops and splitting functions with side effects into a state transformer plus a pure function that returns a value. This resulted in a shallow embedding of the C++ sources in PVS.

4.1   Key Abstractions

In a real system executing on the Fiasco microkernel, many threads can run in parallel, and each one can start an IPC system call. Therefore, the IPC code in the kernel potentially runs in parallel with itself many times. In order to obtain a sequential model that can be easily described in PVS, we applied the preemption abstraction as explained in Section 2.

---

[1] An exception are interrupts that are mapped into an IPC message to the thread that registered for that interrupt. In this case the receiving thread is active. However, interrupt IPC is not considered throughout this paper.

As the first step we identified the set of side effects SE. When a thread t performs an IPC operation other threads can modify the state of t in the following way: (1) the thread t can be killed, (2) a timeout can occur meaning that t should not wait any longer for an IPC partner to become ready, (3) the IPC operation of t can be canceled or (4) a receiver can become ready, meaning that t can proceed with the send part of the IPC. The side effects are modeled in PVS with the type PreemptionAction and the function doPreemptionAction, as we will explain in Section 4.2 below.

As a second step we focused on the IPC code of just one thread, ignoring the rest of the system. The preemption points are replaced by the preemption-point function, which is formalized in PVS by preemptionPoint, see Section 4.2 below. Note, that after applying the preemption abstraction there is no scheduler left in the model. The only effect the scheduler could have is that our thread t remains for a longer time in some preemption point and that therefore some more side effects accumulate.

Independently from the preemption abstraction, we decided to focus on the core functionality of IPC. We only model short IPC between real threads (no preemption IPC, no interrupt IPC, no long IPC). Note that we do model timeouts in an abstract way without any notion of time in the model: A timeout side effect can occur in any preemption point.

4.2   PVS Specification

In PVS a theory is a module that encapsulates definitions and properties. It provides a means to hierarchically decompose a specification. Our work is composed of several theories with simple dependencies among them. The theories state and ipc contain the model and will be discussed in this section. For reasons of clarity and space, we will restrict ourselves to some relevant, slightly simplified extracts of our model. The complete specification can be obtained via http://www.cs.ru.nl/~tamalet/.

We define ThreadPointer as an uninterpreted type, which essentially represents an arbitrary set. This set should have at least two elements, which will be enforced by an axiom. We say that null is a ThreadPointer, and declare NonNullTP as the set of non-null thread pointers. The nil_thread_ptr constant points to the special nil thread (see Section 3), used to encode send-only or receive-only IPCs

```
ThreadPointer: TYPE
not_empty_or_single: AXIOM ∃ (tp1,tp2: ThreadPointer): tp1 ≠ tp2
null: ThreadPointer
NonNullTP: TYPE = { tp:ThreadPointer | tp ≠ null }
nil_thread_ptr: NonNullTP
```

Fiasco stores the status of a thread in a bit vector. We have represented the flags of this vector that are relevant to our model as a record with boolean fields. A complete description of the status flags can be found in [Hoh02].

```
ThreadStatus: TYPE = [# ready, cancel, dead, busy, invalid,
    polling, receiving, ipc_in_progress,
    send_in_progress, transfer_in_progress: bool #]
```

Each thread is composed of a status, a partner to engage with in IPC and a list of senders (named senders_waiting) containing the senders that are queued if the receiver is busy. As explained in Section 3, the sender is the active part in an IPC, and one of the actions a sender performs is locking the receiver. In our abstract model, it is sufficient to know which sender owns the lock. This results in the following representation of threads.

```
Thread: TYPE = [# status: ThreadStatus,
    partner,lock: ThreadPointer, senders_waiting: list[NonNullTP] #]
```

Though the status flags can be set/cleared individually, one usually considers a certain combination of flags to check whether a thread is in a specific state. For instance, to determine whether two threads are engaged in IPC, the following tests are necessary:

```
inIpc(snd, rcv: NonNullTP)(s : System): bool =
    LET rcv = s'threads(rcv), rcv_stat = rcv'status IN
        rcv_stat'transfer_in_progress ∧ rcv_stat'ipc_in_progress ∧
            ¬ rcv_stat'cancel ∧ rcv'partner = snd
```

PVS-functions are explicitly parameterized with a System object representing the global state of the machine. Moreover, each function will produce the modified global state as a result. This state is defined as follows:

```
System: TYPE = [# current: NonNullTP, threads: [NonNullTP →
Thread],
    error, timeout, fail: bool, seed: nat #]
```

The field current is a pointer to the active thread, threads is a 'dereference' function yielding the threads of the system, error and timeout indicate if an error or a timeout occurred, respectively, and fail is set if one of the assertions failed. The field seed is explained below.

The manipulation of state information makes specifications needlessly complex. However, with a suitable set of helper functions, one can easily avoid an explicit state object. Particularly, the following composition operation appears to be convenient in our description.

```
SystemFun: TYPE = [System → System]

≫(s1, s2: SystemFun): SystemFun = λ (s: System):
    LET s1s = s1(s) IN IF s1s'error THEN s1s ELSE s2(s1s) ENDIF
```

This operation resembles standard function composition. Observe that the second function will not be applied if the first one resulted in an error.

In the first step of our approach the set SE of possible side effects is identified. This was done by careful examination of the possible effects concurrent threads can have on a each other, resulting in the following set of preemption actions:

```
PreemptionAction : TYPE =
{ kill,                    % The partner is killed
  timeout,                 % A timeout occurs
  ipc_cancelled,           % IPC has been canceled
  receiver_ready }         % The receiver becomes ready
```

Next, all preemption points are replaced by non-deterministically chosen list of preemption actions that are executed. Since PVS does not directly support non-determinism, we introduce the following auxiliary function:

```
generatePAs(n: nat): list[PreemptionAction]
```

This function is not further specified. In a proof, this means that we cannot assume anything about the actions appearing in the result list, hence it has to be considered as arbitrary. The argument **n** is necessary for technical reasons: by using different argument values each time **generatePAs** is called, different result lists will be produced. For, had we omitted this argument, **generatePAs** would have been treated as a constant, yielding the same unspecified list of preemption actions everywhere it is called. This explains the existence of the **seed** field in the system state. At each preemption point, the seed is passed to **generatePAs**, and it is incremented.

The effect of preemption actions on the system state is specified by the function doPreemptionAction:

```
doPreemptionAction(partner: NonNullTP, allow_timeout: bool)
      (act: PreemptionAction, s:System): System =
  CASES act OF
    ipc_cancelled: sysThreadExRegs(s'current)(s),
    timeout:       IF allow_timeout THEN timeOut(s'current)(s)
                   ELSE s ENDIF,
    kill:          kill(partner)(s),
    receiver_ready: IF s'current = partner THEN s
                    ELSE receiverReady(s'current, partner)(s) ENDIF
  ENDCASES
```

The functions sysThreadExRegs and kill basically set the cancel and dead flags of the thread status vector, respectively, while timeOut sets the timeout flag of the system state. The function receiverReady sets the ready and transfer_in_progress bits on the sender and unsets ready on the receiver. Ensuring that the sender and the receiver are not the same whenever receiverReady is called was necessary to prove certain properties; see Section 5. In Fiasco, this is implicit since it doesn't make sense for a thread to engage in IPC with itself[2].

Finally, we define **preemptionPoint** as the preemption-point function that executes a list of preemption actions.

```
preemptionPoint(partner: NonNullTP, allow_timeout: bool)
      (s:System): System =
```

---

[2] And if it tries to, it will get deadlocked waiting for itself to become ready.

```
doPAs(partner, allow_timeout)(generatePAs(s'seed))(newSeed(s))

newSeed(s: System): System = s WITH [seed := s'seed + 1]

doPAs(partner: NonNullTP, allow_timeout: bool)
   (pas: list[PreemptionAction])(s: System): System =
      reduce(s, doPreemptionAction(partner, allow_timeout))(pas)
```

The function reduce is a predefined list function, similar to fold or fold_left in other languages. In essence, doPAs composes the effects of the preemption actions occurring in the list.

These and other basic definitions form the state theory. The ipc theory contains the model of the C++ functions that implement Fiasco's IPC mechanism. The main function of this theory is

```
doIpc(rcv,snd: NonNullTP, has_rcv,has_snd: bool)(s:System):System =
   IF has_snd∧ has_rcv
   THEN doIpcSend (rcv,TRUE) ≫ doIpcReceive(snd)(s)
   ELSIF has_snd THEN doIpcSend(rcv, FALSE)(s)
   ELSIF has_rcv THEN doIpcReceive(snd)(s)
   ELSE s ENDIF
```

A few details of doIpcSend will be discussed later; the definition of doIpcReceive is unimportant for this paper.

5   Validating Some Properties

This section in based on the PVS theories prop_wakeup, prop_locks, and prop_assertions containing our properties of interest.

Property 1: Receiver woken. Consider the send part of an IPC call of a thread t_s that transfers data to a partner thread t_r. In Fiasco the sender is the active part, that is, t_r is sleeping during its receive operation. Sleeping here means that the ready flag of t_r is false, causing the scheduler to never select t_r. It is therefore essential that, after the send has been finished, the thread t_s wakes up its partner t_r, such that t_r can be scheduled again. This property is formalized as follows:

```
receiver_woken: LEMMA
   ∀ (partner: Non_Null_TP)(s: System):
      LET sSend = doIpcSend(partner)(s) IN
         ¬ sSend'error∧ inIpc(sSend'current, partner)(sSend)
            ⇒ sSend'threads(partner)'state'ready
```

The property states that if after the execution of doIpcSend there is no error on the system state and the sender and the receiver are still engaged, then the ready bit of the receiver is set. The proof posed no difficulty and it consisted mainly of definition unfoldings and case distinctions.

Property 2: Lock removed. Consider again a thread t_s that wants to engage in a send operation with t_r as receiver. Before actually starting the send, t_s obtains the lock of t_r to make sure that it is the only thread sending to t_r. After the send the lock must of course be released again.

```
lock_removed: LEMMA
  ∀ (rcv_ptr: NonNullTP)(s: System):
      ¬s'error ∧  ¬s'threads(rcv_ptr)'status'invalid ∧
      rcv_ptr ≠ nil_thread_ptr ⇒
        LET new_state = doIpcSend(rcv_ptr)(s) IN
            new_state'threads(rcv_ptr)'lock = null
```

The property has three requirements, namely, the state of the receiver must be valid, the receiver must not be the nil thread and there should be no error flagged on the initial system state. Under these conditions we were able to prove that after the execution of `doIpcSend`, the lock on the receiver is free.

To reduce the complexity of the proof, five lemmas were created. They assert that the lock is released on each of the possible path taken by `do_ipc_send`. This decomposition was also very helpful in making the proof more resistant to changes in the model.

Property 3: Assertions passed. The Fiasco sources contain some assertions. When an assertion in the kernel is violated, the system simply halts. We included all the assertions that were expressible in our model, but some referred to things we had abstracted from, like the CPU lock, and thus were omitted. In total nine assertions were checked and it was in one them where the bug was found.

To find out if any of them could fail during a call to `sysIpc`, we added the field `fail` to the system state and we defined:

```
assert(b: bool)(s: System): System =
  IF b THEN s ELSE s WITH [fail := TRUE] ENDIF
```

Then the property was stated as shown next.

```
assertions_passed: LEMMA
  ∀ (rcv, snd: NonNullTP, has_rcv,has_snd: bool, s:System):
      ¬doIpc(rcv, snd, has_rcv, has_snd)(s)'fail
```

The function `doIpcSendPart` contained the assertion causing the failure.

```
doIpcSendPart(partner: NonNullTP, b: bool): SystemFun =
  tryHandshakeReceiver(partner) ≫
  λ(s:System): assert(¬s'threads(s'current)'status'polling) ≫
  [...]
```

The problem found is related to the `polling` bit, which is set on the sender when it has to wait for the receiver to become ready. Essentially, the sender *polls* the receiver at intervals to see if it has become ready. Once the receiver is ready and the handshake finishes successfully, this bit should be cleared.

When trying to prove that after a (successful) call to `tryHandshakeReceiver`, the `polling` bit is cleared, we found an execution path in the `doSendWait` function (invoked by `tryHandshakeReceiver`) that did not clear it. After careful examination of the model, the author of that code was contacted and it was confirmed that indeed we had found an error.

But this was not the only complication we faced. There was also an assertion that could not be completely verified within our model due to the abstractions made on the sender. Since we did not model the sender as a separate thread, we could not prove that `inIpc` is commutative, that is, if the sender is engaged in IPC with the receiver, then the receiver is engaged with the sender. An axiom was added to overcome this problem.

Proving this property was quite laborious; 78 other lemmas were used directly or indirectly. The proofs were not intrinsically hard but cumbersome. The unfolding of some definitions resulted in proof sequents spanning hundreds of lines in the PVS prover. The following simple pattern can be identified in many of the proofs: unfold definitions and give names to intermediate states (to reduce the size of a sequent) as needed, then prove each branch using other lemmas if needed. Thanks to our lightweight approach to model concurrency, the number of branches was amenable to interactive theorem proving. The only proofs that needed induction were the ones concerning the list of actions that occur at a preemption point and the proofs dealing with the list of senders in the receiver.

6   Case Study Evaluation

In this section we share some reflections and lessons learned from our case study. We also comment on possible directions for future work.

Main lessons learned. The case study has validated the applicability of the preemption abstraction approach as a lightweight formal proof method for concurrent code.

Using the proof asistant PVS, we modeled `sys_ipc`: the function that handles all inter-process communication focusing on the interaction between senders and receivers. While constructing the model we followed the source code (its structure and names) as much as possible. We focused both on a few key properties and on the assertions that were contained in the code. Furthermore, we abstracted from some important parts of the system, such as scheduling and Long IPC. Therefore, this case study cannot give a full formal proof of the studied system. However, the proofs of the studied properties significantly increased the confidence in the studied code and, when we found the bug, we could easily point out the corresponding place in the source code where the error occurred.

The code that was analyzed is about 3000 lines. The PVS model is about 2000 lines and the proof scripts are another 5000 lines long. Developing the proofs took 2 man-months but checking the proofs takes just a few minutes.

We want to emphasize the fact that the bug was found thanks to an assertion in the code. One usually thinks of assertions as just a runtime check mechanism, but they are more than that: they describe the intended behavior of the code. We used them to generate properties of our model of the system. Had the code not been instrumented with assertions, we would have probably missed the bug.

The soundness of our approach to model concurrency depends of course on the completeness of the list of actions that may occur at preemption points. We determined the possible events that the environment could have on thread at a preemption point by studying the source code. We are fairly confident that our list is exhaustive, however, a fully formal proof would also verify this assertion.

Applicability to systems without explicit preemption points. The applicability of the preemption abstraction does not depend on the presence of explicit atomic blocks and preemption points in the software. On conventional hardware memory access is atomic, even in systems with multiple processors. For the preemption abstraction it is therefore not relevant whether there are possibly several threads running truly in parallel on several CPU's or not. The important point is, that at the level of memory access, all activity in the system is sequentialized. Therefore, one can think of a memory access as an atomic block with preemption points between memory accesses.

Under this interpretation, the number of preemption points will truly be tremendous. One clearly has to formulate the abstract model without writing out every invocation of the preemption-point function. This can easily be achieved with a higher-order combinator that inserts the preemption-point function after each memory access. A legitimate question is, whether it is still possible to verify any property in such a model. In general, the situation is admittedly hopeless. However, systems that have been designed to run in a truly parallel environment without the use of locks are far from the general case.

As an example let us consider a predecessor version of Fiasco that was fully preemptable. There, a timer interrupt could occur after each assembly instruction and induce the scheduling of a different thread. This new thread could potentially modify the state of the interrupted thread. This predecessor version of Fiasco was written in the lock-free programming style [HH01]: To modify a kernel data structure, a thread would first make a private copy, modify this private copy and finally write back the new version in an atomic way (for instance by using the compare-and-swap instruction). If the original data structure has been modified in between, it tries the same procedure again. This way, large portions of the code cannot be affected by parallel running threads, because it only operates on data structures that the other threads do not modify. The calls to the preemption-point function in the abstract model of such code can therefore be treated automatically in the verification environment.

Future Work. A logical next step could be to extend the model and prove more properties. We would start by adding preemption and interrupt senders as well as long IPCs. It would also be interesting to prove the completeness of the set of preemption actions. This could be done by modelling all system calls and showing that any effect these calls can have on a running thread has already been considered. During the first phase of this work, we would have benefited from having a tool that, once configured, semi-automatically produces an abstract model. How to create a general tool that yields different models depending on the user's needs, is an interesting research topic with much potential.

7   Related Work

This work is based on the master's thesis of Erik Schierboom [Sch07], in which a first version of the model was developed and the error was spotted.

Fiasco, and in particular its IPC subsystem, has been the subject of several case studies in the application of formal methods to real-world software. In her master's thesis, Endrawaty [End05] modelled the same subsystem of an earlier Fiasco version. She used Promela as specification language and the SPIN model checker [HPV00] to perform simulations and to verify some simple properties. Annamalai [Ann05] extended Endrawaty's model by adding timeouts among other things, and proved more properties, some of which were liveness properties. Instead of having a lightweight approach to concurrency, they run complete threads in parallel in the model checker leading to huge state spaces. Modelling only two threads where each does only 1 IPC, proving a property took about 8 hours, 2GBs of RAM and 8GBs of hard disk. Proving properties about several IPCs or more than two threads was unfeasible. None of these studies found any error in the code. The bug that we found was only introduced later, when René Reussner rewrote Fiasco's IPC in his master thesis [Reu05].

Kolanski and Klein worked closely with the L4 development team to obtain a formalization of the kernel's application programming interface (API) using the B method [KK06]. Concurrency is modeled using B's parallel composition, hence it is not explicit in their abstract model.

One of the authors of this paper was involved in both the VFiasco and the Robin projects [HT05, TVW09, Tew07]. In both projects the verification of operating-system kernels was attempted, for VFiasco it was the Fiasco microkernel, for Robin it was the Nova micro-hypervisor. At the time of the VFiasco project the Fiasco microkernel was fully preemptable. The Nova micro-hypervisor consists of atomic code blocks with preemption points in between. Both projects concentrated on the modelling and the semantics of certain aspects of the execution environment of these kernels. The verification of larger portions of code was not attempted. Therefore no solution on how to deal with parallelism has been developed in these two projects.

The l4.verified project [Kle09, EKE08, CKS08, Tuc09] attempts the verification of the seL4 kernel. While l4.verified has good chances to finish the first complete verification of a realistic operating-system kernel, we are not aware of any published information about the interruptability of the seL4 kernel or the treatment of parallelism in the verification.

Coyotos [SDSM04] is a secure, microkernel-based operating system built in a new systems programming language (BitC) with a well-defined, mechanically-specified semantics. Singularity [HLA+05] is a research operating system at Microsoft Research that aims to build a dependable operating system written in a type-safe language like C# and specified in Sing#, a Spec# extension. These projects are far more comprehensive and long term than our case study.

The Verisoft project [AHL+08, DDB08, HP08] aims at the complete verification of a computer system from an e-mail client down to the gate level of the processor. For the verification of their ATAPI disk driver the Verisoft project used a model in which processor steps are interleaved with the steps of the ATAPI device. To simplify the reasoning the interleaved steps are reordered into larger non-interleaved chunks as much as possible.

8 Conclusions

This work presented a lightweight approach to model concurrency which avoids the need of setting up an interleaving semantics and allows one to reason in a non-parallel fashion. This technique is best suited for systems where a component can be affected by its environment at specific points and by well identified actions.

This approach was applied in the modelling of the IPC subsystem of Fiasco microkernel. It enabled proving some properties of the model with reasonable effort. Under the assumption that our high-level model is faithful and that the identified list of actions is exhaustive, we can ensure that the code honours the properties here studied. During this process we spotted a programming error that, due to its concurrent nature, was hard to be found by testing techniques.

Acknowledgements. We would like to thank the operating-systems group at TU Dresden for their support, in particular Rene Reussner and Michael Hohmuth for answering many questions about IPC in Fiasco.

References

[AHL⁺08]   Alkassar, E., Hillebrand, M.A., Leinenbach, D., Schirmer, N.W., Starostin, A.: The Verisoft approach to systems verification. In: Shankar, N., Woodcock, J. (eds.) VSTTE 2008. LNCS, vol. 5295, pp. 209–224. Springer, Heidelberg (2008)

[Ann05]   Annamalai, S.: Verification of the Fiasco IPC implementation. Master's thesis, Dresden University of Technology (December 2005)

[CKS08]   Cock, D., Klein, G., Sewell, T.: Secure microkernels, state monads and scalable refinement. In: Mohamed, O.A., Muñoz, C., Tahar, S. (eds.) TPHOLs 2008. LNCS, vol. 5170, pp. 167–182. Springer, Heidelberg (2008)

[DDB08]   Daum, M., Dörrenbächer, J., Bogan, S.: Model stack for the pervasive verification of a microkernel-based operating system. In: Beckert, B., Klein, G. (eds.) 5th International Verification Workshop, CEUR Workshop Proceedings, vol. 372, pp. 56–70 (2008), CEUR-WS.org

[EKE08]   Elkaduwe, D., Klein, G., Elphinstone, K.: Verified protection model of the seL4 microkernel. In: Shankar, N., Woodcock, J. (eds.) VSTTE 2008. LNCS, vol. 5295, pp. 99–114. Springer, Heidelberg (2008)

[End05]   Endrawaty: Verification of the Fiasco IPC Implementation. Master's thesis, Dresden University of Technology (March 2005)

[HH01]   Hohmuth, M., Härtig, H.: Pragmatic nonblocking synchronization for real-time systems. In: Proceedings of the General Track: 2002 USENIX Annual Technical Conference, Berkeley, CA, USA, pp. 217–230. USENIX Association (2001)

[HHW98]   Hartig, H., Hohmuth, M., Wolter, J.: Taming linux. In: Proceedings of the 5th Annual Australasian Conference on Parallel And Real-Time Systems, PART 1998 (1998)

[HLA+05]   Hunt, G., Larus, J.R., Abadi, M., Aiken, M., Barham, P., Fähndrich, M., Hawblitzel, C., Hodson, O., Levi, S., Murphy, N., Steensgaard, B., Tarditi, D., Wobber, T., Zill, B.D.: An overview of the Singularity project. Technical report, Microsoft Research (October 2005)

[Hoh98]   Hohmuth, M.: The Fiasco kernel: Requirements definition. Technical Report TUD-FI98-12, TU Dresden (1998), http://os.inf.tu-dresden.de/fiasco/doc.html

[Hoh02]   Hohmuth, M.: Pragmatic nonblocking synchronization for real-time systems. PhD thesis, TU Dresden, Fakultät Informatik (September 2002)

[HP01]   Hohmuth, M., Peter, M.: Helping in a multiprocessor environment. In: Proceeding of the Second Workshop on Common Microkernel System Platforms (2001)

[HP08]   Hillebrand, M.A., Paul, W.J.: On the architecture of system verification environments. In: Yorav, K. (ed.) HVC 2007. LNCS, vol. 4899, pp. 153–168. Springer, Heidelberg (2008)

[HPV00]   Havelund, K., Penix, J., Visser, W. (eds.): SPIN 2000. LNCS, vol. 1885. Springer, Heidelberg (2000)

[HT05]   Hohmuth, M., Tews, H.: The VFiasco approach for a verified operating system. In: Proceedings of the 2nd ECOOP Workshop on Programming Languages and Operating Systems, Glasgow (2005)

[KK06]   Kolanski, R., Klein, G.: Formalising the L4 microkernel API. In: CATS 2006: Proceedings of the 12th Computing: The Australasian Theroy Symposium, Darlinghurst, Australia, pp. 53–68 (2006)

[Kle09]   Klein, G.: Operating system verification—an overview. Sādhanā 34(1), 27–69 (2009)

[OSRS01]   Owre, S., Shankar, N., Rushby, J.M., Stringer-Calvert, D.W.J.: PVS language reference (version 2.4). Technical report, Computer Science Laboratory, SRI International, Menlo Park, CA (November 2001)

[Reu05]   Reusner, R.: Implementierung eines Echtzeit-IPC-Pfades mit Unterbrechungspunkten für L4/Fiasco. Master's thesis, TU Dresden (July 2005)

[Sch07]   Schierboom, E.G.H.: Verification of the Fiasco IPC Implementation. Master's thesis, Radboud University, Computing Science Department (2007)

[SDSM04]   Shapiro, J., Doerrie, M., Sridhar, S., Miller, M.: Towards a verified, general-purpose operating system kernel. In: Proc. NICTA OS Verification Workshop 2004, Sydney, New South Wales, Australia (October 2004)

[Tew07]   Tews, H.: Formal Methods in the Robin project: Specification and verification of the Nova microhypervisor. In: Tews, H. (ed.) Proceedings of the C/C++ Verification Workshop, July 2007, pp. 59–68 (2007); Technical eport ICIS-R07015, Radboud University Nijmegen

[Tuc09]   Tuch, H.: Formal verification of C systems code: Structured types, separation logic and theorem proving. Journal of Automated Reasoning: Special Issue on Operating System Verification, 59 (to appear, 2009)

[TVW09]   Tews, H., Völp, M., Weber, T.: Formal memory models for the verification of low-level operating-system code. Journal of Automated Reasoning 42(2-4), 189–227 (2009)

A Rigorous Methodology for Composing Services

Kenneth J. Turner and Koon Leai Larry Tan

Computing Science and Mathematics, University of Stirling, Stirling FK9 4LA, UK
{kjt,klt}@cs.stir.ac.uk

Abstract. Creating new services through composition of existing ones is an attractive option. However, composition can be complex and service compatibility needs to be checked. A rigorous and industrially-usable methodology is therefore desirable for creating, verifying, implementing and validating composed services. An explanation is given of the approach taken by CRESS (Communication Representation Employing Systematic Specification). Formal verification and validation are performed through automated translation to LOTOS (Language Of Temporal Ordering Specification). Implementation and validation are performed through automated translation to BPEL (Business Process Execution Logic) and WSDL (Web Services Description Language). The approach is illustrated with an application to grid service composition in e-Social Science.

1 Introduction

1.1 Motivation

Workflows have been widely adopted to create new services by composing existing ones. Grid services are similar to web services, so it is not surprising that common mechanisms can be used with both to combine services. Such composite services are becoming increasingly common in commercial and scientific applications. They can require complex logic to combine independently designed services. Compatibility with third-party services can also be an issue.

It is therefore desirable to have a rigorous methodology for creating and analysing composed services. However, formal approaches are mostly restricted to computer scientists and are hard to sell to industry. This paper reports on work to encourage use of formal methods in the field of grid and web services:

- an accessible graphical notation is used to describe composite services
- formal models are automatically created, validated and verified without requiring detailed knowledge of formal methods
- implementations are automatically created and deployed once services have been validated and verified.

1.2 Composing Services

Grid computing allows heterogeneous systems and resources to interoperate following the paradigm of SOA (Service Oriented Architecture). New services can be created by combining existing ones. The terms 'composition', 'orchestration' and 'workflow' are

M. Alpuente, B. Cook, and C. Joubert (Eds.): FMICS 2009, LNCS 5825, pp. 165–180, 2009.

all very similar, and are used interchangeably in this paper. BPEL (Business Process Execution Language [1]) is a standardised approach for orchestrating *web* services. The authors and others have investigated techniques for orchestrating *grid* services.

Service composition raises a number of issues. The logic that combines services can become complex. Sophisticated error handling may also be required. Compatibility of component services may be a concern, especially if the services are defined using only WSDL (Web Services Description Language). Since WSDL describes just interface syntax and not semantics, deeper issues of compatibility can arise.

A methodology is hence desirable for developing composed services. Defining compositions should be made straightforward since the developer may well have a limited computing background. Verification ('doing the thing right') should allow the service composition to be automatically checked against desirable properties. Once confidence has been built in the design, implementation and deployment should be fully automatic. Validation ('doing the right thing') should be possible during specification (to build confidence in the design) and also after implementation (to check non-functional properties such as performance and dependability).

Grid and web services differ in their emphasis on use of resources, e.g. for processing, distributed data and specialised devices. Resources are often used by grid services to offer stateful services to clients. It is therefore necessary to formally model interactions with dynamic resources in grid service composition. For flexibility, it should also be possible to dynamically allocate the partners that support a composite service. Partners are third-party services that are combined through workflow logic to offer a new, composite service.

1.3   Service Composition Methodology

Surprisingly little attention has been given to rigorous composition of grid services (though more has been done on composed web services). Even where this has been studied, formal models are usually developed separately from their implementations. In contrast, the work reported here is a complete methodology that handles all aspects of service creation, from initial design through to system testing. This approach is called CRESS (Communication Representation Employing Systematic Specification, *www.cs. stir.ac.uk/~kjt/research/cress.html*). In fact, CRESS was designed for modelling many kinds of services and has been applied in many domains. For grid and web services, CRESS can be viewed as a workflow language for specifying composite behaviour.

Early work by the authors demonstrated that grid service composition could be achieved by adapting BPEL. However, there were significant limitations in BPEL that required work-arounds (e.g. for EndPoint References). Composed grid services were also not much more than simple web services, e.g. there was no support for service resources and dynamic partners in the style that grid services commonly use. Only formal validation was supported. The new work reported in the present paper has resulted in a rounded methodology for orchestrating services. Formalisation has been extended to deal with full grid services. Formal verification and implementation validation have also been added to the methodology.

There are several advantages to this approach. A composite service need be described only once, using an accessible graphical notation. The formal specification and the implementation code can then be automatically generated from this single description. Automatic formal verification and formal validation can be used to ensure that the service composition is functionally correct. Errors at the design stage can be cheaply corrected by modifying how the composition is described. Implementation and deployment are then fully automatic. Although further checking might appear unnecessary, a range of practical issues make implementation validation desirable. For example performance bottlenecks may arise, or factors such as dependability and reliability might need attention. Although the methodology described here supports all aspects of composing services, the emphasis in this paper is on a new and distinct facet: how formal verification and validation can be supported.

1.4   Relationship to Other Work

Specifying Composed Services. Several visual programming tools can be used to design workflows, e.g. jABC (Java Application Building Center, *jabc.cs.tu-dortmund.de/opencms/en*) and Triana (*www.trianacode.org*). However, these are rather generalised and not specifically focused on web/grid services and their standards. Formalising *web* services has, however, been studied by the formal methods community.

LTSA-WS (Labelled Transition System Analyser for Web Services [8]) is a finite state method. Abstract service scenarios and actual service implementations are generated through behavioural models in the form of state transition systems. Verification and validation are performed by comparing the two systems. The approach is limited to handling data types but not their values. This restricts the formal analysis of service composition since data values are often used in conditions that influence behaviour. CRESS differs in generating the formal model and the service implementation from a single abstract description. CRESS uses LOTOS (Language Of Temporal Ordering Specification [12]) to model service composition, and can therefore model data types as well as their values.

Temporal business rules have been used to synthesise composite service models [21]. The pattern-based specification language PROPOLS (Property Specification Pattern Ontology Language for Service Composition) expresses these rules. Each rule has a predefined finite state automaton to represent it. A behavioural model is then generated by composing the rules using their respective finite state automata. This can be further iterated with additional rules until a satisfactory model is generated. The process model can then be transformed into BPEL, although this aspect appears to be under development. The approach does not, however, deal with data types. CRESS differs in generating both the implementation and the formal specification from the same CRESS description, dealing fully with data types and values.

WSAT (Web Services Analysis Tool [9]) is used to analyse and verify composite web services, particularly focusing on asynchronous communication. Specifications can be written bottom-up or top-down, finally being translated into Promela and model-checked using SPIN. For composite web services that interact asynchronously, WSAT is able to verify the concepts of synchronisability and realisability. However, the tool does not support the full range of capabilities found in standards such as BPEL. A composite web service specification often deals with error handling, compensation and correlation – things that are not yet handled by WSAT.

[4,7] use a process algebraic approach to automate translation between BPEL and LOTOS. CRESS differs in that no specification is required of either BPEL or LOTOS. Instead a graphical notation, accessible to the non-specialist, supports abstract service descriptions that are translated into BPEL and LOTOS automatically. This is an advantage as the service developer may well not be familiar with either BPEL or LOTOS.

Implementing Composed Services. Web service orchestration has been actively studied and supported in a number of pragmatic developments (e.g. IBM WebSphere Process Server, Oracle Business Process Server). There are several implementations for modelling and executing service workflows, but they lack formal analysis.

JOpera [14] is a service composition tool for building new services by combining existing ones. It provides a visual composition language and also a run-time platform to execute services. JOpera claims to offer greater flexibility and expressivity than BPEL. Although JOpera initially focused on web services, support for grid service composition has also been investigated.

Taverna [13] was developed to model web service workflows – specifically for bioinformatics. It introduced SCUFL (Simple Conceptual Unified Flow Language) to model grid applications in a specialised workflow language.

BPEL has been investigated by several researchers for orchestrating grid services. [16] developed BPEL extensibility mechanisms to orchestrate services based on OGSI (Open Grid Service Infrastructure) and WSRF (Web Services Resource Framework [11]). [22] used specialised constructs to achieve interoperability with WSRF services. These efforts showed that grid service orchestration was possible, but restricted.

Since web services may vary dynamically, partner services may become inconsistent with respect to workflows that rely on them. ALBERT (Assertion Language for BPEL Process Interactions [2]) is a language for expressing (non)-functional properties of workflows. The continued validity of these properties can be monitored at run time.

OMII-BPEL (Open Middleware Infrastructure Institute BPEL [19]) aims to support the orchestration of scientific workflows with a multitude of service processes and long-duration process executions. It provides a customised BPEL engine, and supports a set of constructs desirable for specification of scientific workflows.

The OMII-BPEL work is the closest to CRESS. The authors strongly believe that implementations should be created in standard languages (BPEL, WSDL, XSD) which are already widely used. For example, this allows the use of a variety of orchestration engines. CRESS differs from similar BPEL approaches in taking a more abstract (and language-independent) view. Specification, implementation and analysis can therefore be integrated in a single methodology.

2   Background

2.1 Service Composition and Grid Services

SOA (Service Oriented Architecture) treats capabilities or functions as individual services. Service composition is a key feature of SOA for creating new services by combining the behaviour of existing ones. BPEL (Business Process Execution Language

[1]) is one of the most popular languages for specifying composite *web* services. Although early work on composing *grid* services using BPEL showed promise, this was not straightforward. Fortunately, the latest standard for BPEL supports WSRF (Web Services Resources Framework [11]) and is hence appropriate for grid services.

WSRF allows a service instance to be associated with arbitrary numbers and types of resources. 'Resource pairs' are identified by an EPR (EndPoint Reference [20]). Grid services promote virtual collaboration among users of distributed systems. A grid environment can be highly dynamic, with resources, partners and services being created, added, shared and removed over time.

Grid computing initially developed through applications in the physical sciences. The trend is now towards use in other areas such as e-Social Science, which has been recognised as a promising application of grid computing. The authors are formalising support for workflows on the DAMES project (Data Management through e-Social Science, *www.dames.org.uk*).

To illustrate the methodology for developing workflows, this paper tackles a common task performed by social scientists: representing occupations in different classification schemes. Occupational data researchers are interested in analysing questions such as how jobs affect social position, social interaction patterns, etc. There are many occupational classification schemes, some of them international standards. As each classification scheme favours certain types of analysis, occupational researchers have to map datasets to particular schemes to perform the analysis. This might involve several intermediate mappings to arrive at the desired encoding. As a result, translation is often performed using computer scripts or paper indexes that map between (usually) two schemes. Sections 3 and 4 discuss how an occupational translation service was rigorously developed using service composition.

2.2 CRESS

CRESS is a domain-independent graphical notation for describing services. CRESS takes an abstract approach in which a high-level service description automatically generates a formal specification and an executable implementation. In other work, it has been used to describe a variety of voice services and also web services. CRESS can be used as a graphical workflow notation for grid and web services.

CRESS service descriptions are graphical, making the approach accessible to non-specialists. The focus is on high-level description, abstracting away the technical details required in an actual implementation. CRESS is designed as an extensible framework where support for new domains and target languages can be added like plug-ins.

The CRESS representation for service composition is intentionally close to BPEL. A brief description of the notation subset used in this paper is given here. Refer to figures 1 and 2 for the examples cited below.

A CRESS diagram typically includes a rule box, numbered nodes, and arcs that link nodes. A rule box is a rounded rectangle which (for grid and web services) defines variables and their types, as well as dynamic partners. Complex data structures can be defined, e.g. '{...}' for records. As an example, the following defines two variables *mapping1* and *mapping2* whose type is a record with two string fields:

{ **String** job **String** scheme } mapping1:ALLOCATOR, mapping2:ALLOCATOR

Variables and their types are normally associated with the diagram that defines them. A variable can be qualified by its owning diagram (*Allocator* above).

A rule box can also indicate which other services are required, e.g. '/ Allocator' in the description of the *Lookup* service shows it depends on the *Allocator* service.

The activities in a composed service are described in numbered ellipses. A typical composition starts with **Receive** as an incoming request that specifies the service, port and operation names, as well as the input variable. A typical composition ends with a **Reply** as an outgoing response that returns an output variable or a fault. There can be alternative **Reply** activities for one **Receive**, and even several **Receive** activities. **Invoke** is used to call an external partner by service, port and operation. Invocation specifies an output variable, an optional input variable, and optional faults that may be thrown. (A one-way invocation is useful for long-running transactions.) Some examples are:

> **Receive** lookup.job.translate schemes   (input *schemes*)
> **Reply** lookup.job.translate codes   (output *codes*)
> **Reply** lookup.job.translate allocatorError.reason   (fault *allocatorError.reason*)
> **Invoke** allocator.job.translate mapping1 code1   (output *mapping1*, input *code1*)

Faults can be defined with just a name (*allocatorError*), with just a value (*.reason*), or with both elements.

Other activities include **Terminate** (to end behaviour), **Compensate** (to undo work following a failure), and **Fork/Join** (for concurrency). For the latter, a fine degree of control over concurrency can be specified. In general, each activity may complete successfully or may fail. A join condition such as '3 && 4' means that activities 3 and 4 must succeed before behaviour continues. Activities as well as arcs can contain assignments such as '/ mapping1.job <− schemes.job'.

Branches in CRESS diagrams normally represent choices. A deterministic choice has labels on arcs for conditions that govern which path is followed. A non-deterministic choice has unlabelled arcs. Event choices are not made immediately, but rather when some event happens. For example, a '**Catch** *.reason*' branch is followed only when a fault with some *reason* value occurs. A **Compensation** branch is taken only when a **Compensate** activity is used to undo previous work. Typically, compensation is defined after an **Invoke** since a failure may mean that changes already made have to be undone.

3   Formal Specification and Analysis of Composed Grid Services

3.1   Describing Service Composition

The service developer starts by drawing a CRESS diagram that describes the logic used to combine the functions of external service partners. Typically these partners have already been created by others, though new partner services might also be created for the purposes of the orchestration. In a complex development, a number of CRESS diagrams may be defined to realise the orchestration. CRESS also supports feature diagrams for common functions that can be added automatically to service descriptions.

During the work reported in this paper, CRESS was extended to treat EPRs (EndPoint References) as first-class values, to support grid resources fully, to handle dynamic

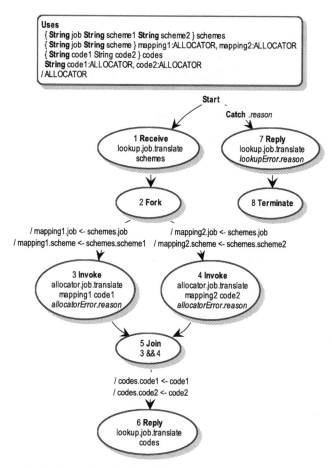

Fig. 1. CRESS Description of The Occupation Lookup Service

service partners, to formally verify properties, and to validate implementations. These aspects are all illustrated using the following example.

The diagrams in figures 1 and 2 show the use of CRESS to describe an e-Social Science workflow. This supports the classification of occupations mentioned in section 2.1. The services involved in this example are as follows:

Lookup: This is the top-level workflow that takes a request to translate a job title into two occupational schemes. It uses the *Allocator* partner to perform these translations in parallel, and returns the combined result.

Allocator: This partner service is itself a workflow that takes a request to map an occupation into some scheme. It uses the *Factory* partner to find a suitable resource (i.e. a *Mapper* service), perform the translation, and then return the occupation code.

Factory: This partner service accepts a request to find an occupational classification translator. It dynamically allocates a resource for performing this task, and returns a reference to it. If no suitable resource can be allocated, a fault is thrown.

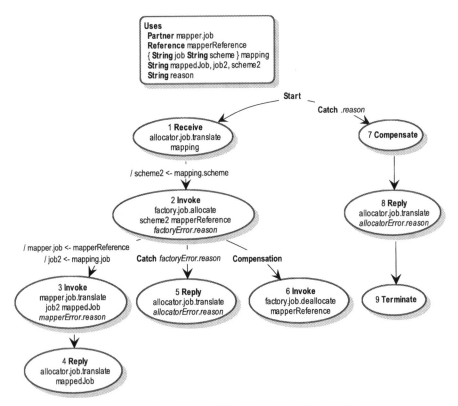

Fig. 2. CRESS Description of The Occupation Allocator Service

Mapper: This partner service is selected dynamically, so it represents a class of translation services. The given job title is translated into a particular occupational scheme.

Lookup Service. The service in figure 1 defines translation logic that makes use of
the partner *Allocator* service. Initially the service proceeds along the arc from **Start**
to node 1. The service then accepts a request to translate a job title into two specified
schemes (node 1). The translations may be automated (e.g. through an online service)
or may be manual (e.g. requiring a researcher to look up a classification scheme). Since
the delay in translation for each scheme is unknown, both translations are performed in
parallel (node 2 to node 5).

  Both parallel branches are similar. For example, the left-hand branch copies the *job*
and *scheme* names into the *mapping1* structure (arc from node 2 to node 3). The *Allocator* service is then called to translate this into a job code (node 3). This service may
give rise to a fault if the translation cannot be performed (fault name *allocatorError*,
fault value *reason*). Both parallel branches require to complete successfully before further action is taken, as specified by the join condition in node 5. At this point, the two
job codes are combined into a *codes* structure (arc from node 5 to node 6). The *Lookup*
service ends by sending this to its caller (node 6).

  Concurrency requires proper handling of faults. For example, if one of the parallel
branches fails then the other cannot be left hanging. The top-level error handler (arc

from **Start** to node 7) catches a fault from either parallel invocation. It replies to the caller with the reason why the *Allocator* failed, and terminates the whole workflow.

Allocator Service. The service in figure 2 initially proceeds along the arc from **Start** to node 1. Here it accepts a request for a particular job mapping. The classification scheme is extracted into *scheme2* (arc from node 1 to 2). Since it is necessary to find a suitable translation service, the *Factory* partner is called to find one for the particular scheme (node 2). This returns a *Mapper* reference for a suitable service instance. If no suitable service is found, a fault is thrown.

The *Allocator* then dynamically sets the partner (*mapper.job*) for the *Mapper* service, and extracts the job title into *job2* (arc from node 2 to node 3). When the *Mapper* is called to translate the job title, this dynamic partner is used (node 3). In normal circumstances, the *Allocator* replies with the job code (*mappedJob*) to its caller (node 4).

Various error conditions are handled by the *Allocator*. If the *Factory* invocation in node 2 fails, the error is caught in the local scope and returned to the caller (node 5). A mapping failure in node 3 needs to be handled differently. Since no fault handler is defined for this invocation, the global fault handler is used (arc from **Start** to node 7). This requires compensation because simply terminating the *Allocator* would leave the translation resource allocated. **Compensate** in node 7 requests global compensation. All subsidiary compensation activities are then called in reverse order of completion. In this example, there is only one such activity (arc from node 2 to node 6). The effect is to deallocate the service instance (*mapperReference*) that the *Factory* had allocated (node 6). Following compensation, the *Allocator* returns the fault *reason* to its caller and terminates the workflow (nodes 8 and 9).

Collectively, figures 1 and 2 define a composite service with four partners. However, a client of the whole translation service sees just a single grid service; the internal design of this is intentionally hidden, and could be changed in future.

3.2 Formalising Service Composition

A CRESS diagram is automatically translated into LOTOS (Language Of Temporal Ordering Specification [12]), including support for diagram-defined data types and behaviour. (A number of formal approaches to grid or web services support only elementary data types such as booleans and integers.) Service behaviour is represented by interacting LOTOS processes. As the focus is on service composition, CRESS fully specifies the logic that combines external partner services. CRESS does not normally have enough information to specify these partners, and instead defines only their interfaces. However if a partner service is itself a composition, CRESS will specify it fully.

Since partner services are usually defined by others, it is likely that no formal specification exists of them. Indeed, the design of a partner service may be proprietary and hidden. The automated interface specifications generated by CRESS are sufficient for basic compatibility checks with partners. For a more thorough analysis it is desirable to have more complete (though still abstract) specifications of partner services. These specifications have to be created manually, by the developer of the partner service or by the developer of the composite service. However, having a formal specification of all services is good practice anyway.

Handling of dynamic resources in LOTOS has been added for the work reported here. For static service partners, interactions between a composite service and a service partner are via LOTOS events that specify the service, port and operation. For dynamic service partners, synchronisation is specified with a resource prior any interaction. This is reasonable as an actual implementation also does the same thing.

The **Partner** type in CRESS is a unique key that identifies a resource pair. An assignment to *partner.port* is performed prior to invoking a dynamic partner. In LOTOS, this is translated as an assignment to the corresponding EndPoint Reference variable. Synchronisation with a dynamic partner specifies the EPR required. It is only after this that a dynamic partner instance can be invoked.

Figure 3 shows how the various specification elements are combined in the CRESS methodology. The generated specification of the composite service normally dominates the specifications of its partner services. The composite LOTOS specification that results is sufficient for use with several LOTOS tools, e.g. LOLA (LOTOS Laboratory [15]). However, some LOTOS tools such as CADP (Construction and Analysis of Distributed Processes [10]) require the specification to be preprocessed first.

A CRESS service description is rigorously analysed through formal validation and verification of the automatically generated LOTOS. Once the composition has been checked to have the desired properties, an implementation can be created automatically.

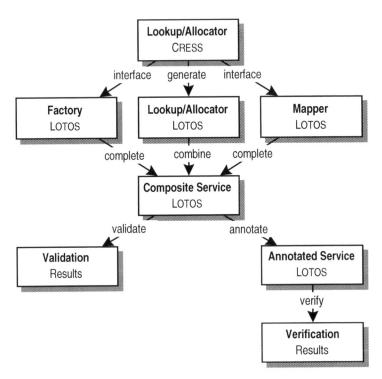

Fig. 3. Formal Validation and Verification with CRESS

3.3 Validating Service Compositions

Formal validation can be directly performed on the composite specification produced by CRESS. This makes use of a test notation and tool called MUSTARD (Multiple Use Scenario Test and Refusal Description [18]). MUSTARD can be used to test partner services as well as service compositions.

As a simple example of validation with MUSTARD, the following acceptance test checks the translation of job title 'nurse' into the SOC2000 and SIC92 classifications (codes '3211' and '95.14' respectively). The test succeeds if it is possible to send a translation request and then to read the expected response. Strings in MUSTARD are preceded by a single quote.

```
test(Nurse_Translation,
  succeed(
    send(lookup.job.translate, schemes('Nurse,'SOC2000,'SIC92)),
    read(lookup.job.translate, codes('3211,'95.14))))
```

Acceptance tests check only what a system must do. MUSTARD is also used to define refusal tests that check what a system must not do. Concurrent behaviour can be checked as well. In the following test, parallel requests are performed to translate a job title using different occupational schemes:

```
test(Parallel_Translation,
  succeed(
    interleave(
      sequence(
        send(lookup.job.translate, schemes('Cab Driver,'SOC2000,'SIC92)),
        read(lookup.job.translate, codes('8214,'60.22))),
      sequence(
        send(lookup.job.translate, schemes('Private Detective,'SIC92,'SOC2000)),
        read(lookup.job.translate, codes('74.60/1,'9241))))))
```

MUSTARD translates such tests into LOTOS, adds them to the composite specification generated by CRESS, and uses the validation facilities of LOLA to formally check that the specification passes its tests. This is achieved through abstract execution of the specification, constrained by the test behaviours. The tests above are simple examples. In practice, MUSTARD is used for a variety of tests that may include alternatives, conditions, non-determinism, variables, wild-card values, service dependencies (whether a particular service is deployed), fixtures (common preambles for tests), and reset actions (to put a service into a known state). As will be seen in section 4, the same MUSTARD tests are used to validate implementations as well as specifications.

Although such validation is formally based, testing is necessarily limited. Its main advantage is that validation is practical: automated validation of even a complex service is performed in seconds or minutes. However, formal verification is desirable as a complement to this. Rather than showing that the specification exhibits desirable behaviour on certain test cases, it is preferable to prove properties in general for classes of tests.

3.4 Annotating LOTOS

For formal verification of LOTOS, the toolset of choice is CADP (Construction and Analysis of Distributed Processes [10]). However, CADP places a number of restrictions on the form of LOTOS that it will accept. In particular, data types need to be extensively annotated. Verification is performed only after an automated CRESS step to annotate a LOTOS specification for CADP. This requires a tool that knows about standard LOTOS data types as well as the data types that CRESS generates.

CADP does not allow parameterised data types, so they must be instantiated first. The authors have developed a tool to 'flatten' and annotate data types: all data types are collapsed into one, and CADP pragmas are inserted. CADP also does not support infinite sorts. Annotations in the form of special LOTOS comments are therefore added to a specification prior to verification, e.g. to identify constructor operations and external implementations of data types.

CADP can verify a LOTOS specification through model checking. Abstract data types with infinite values have to be limited to a finite range for verification. Most data types in grid and web services have finite (although possibly large) ranges whose size may depend on the programming language or platform. Several CRESS library data types such as *Number* have an infinite range.

In previous work, finite ranges were manually specified for CRESS data types (e.g. *Char*, *Number*, *Text*). In the work reported here, the automated annotation tool also deals with restricting ranges. C implementation skeletons are created automatically for user-defined data types (e.g. record structures in CRESS). For the occupation translation example, C skeleton files are created automatically for CRESS types like *schemes* and *mapping*. As it happens, this particular example does not need any special implementations for data types – CADP supplies default implementations. However, specific implementations can be created manually to replace the default ones.

Roughly speaking, each CRESS diagram node corresponds to a LOTOS process. A LOTOS process communicates using events at gates. Processes synchronise their communications at gates, which may be selectively hidden from external view. Processes may run independently in parallel or may synchronise on specific gates.

Factory and *Mapper* are normal partners, and are instantiated where they are used inside the definition of *Allocator*. The *Allocator* is actually instantiated twice: once inside *Lookup*, where it is used, and again at the global level. This is because *Allocator* is a composite service that can also be used in its own right. A *Resource* partner implicitly represents the set of dynamic resources that may be allocated by the *Factory*. In implementation terms, this is called the 'resource home'. In CRESS terms, *Resource* is a 'phantom partner' that is instantiated at the global level for use by all services.

3.5   Verifying Service Compositions

Verification allows general properties to be checked, whereas validation can check only specific cases (though these are usually selected to be the critical ones). Model checking requires a finite (though possibly large) state space, and so will not be practicable in some cases. Validation can deal with very large or infinite state spaces. The two techniques are therefore complementary, and help to ensure that the methodology for service development is both rigorous and practical.

Service properties are verified using the notation and tool called CLOVE (CRESS Language-Oriented Verification Environment). This supports the high-level formulation of properties, and provides a simple way of using the actual verification tools. To some extent, CLOVE is oriented towards the needs of verifying grid or web services. Verification is normally undertaken only by specialists. To fit in with the pragmatic aims of CRESS, CLOVE is designed for use by those with limited knowledge of formal methods. For example, common properties of services are automatically checked, and property templates are also supported. This allows the domain specialist the verify correctness of service descriptions.

The specification patterns repository (*patterns.projects.cis.ksu.edu*) builds on the fact that verification properties are often common across many application domains. This makes it possible to develop template properties that can be supported by different formal methods [6]. CLOVE supports this approach by embedding and extending these properties, using the LOTOS representations developed by Mateescu (*www.inrialpes. fr/vasy/cadp/resources/evaluator/rafmc.html*). In addition, CLOVE supports common properties such as freedom from deadlock and livelock, as well as specialised properties that are appropriate for services.

As examples, the following properties are desirable for the occupational translation service in figures 1 and 2:

− The service should always be available, i.e. free from deadlocks (a safety property).
− If the service receives a request, it must able to accept a new request at a future point (a liveness property).
− For correct service requests, the client should receive the translated job title or a fault due to partner failure.
− For incorrect service requests (an unknown job title or classification scheme), a fault must be reported to the client.
− If an occupation translator cannot be found, a fault must be reported to the client.

As a concrete example, the following CLOVE property deals with service requests and responses. A request to translate an occupation into some schemes must always ('global') must result in the occupation codes or a lookup error with a string message. ('?' means any value of the given type.) If this property does not hold of the service description, the cause of the failure is analysed.

```
property(General_ Response,
  response(global,
    signal(lookup.job.translate,?schemes),
    or(
      signal(lookup.job.translate,?codes),
      signal(lookup.job.translate,lookupError,?string))))
```

The *Nurse_ Translation* example in section 3.3 runs only one test. The following CLOVE property asserts that translating job title 'nurse' into the SOC2000 and SIC92 classifications should yield the correct result in all cases.

```
property(Nurse_ Response,
  response(global,
    signal(lookup.job.translate,schemes('Nurse,'SOC2000,'SIC92)),
    signal(lookup.job.translate,codes('3211,'95.14))))
```

Common service properties (e.g. deadlock freedom) are automatically verified without having to be specified explicitly. In addition, service-specific properties like the above can be formulated by the developer. The CLOVE notation is intended to be more accessible than the underlying formalism (μ-calculus). CLOVE is also designed to be similar to MUSTARD, allowing the developer to verify and validate services in a similar way. Although these example properties are simple, they are typical of service verification practice. CLOVE also supports other types of property, e.g. for safety or liveness.

Behind the scenes, CLOVE automatically translates the properties into μ-calculus [5] – a temporal logic that allows branching-time properties to be checked. CLOVE then invokes CADP to carry out property verification. The goal for verifying CRESS service descriptions is to make this as 'push button' as possible, especially since the service developer is unlikely to be a formal methods expert. In fact it is possible for the developer to compose services without leaving the CRESS diagram editor. A service composition can be described graphically, validated, verified, implemented and deployed from within this graphical tool.

The CADP tools used for verification are CAESAR (behaviour compiler), CAESAR.ADT (data type compiler) and Evaluator. CAESAR.ADT generates a C header file from the LOTOS specification, including references to the C skeleton files generated by CRESS. CAESAR is then used to generate a BCG (Boundary Components Graph) for the specification. The Evaluator tool verifies properties of a specification in LOTOS or BCG form. Verification steps are defined by an automated script written in SVL (Script Verification Language). Desirable properties include deadlock freedom, consistency of service behaviour, and reachability of service states.

The CRESS specification generated from figures 1 and 2 was successfully verified against these properties after some corrections. For example, the original description would deadlock if a request contained an invalid occupational scheme. As a result, there was no response to the client request.

4   Implementing and Deploying Composed Grid Services

The main emphasis of this paper is on formal aspects, so the automated implementation will be described only briefly. The *same* CRESS description as used for specification is automatically implemented through translation into BPEL/WSDL and is packaged for deployment. Services that are part of the composition have their interfaces and data types generated in WSDL and XSD respectively. The BPEL, WSDL interface, WSDL catalogue, deployment descriptor and common definitions are automatically generated for the composite service and its partners. CRESS generates outline implementations of partners that are completed manually for use in the final implementation.

Service orchestration (for *Lookup* and *Allocator* in this example) is performed by the ActiveBPEL engine (*www.activebpel.org*). The composed service is automatically created and deployed as a BPEL archive. If orchestration makes use of partner *web* services, these are also deployed in ActiveBPEL. More typically, the partners are *grid* services (*Factory* and *Mapper* here). These are automatically packaged and deployed as grid service archives using the Globus Toolkit (*www.globus.org*).

ActiveBPEL, Globus Toolkit, the composite service and its partners can all run on one system, though more typically they are distributed. This is defined by a CRESS configuration diagram (not shown here) that defines the locations and deployment characteristics of all services. The running implementation can then be validated again using the *same* MUSTARD tests as were used for the specification (section 3.3). In particular, this evaluates non-functional properties such as performance, dependability and reliability. This time, MUSTARD is translated into an intermediate form that is suitable for use in testing an implementation. MINT (MUSTARD interpreter) executes these tests in a similar kind of way as LOLA does for LOTOS. However, MINT has additional capabilities for evaluating an implementation. For example, it can perform stress testing by running many tests concurrently or sequentially to check implementation performance.

5   Conclusion

The CRESS methodology for composing services has now been rounded out to handle all the key characteristics of grid services. For example, service resources, EndPoint References and dynamic partner assignments are now fully handled in both the specification and implementation phases of CRESS. Formal validation of the generated LOTOS specifications was already possible using MUSTARD. New work has added automatic verification of desirable specification properties, allowing properties of a composite service to be proven in general. Automatic validation of the generated implementation is also now possible, using MINT to check (non-)functional characteristics.

Verification through model checking requires a finite state space. This is a reasonable restriction since the data types of an actual grid service implementation are finite. Though the state space can grow very large, the size of it can be constrained by using subsets of data values and by choosing significant values for verification. However, validation still has a useful role. For example, it can be used with infinite state spaces, can check specific cases, and can be used for stress-testing the implementation.

Support for automated formal analysis will be further improved. It is planned to allow data types to be annotated in CRESS with regard to useful ranges and interesting values. A possible approach here is to use PCL (Parameter Constraint Language [17]) to specify significant values for validation and verification. This would allow MUSTARD test cases to be automatically defined.

A rigorous methodology for developing composite grid services has been presented. This uses an accessible graphical notation and a high degree of automation to make it attractive to industry. An occupational classification service has been used to explain how interactions with dynamic resources and dynamic partners are supported by CRESS. Abstract CRESS descriptions are automatically translated into LOTOS for formal verification of desirable properties, and also for formal validation of significant test cases. These are almost 'push button' procedures. The CRESS descriptions can then be automatically translated into implementations with confidence. The same MUSTARD tests can again be used to check the performance characteristics of these implementations.

Acknowledgements

Larry Tan was supported by an Overseas Research Studentship, by the University of Stirling, and by the Economic and Social Research Council (grant RES-149-25-1066).

References

1. Arkin, A., et al. (eds.) Web Services Business Process Execution Language, Version 2.0. Organization for The Advancement of Structured Information Standards (April 2007)
2. Baresi, L., et al.: Validation of web service compositions. Software 1(6), 219–232 (2007)
3. Bolognesi, T., Brinksma, E.: Introduction to the ISO specification language Lotos. Computer Networks 14(1), 25–59 (1988)
4. Chirichiello, A., Salaün, G.: Encoding abstract descriptions into executable web services: Towards a formal development. In: Proc. Web Intelligence 2005, December 2005. IEEE, Los Alamitos (2005)
5. Clark, E.M., Grumberg, O., Peled, D.A.: Model Checking. MIT Press, Cambridge (2000)
6. Dwyer, M.B., Avrunin, G.S., Corbett, J.C.: Patterns in property specifications for finite-state verification. In: Proc. 21st Int. Conf. on Software Engineering, pp. 411–420 (1999)
7. Ferrara, A.: Web services: A process algebra approach. In: Proc. 2nd Int. Conf. on Service-Oriented Computing, pp. 242–251. ACM Press, New York (2004)
8. Foster, H.: A Rigorous Approach to Engineering Web Service Compositions. PhD thesis, Imperial College, London (January 2006)
9. Fu, X., Bultan, T., Su, J.: Analysis of interacting BPEL web services. In: Proc. 13th. Int. World Wide Web Conf., pp. 621–630. ACM Press, New York (2004)
10. Garavel, H., Lang, F., Mateescu, R.: An overview of CADP 2001. European Association for Software Science and Technology Newsletter 4, 13–24 (2002)
11. Graham, S., et al.: Web Services Resource. Version 1.2. Organization for The Advancement of Structured Information Standards (April 2006)
12. ISO/IEC. LOTOS – A Formal Description Technique based on the Temporal Ordering of Observational Behaviour. ISO/IEC 8807 (1989)
13. Oinn, T., et al.: Taverna: A tool for the composition and enactment of bioinformatics workflows. Bioinformatics 20(17), 3045–3054 (2004)
14. Pautasso, C.: JOpera: An agile environment for web service composition with visual unit testing and refactoring. In: Proc. IEEE Symp. on Visual Languages and Human Centric Computing. IEEE, Los Alamitos (2005)
15. Pavón Gomez, S., Larrabeiti, D., Rabay Filho, G.: Lola user manual (version 3R6). Technical report, Polytechnic University of Madrid (February 1995)
16. Slomiski, A.: On using Bpel extensibility to implement OGSI and WSRF grid workflows. In: Proc. Global Grid Forum 10, Berlin (March 2005)
17. Turner, K.J.: Test generation for radiotherapy accelerators. Software Tools for Technology Transfer 7(4), 361–375 (2005)
18. Turner, K.J.: Validating feature-based specifications. Software Practice and Experience 36(10), 999–1027 (2006)
19. Wassermann, B., et al.: Sedna: A Bpel-based environment for visual scientific workflow modelling. In: Workflows for E-Science, pp. 428–449. Springer, Heidelberg (2007)
20. W3C. Web Services Addressing (WS-Addressing). World Wide Web Consortium (May 2006)
21. Yu, J., et al.: Using temporal business rules to synthesize service composition process models. In: Proc. 1st Int. Workshop on Architectures, Concepts and Technologies for Service Oriented Computing, July 2007, pp. 86–95. INSTICC Press (2007)
22. Zager, M.: SOA/web services – Business process orchestration with BPEL (October 2008), http://webservices.sys-con.com/read/155631_1.htm

A Certified Implementation on Top of the Java Virtual Machine*

Javier de Dios and Ricardo Peña

Departamento de Sistemas Informáticos y Computación
Universidad Complutense de Madrid
jdcastro@aventia.com, ricardo@sip.ucm.es

Abstract. Safe is a first-order functional language with unusual memory management features: memory can be both explicitly and implicitly deallocated at some specific points in the program text, and there is no need for a runtime garbage collector. The final code is bytecode of the Java Virtual Machine (JVM), so the language is useful for programming small devices based on this machine.

As an intermediate stage in the compiler's back-end, we have defined the *Safe Virtual Machine* (SVM), and have implemented this machine on top of the Java Virtual Machine (JVM). The paper presents the certified implementation of the SVM on top of the JVM. We have used the proof assistant Isabelle/HOL for this purpose.

1 Introduction

Safe[1] [20,15] was introduced as a research platform for investigating the suitability of functional languages for programming small devices and embedded systems with strict memory requirements. Its final aim is to be able to infer and certify —at compile time— safe upper bounds on memory consumption in a Proof Carrying Code environment [17]. Two features make *Safe* different from conventional functional languages: (1) Its region-based memory management system does not need a garbage collector; and (2) The programmer may ask for explicit destruction of memory cells, so that they could be reused by the program. The compiler produces as target language Java bytecode. These characteristics, together with the formal certification of memory safety properties, would make *Safe* useful for programming small devices.

Regions in *Safe* are inferred by the compiler and their allocation and deallocation are implicit. However, cell destruction, if desired, is explicit in the text and it is expressed as a special form of pattern matching. This is a dangerous feature which could result in having dangling pointers at runtime. The *Safe* compiler is at present equipped with a battery of static analyses, which taken as a whole infer the important property of absence of dangling pointers [20,15,14,16]. These

---

* Partially supported by the Spanish and Madrid Region Government grants S-0505/TIC/0407 (PROMESAS), and TIN2008-06622-C03-01/TIN (STAMP).
[1] http://dalila.sip.ucm.es/safe

M. Alpuente, B. Cook, and C. Joubert (Eds.): FMICS 2009, LNCS 5825, pp. 181–196, 2009.

analyses are conveyed on an intermediate language called *Core-Safe* (explained in Sec. 2.1), obtained after type-checking and desugaring the source language called *Full-Safe*. The back-end comprises two more phases:

1. A translation from *Core-Safe* to the bytecode language of an imperative abstract machine of our own, called the *Safe Virtual Machine* (SVM). This language is explained in Sec. 2.2.
2. A translation from SVM to the bytecode language of the *Java Virtual Machine* (JVM) [13].

We have decided to provide certificates on the absence of dangling pointers and (future certificates) on memory consumption at the *Core-Safe* level. The main reason for that is avoiding translating the certificates down to the JVM level, in parallel with the code. We also conjecture that this latter approach would result in huge certificates and huge checking times. For this reason, we prove instead that the translation does not destroy the certified properties. In particular, that the heap structure and the number of active cells are correctly mapped to the low level machine. Otherwise, absence of dangling pointers or memory consumption would not be preserved.

In a previous work [5], we certified the translation from *Core-Safe* to SVM. The main proof technique used there was structural induction on *Core-Safe* expressions. The distance between *Core-Safe* and the SVM was not so long as both languages shared the same heap definition, and the main emphasis was on proving that the resources 'consumed' at the *Core-Safe* level were the same that at the SVM level. Here we present the certification of the last translation step. The proof technique is different because here both languages are imperative. In essence we show that the JVM correctly simulates the SVM. The distance between both machines is so long (there is an expansion factor of around 20 between an SVM instruction and its translation to JVM) that the proofs are huge, although not difficult. The hardest part is showing that the final states in both machines preserve the simulation relation.

Machine-assisted compiler certification has been developed by several authors in the last few years. In Sec. 6 we review some of these works. As it is argued in [10,11], mechanised certification is superior to manual verification and of course to plain testing. For the certification being really trustable, the code running in the compiler's back-end should be *exactly the same* which has been proved correct by the proof-assistant. Fortunately, modern proof-assistants such as Coq [2] and Isabelle/HOL [19] provide code extraction facilities which deliver code written in some widely used languages such as Caml or Haskell. Of course, one must trust the translation done by the proof-assistant.

Isabelle/HOL is a well-known proof assistant, allowing to express definitions and properties in a formal language and to prove them with some human help. We have formalised in Isabelle/HOL the semantics of our abstract machine SVM, its translation to the JVM, and the JVM itself by extending a previous formalisation by G. Klein [7]. This was needed because Klein's machine was a rather small subset of the actual JVM and it did not cover some features needed by our implementation. This infrastructure allowed us to formally state and prove the correctness theorem.

The plan of the paper is as follows: In Section 2 we summarise our language *Safe* and formalise in Isabelle/HOL the semantics of the SVM; Section 3 presents the JVM formalisation made by Klein and our extension; in Section 4, we explain our design for mapping our machine to the JVM, and present the main code generation functions; the certification itself is summarised in Section 5: we define a simulation relation and prove that the pair formed by the instructions translation and our memory management system, correctly simulates the SVM semantics; there is finally a conclusions and related work section.

The paper is a summary of a rather large development whose full details can be found at `http://dalila.sip.ucm.es/safe/certifsvm2jvm`, where all the Isabelle/HOL theories containing the code generation functions, the lemmas, and the proofs are available.

2   The *Safe* Language

Safe [20,15,14,16] is a first-order eager language with a syntax similar to Haskell's. Its runtime system uses *regions*, i.e. disjoint parts of the heap where the program allocates data structures. The smallest memory unit is the *cell*, a contiguous memory space big enough to hold a data construction. A cell contains the mark of the constructor and a representation of the free variables to which the constructor is applied. These may consist either of basic values, or of pointers to other constructions. It is allocated at constructor application time. A *region* is a collection of cells. It is created empty and it may grow and shrink while it is active. Region deallocation frees all its cells. The allocation and deallocation of regions is bound to function calls. A *working region* is allocated when entering the call and deallocated when exiting it. Inside the function, data structures not belonging to the output may be built there. When a function body is executing, the *live* regions are the working regions of all the active calls leading to this one. Not all live regions are in scope: they are (for reading, or for cell destruction) those regions where the arguments live, also (for reading, destruction, or insertion) the regions received as additional arguments, and the *self* working region. The region arguments are explicit in the intermediate code but not in the source, since they are inferred by the compiler. The following list sorting function builds and intermediate tree not needed in the output:

```
treesort xs = inorder (makeTree xs)
```

After region inference [14], the code is annotated with region arguments (those occurring after the @):

```
treesort xs @ r = inorder (makeTree xs @ self) @ r
```

so that the tree is created in `treeSort`'s *self* region and deallocated upon termination. The destruction facilities are associated to pattern matching. For instance, we show here a constant space function appending two lists:

```
append []!    ys  = ys
append (x:xs)! ys = x : append xs ys
```

The ! mark is the way programmers indicate that the matched cell must be destroyed. The constant space consumption is due to that, at each recursive call, a cell is deleted by the pattern matching while a new one is allocated by the (:) construction.

2.1   *Core-Safe* and Its Translation to SVM

The *Safe* front-end desugars *Full-Safe* and produces a bare-bones functional language called *Core-Safe*. The transformation starts with region inference and continues with Hindler-Milner type inference, pattern matching desugaring into **case** expressions, transforming **where** clauses into **let** expressions, and some others. A *Core-Safe* program is a sequence of possibly recursive polymorphic data and function definitions followed by a main expression e whose value is the program result. Destructive pattern matching is transformed into **case!** expressions, and only constants or variables are allowed in function and constructor applications. Also, only variables are allowed in **case/case!** discriminants and in copy and reuse expressions. Region arguments are explicit in constructor and function applications and in the copy expression. Function definitions have additional region arguments $r_1, \ldots, r_m$ where the function is allowed to build data structures. As an example, we show the *Core-Safe* version of the above **append** function, and a main program invoking it:

$$append\ xs\ ys\ @\ r = \textbf{case!}\ xs\ \textbf{of}$$
$$[\,] \quad \rightarrow \quad ys$$
$$x : xx \quad \rightarrow \quad \textbf{let}\ yy = append\ xx\ ys\ @\ r\ \textbf{in}$$
$$\textbf{let}\ zz = (x : yy)\ @\ r\ \textbf{in}\ zz;$$
$$\textbf{let}\ l = [\,]\ @\ self\ \textbf{in}\ append\ l\ l\ @\ self$$

2.2   The Safe Virtual Machine

The *Safe* compiler translates *Core-Safe* into a set of sequences of imperative SVM instructions. These belong to the instruction set of the SVM, whose semantics in terms of configuration transitions is shown Fig. 1. A configuration of the SVM consists of the six components $(is,\ \Delta,\ k_0,\ k,\ S,\ cs)$, where is is the current instruction sequence, Δ is the heap, k and k_0 are machine registers respectively denoting the topmost region in the heap and the topmost region that must be preserved upon reaching a normal form, S is the stack and cs is the code store where the instruction sequences are kept. For example, the *Core-Safe* **append** program of Sec. 2.1 generates the code store of Fig. 2.

A heap Δ is a function from pointers to construction cells w of the form $(j, C\ \overline{b_i}^n)$, meaning that the cell is located in region j, that C is the data constructor and the b_i are its arguments. Regions are stacked as functions are invoked. Region identifiers j are natural numbers indicating the position of the region in the region stack. By $\Delta \mid_k$ we denote the heap obtained by deleting from Δ those

Initial/final configuration	Condition
(DECREGION $: is$, Δ, k_0, k, S, cs) $\Rightarrow$ (is, $\Delta\vert_{k_0}$, k_0, k_0, S, cs)	$k \geq k_0$
([POPCONT], Δ, k, k, $b : (k_0, p) : S$, $cs[p \mapsto is]$) $\Rightarrow$ (is, Δ, k_0, k, $b : S$, cs)	
(PUSHCONT $p : is$, Δ, k_0, k, S, $cs[p \mapsto is']$) $\Rightarrow$ (is, Δ, k, k, $(k_0, p) : S$, cs)	
(COPY $: is$, $\Delta[b \mapsto (l, C\,\overline{b_i}^n)]$, k_0, k, $b : j : S$, cs) $\Rightarrow$ (is, Θ, k_0, k, $b' : S$, cs)	$(\Theta, b') = copy(\Delta, j, b)$ $j \leq k$ $fresh(b')$
(REUSE $: is$, $\Delta \uplus [b \mapsto w]$, k_0, k, $b : S$, cs) $\Rightarrow$ (is, $\Delta \uplus [b' \mapsto w]$, k_0, k, $b' : S$, cs)	
([CALL p], Δ, k_0, k, S, $cs[p \mapsto is]$) $\Rightarrow$ (is, Δ, k_0, $k + 1$, S, cs)	
(PRIMOP $\oplus : is$, Δ, k_0, k, $c_1 : c_2 : S$, cs) $\Rightarrow$ (is, Δ, k_0, k, $c : S$, cs)	$c = c_1 \oplus c_2$
([MATCH l $\overline{p_j}^m$], $\Delta[S!l \mapsto (j, C_r^m\,\overline{b_i}^n)]$, k_0, k, S, $cs\overline{[p_j \mapsto is_j}^m]$) $\Rightarrow$ (is_r, Δ, k_0, k, $\overline{b_i}^n : S$, cs)	
([MATCH! l $\overline{p_j}^m$], $\Delta \uplus [S!l \mapsto (j, C_r^m\,\overline{b_i}^n)]$, k_0, k, S, $cs\overline{[p_j \mapsto is_j}^m]$) $\Rightarrow$ (is_r, Δ, k_0, k, $\overline{b_i}^n : S$, cs)	
([MATCHN l v m $\overline{p_j}^m$], Δ, k_0, k, S, $cs\overline{[p_j \mapsto is_j}^{m+1}]$) $\Rightarrow$ (is_r, Δ, k_0, k, S, cs)	$r = S!l - v + 1 \wedge 1 \leq r \leq m$
([MATCHN l v m $\overline{p_j}^m$], Δ, k_0, k, S, $cs\overline{[p_j \mapsto is_j}^{m+1}]$) $\Rightarrow$ (is_{m+1}, Δ, k_0, k, S, cs)	$r = S!l - v + 1 \wedge \neg(1 \leq r \leq m)$
(BUILDENV $\overline{K_i}^n : is$, Δ, k_0, k, S, cs) $\Rightarrow$ (is, Δ, k_0, k, $\overline{Item_k(K_i)}^n : S$, cs)	(1)
(BUILDCLS C_r^m $\overline{K_i}^n$ $K : is$, Δ, k_0, k, S, cs) $\Rightarrow$ (is, $\Delta \uplus [b \mapsto (Item_k(K), C_r^m\,\overline{Item_k(K_i)}^n)]$, k_0, k, $b : S$, cs)	$Item_k(K) \leq k$, $fresh(b)$ (1)
(SLIDE m $n : is$, Δ, k_0, k, $\overline{b_i}^m : \overline{b_i}^n : S$, cs) $\Rightarrow$ (is, Δ, k_0, k, $\overline{b_i}^m : S$, cs)	

$$(1) \quad Item_k(K) \stackrel{\text{def}}{=} \begin{cases} S!j & \text{if } K = j \in \mathbb{N} \\ c & \text{if } K = c \\ k & \text{if } K = self \end{cases}$$

Fig. 1. The abstract machine SVM

regions above region k. We will use $p, q, \ldots$ to denote code labels solved by cs, and $b, b_i, \ldots$ to denote either cell pointers solved by Δ, or basic constants. By C_r^m we denote the data constructor which leads to the r-th alternative out of m of a **case**. By $S!j$ we denote the j-th element of the stack S counting from the top and starting at 0 (i.e. $S!0$ is the top element).

We do not show the translation functions from *Core-Safe* to SVM here but, in order to understand the machine behaviour, we give some hints about it:

- **let** $x_1 = e_1$ **in** e_2 is translated into pushing a continuation for e_2 in the SVM stack (PUSHCONT instruction), followed by the instructions of e_1. If e_1 is a constructor application, a new cell is allocated for it (BUILDCLS instruction) and the execution proceeds with e_2.
- **case** expressions are translated into a MATCH/MATCH!/MATCHN instruction jumping to the appropriate alternative. Each one is a separate sequence.
- The translation of function application consists of pushing the arguments in the SVM stack (BUILDENV instruction), and then jumping to the function body (CALL instruction). Function calls are always tail recursive, so there is no need for a return instruction.

$P_1 \mapsto [BUILDCLS\ Nil_0^2\ [\ ]\ self,\ BUILDENV\ [0,0,self],\ SLIDE\ 3\ 1,\ CALL\ P_2]$
$P_2 \mapsto [MATCH!\ 0\ [P_3, P_4]]$
$P_3 \mapsto [BUILDENV\ [1],\ SLIDE\ 1\ 3,\ DECREGION,\ POPCONT]$
$P_4 \mapsto [PUSHCONT\ P_5, BUILDENV\ [3,\ 5,\ 6], SLIDE\ 3\ 0, CALL\ P_2]$
$P_5 \mapsto [BUILDCLS\ Cons_1^2\ [1,\ 0]\ 5, BUILDENV\ [0], SLIDE\ 1\ 6, DECREGION, POPCONT]$

Fig. 2. Imperative code for the *Core-Safe* **append** program

- When a normal form is reached: (1) the current environment is discarded from the stack (SLIDE instruction); (2) some regions may be deallocated, since a tail recursive call chain terminates (DECREGION instruction); and (3) a continuation sequence is looked for in the stack (POPCONT instruction).
- The copy $x@r$, reuse $x!$, and primitive operation $a_1 \oplus a_2$ expressions are respectively translated into sequences containing a COPY, a REUSE, and a PRIMOP instructions.

We now explain more closely each individual instruction: DECREGION deletes from the heap all the regions between the current region k and region k_0, excluding the latter; POPCONT pops a continuation from the stack or stops the execution if there is none. Notice that b —which will usually be a value— is left in the stack so that it can be accessed by the continuation; PUSHCONT pushes a continuation represented by a region number and a code pointer.

Instruction COPY copies to region j the data structure starting at pointer b on top of the stack; REUSE creates a fresh pointer b' and makes it to point to the data structure pointed to by b on top of the stack; CALL jumps to a new instruction sequence and stacks an empty region $k+1$; PRIMOP operates two basic values located in the stack and replaces them by the result of the operation.

Instruction MATCH does a vectored jump depending on the matched cell constructor; MATCH! additionally destroys the matched cell; MATCHN is used when the **case** discriminant is a basic value. The equations respectively describe what happens when the discriminant is matched by one alternative, and when it is not matched and the default alternative must be taken.

Instruction BUILDENV receives a list of keys K_i and creates a portion of environment on top of the stack: If a key K is a natural number j, the item $S!j$ is copied and pushed on the stack; if it is a basic constant c, it is directly pushed on the stack; if it is the identifier *self*, then the current region number k is pushed on the stack; BUILDCLS allocates fresh memory and constructs a heap cell. It receives a list of keys and the cell constructor C_r^m; SLIDE removes some parts of the stack and it is used to discerd environments when they are no longer needed.

The following invariant is ensured by the Safe compiler: *For every instruction sequence in the code store cs, instruction i is the last one if and only if it belongs to the set {POPCONT, CALL, MATCH, MATCH!, MATCHN}*. It is introduced in Isabelle/HOL as an axiom, since it is needed for proving the correctness theorem.

We have formalised the SVM by first defining in Isabelle/HOL some datatypes for normal form values, and cells:

datatype $Val = Loc\ Location\ |\ IntT\ int\ |\ BoolT\ bool$
types $Cell = Constructor \times Val\ list$

The heap is modelled as a partial function from locations to pairs $(Region, Cell)$, and a nat with the total number of regions. The stack is modelled as a list.

types $HeapMap = Location \rightharpoonup (Region \times Cell)$
$Heap = HeapMap \times nat$
$Stack = StackObject\ list$

where stack objects can be values, region numbers or continuations. The SVM code is modelled by a list of triples, each one consisting of a code label, a SVM instruction sequence, and a function name. The aim is to represent a partial function, but one which can be traversed. A code store provides also information about which labels correspond to continuations.

types $CodeSequence = SafeInstr\ list$
$SVMCode = (CodeLabel \times CodeSequence \times FunName)\ list$
$ContinuationMap = FunName \rightharpoonup CodeLabel\ list$
$CodeStore = SVMCode \times ContinuationMap$

The program counter of the SVM is a pair $(CodeLabel, nat)$ indicating the instruction sequence under execution and the next instruction of the sequence to be executed. The SVM state consists of the heap, the register k_0, the program counter and the stack. Finally, the static part of a SVM program consist of a code store, a constructor table containing constructor static attributes needed at runtime, and a sizes table with sizes for the heap and the stack.

types $PC = CodeLabel \times nat$
$SVMState = Heap \times Region \times PC \times Stack$
$SafeImpProg = CodeStore \times ConstructorTableType \times SizesTable$

We have defined a function $execSVM$ making the SVM to execute the next instruction, or to stop if there is none:

$execSVM :: SafeImpProg \Rightarrow SVMState \Rightarrow (SVMState, SVMState)\ Either$
$execSVM\ ((code, cm), ct, st)\ (h, k0, (l, i), S) =$
$\qquad execSVMInst\ (the\ (map\_of\ code\ l)\ !\ i)\ (map\_of\ ct)\ h\ k0\ (l, i)\ S$

where map_of, defined in Isabelle/HOL, transforms a list of pairs into a partial function. If $execSVM\ P\ s$ gives $Left\ s$, this means that s is a stopping state. Otherwise, it gives $Right\ s'$. There is an equation defining $execSVMInst$ for every SVM instruction. The definitions closely follow the semantics given in Fig. 1.

3   Formalisation of the JVM in Isabelle/HOL

In the past years, there have been some efforts to formally define the JVM in proof assistants in order to verify properties of the machine itself or of applications written in Java bytecode. Concerning Isabelle/HOL, there was some early work by Cornelia Pusch [22] followed by Tobias Nipkow, Gerwin Klein and others in the framework of some EU-funded projects [9,6,8]. As starting point, we

datatype *instr =*

Store nat	| Return	| ArrLoad
| Load nat	| Pop	| ArrStore
| Tableswitch int int (int list)	| Dup	| ArrLength
| Getfield vname cname	| Dup_x1	| ArrNew ty
| Putfield vname cname	| Dup_x2	| Checkcast cname
| Getstatic vname cname	| Swap	| New cname
| Putstatic vname cname	| BinOp op	| LitPush val
| Invoke cname mname (ty list)	| Ifcmpeq int	| Jsr int
| Invoke_static cname mname (ty list)	| Throw	| Ret nat
| Invoke_special cname mname (ty list)	| Goto int	

Fig. 3. Supported instructions of the JVM

have used the definition of the JVM done in 2003 by G. Klein for Microjava, a subset of Java [7], and have extended it with a static heap and some instructions such as **Tableswitch**, **Invoke_static**, binary operators, and others. These extensions are part of the actual JVM and we needed in our implementation.

A JVM program is formalised as a list of class declarations, each one consisting of the class and super-class names, and two lists for field and method declarations.

types $fdecl = vname \times ty$ -- field declaration
      $sig = mname \times ty\ list$ -- signature of a method
      $'c\ mdecl = sig \times ty \times\ 'c$ -- method declaration ($'c$ is the body)
      $'c\ class = cname \times fdecl\ list \times\ 'c\ mdecl\ list$ -- class = superclass, fields, method
      $'c\ cdecl = cname \times\ 'c\ class$ -- class declaration
      $'c\ prog =\ 'c\ cdecl\ list$ -- program

A method's body provides the lengths of the operand stack and of the local variable list, the bytecode instructions, and an exception table.

types $bytecode = instr\ list$
       $jvm\_method = nat \times nat \times bytecode \times exception\_table$
       $jvm\_prog = jvm\_method\ prog$

The supported instructions are listed in Fig. 3. They represent both a subset and an abstraction of the actual JVM instruction set [13].

The dynamic state of the JVM (*jvm_state*) is formed by four components: a possibly raised exception, a static heap (*sheap*), a dynamic heap (*dheap*), an initial heap, and a stack of frames. The second is a partial function from pairs ⟨class, field⟩ to values, and the third is a partial function from locations to either objects or arrays (*heap_entry*). An object contains its class name and a mapping from pairs ⟨field, class⟩ to values. An array consists of its elements type, its length, and a partial mapping from indices to values. A frame (*frame*) is formalised as a tuple containing the operand stack, the local variables (these include the *this* pointer and the method arguments), the class name, the method signature, the program counter, and a tag. This and the initial heap are not present in the actual JVM, and they are related to a proof about the bytecode type system made by Klein.

datatype $heap\_entry =$ $Obj\ cname\ (vname \times cname \rightharpoonup val)$
                 $|\ Arr\ ty\ nat\ (nat \rightharpoonup val)$

types $sheap = cname \times vname \rightharpoonup val$ -- static heap
          $dheap = loc \rightharpoonup heap\_entry$ -- dynamic heap
          $frame = opstack \times locvars \times cname \times sig \times pc \times tag$
          $jvm\_state = val\ option \times sheap \times dheap \times ini\_heap \times frame\ list$

Klein defines a function $exec :: jvm\_prog \times jvm\_state \Rightarrow jvm\_state\ option$, executing the next instruction in the machine, which we have extended to the added
instructions. In addition, he defines the reflexive-transitive closure of the $exec\ P$
relation, for a given program P, as follows:

$exec\_all :: [jvm\_prog, jvm\_state, jvm\_state] \Rightarrow bool$ $(\_ \vdash \_ - jvm \rightarrow \_)$
$P \vdash s - jvm \rightarrow t \equiv (s, t) \in \{(s, t) . exec\ (P, s) = Some\ t\}^*$

4   Implementation of the SVM on Top of the JVM

The JVM provides support for allocating new objects in the heap but not for
releasing them. Instead, there is an automatic garbage collector system which
collects unused objects. On the contrary, the SVM has explicit releasing of cells
and no garbage collector. The JVM provides a frames stack for invoking and
returning from methods. The SVM control flow does not follow the typical
call/return scheme of imperative languages. The SVM is a kind of 'jumping
machine' where the control flow is in part driven by the stack. So, the JVM
stack is not appropriate to be used as the SVM stack. Finally, the SVM stores
code addresses in the stack which are used to jump to the corresponding code.
There is no support instruction in the JVM for this need. Summarising, careful
design decisions are needed in order to correctly map the SVM to the JVM.
First we explain how data structures are mapped, and then how the code is
mapped.

4.1   Mapping the SVM Data Structures

As explained in Sec. 1, one aim of Safe is to statically infer and certify upper
bounds for heap and stack sizes. In order to make the reusing of released cells
easier, we have decided to have fixed-size cells in the heap. The size is determined
at compile time for each particular program, according to the biggest size data
constructor.

The heap is implemented by two classes, `DirectoryCell` and `Heap` providing
a pool of free cells and a stack of regions, each one consisting of a collection of
cells. Before refining this description, let us look at the main interface methods,
which we present in Fig. 4. Following their order of occurrence, they respectively
give support to the SVM instructions `CALL`, `DECREGION` (2 methods), `BUILDCLS`
(2 methods), `MATCH!` and `COPY`.

Notice that access to an arbitrary region is needed in *insertCell* and *copy*,
while *releaseCell* is provided with only the cell pointer as an argument. We have
implemented all the methods (except *decregion*) running in constant time by

void pushRegion ()	-- creates a top empty region
void popRegion ()	-- removes the topmost region
void decregion ()	-- removes the $k - k_0$ topmost regions
cell reserveCell ()	-- returns a fresh cell
void insertCell (p, j)	-- inserts cell p into region j
void releaseCell (p)	-- releases cell p
cell copy (p, j)	-- copies the data structure beginning at p into region j

Fig. 4. The interface of the classes `Heap` and `CellFactory`

representing the regions and the pool as circular doubly-chained lists. Method *decregion* has a cost in $\Theta(k - k_0)$ independently of the number of cells of the deleted regions. The region stack is represented by a static array of dynamic lists and a static field k, so that constant time access to each region is provided. Register k_0 is also a static field of the class `Heap`.

Initially, all the cells and the region array are allocated with sizes provided by the compiler. During program execution, 'allocating' and 'releasing' cells mean moving them from/to the freelist to/from the appropriate region list.

The SVM stack is implemented by a class `Stack` having a static array with a size provided by the compiler. Its only meaningful method is *slide* (m, n), which gives support to the `SLIDE` instruction. The rest of accesses are done by the in-line code emitted by the compiler. We will call RTS (run-time system) to the package consisting of the classes `Heap, DirectoryCell`, and `Stack`.

4.2 Mapping the SVM Code

The code generated by translating a SVM program consists of a single JVM class `PSafe` with a single method `PSafeMain()`. *Core-Safe* functions and the main expression correspond to certain fragments of this method. This decision is forced by the previous one of not using the frames stack of the JVM. Since arguments are pushed to the SVM stack, function calls are implemented by JVM `goto` instructions. A sequence of SVM instructions is represented by a jump-free bytecode sequence. Invocation to RTS methods are allowed in the sequence.

A SVM `MATCH` instruction is implemented by using the JVM `Tableswitch` instruction, which can branch in constant time to any label of a list of static labels. The problem of storing/retrieving code addresses into/from the stack is solved in this way: every continuation label p of every Safe function is given a number $i = cm(p)$ in the range $0, \ldots, totC - 1$, being $totC$ the total number of continuations in the program, which in turn is equal to the number of its non constructor-building **let** expressions —so $totC$ is a static quantity—, and being cm an appropriate bijective function. Instruction `PUSHCONT` p just pushes i to the stack, while `POPCONT` uses a global `Tableswitch` instruction indexed by i to jump to the appropriate static label.

```
[Getstatic Sf stackC,                    ArrLoad,
 Getstatic topf stackC,                  Store 3,            (* local3 <- p *)
 Dup2,                                    LitPush (Intg 2),
 Dup2,                                    BinOp Substract,
 Dup2,                                    Dup,
 ArrLoad,                                 Putstatic topf stackC, (* top <- top - 2 *)
 Store 1,        (* local1 <- b *)        Load 1,
 LitPush (Intg 1),                        ArrStore,           (* S[top] <- b *)
 BinOp Substract,                         Load 2,
 ArrLoad,                                 Putstatic kOf heapC,  (* k0 <- k' *)
 Store 2,        (* local2 <- k' *)       Load 3,               (* jump to continuation *)
 LitPush (Intg 2),                        Goto (trAddr pcc (pc + incPop))]
 BinOp Substract,
```

Fig. 5. The JVM bytecode produced by `POPCONT`

4.3 Translation Functions

As we have said, we have defined in Isabelle the translation from SVM to JVM and used its code extraction facilities to produce the Haskell code actually executed in the compiler. The translation provides, as add-ons, a function mapping the SVM program counters to the JVM program counters corresponding to the translation, a function mapping continuation labels to the small integers mentioned in Sec. 4.2, and a function assigning to each constructor a unique number. These mappings are needed later to define the simulation relation between the states of the SVM and the JVM.

$codeMap :: PC \rightharpoonup pc$
$contMap :: CodeLabel \rightharpoonup nat$
$consMap :: Constructor \rightharpoonup nat$
$trSVM2JVM :: SafeImpProg \Rightarrow jvm\_prog \times codeMap \times contMap \times consMap$

This function creates the initialisation code and the constructor mapping, builds the `SafeMain` class and attaches to it the RTS classes. To produce the bytecode of the only method of that class, it uses the function

$trCodeStore :: [CodeLabel, pc, ContinuationMap, consMap, SVMCode]$
$\qquad \Rightarrow instr\,list \times codeMap \times contMap$

which traverses the SVM code sequences, accumulating the bytecode fragments and the program counter mapping produced by them. It also assigns unique numbers to continuations. In order to translate a sequence, it uses the function

$trSeq :: [contMap, consMap, pc, pc \times codeMap, CodeLabel \times CodeSequence \times FunName]$
$\qquad \Rightarrow (pc \times codeMap) \times instr\,list$

which traverses one SVM sequence, accumulating the bytecode fragments produced by each SVM instruction. It also updates the program counter mapping after each translation. The main translation function, defined by cases on the SVM instruction being translated is

$trInstr :: [pc, codeMap, contMap, consMap, pc, SafeInstr] \Rightarrow instr\,list$

where the first pc is the one corresponding to the first JVM instruction of the translation, and the second one is the program counter of the global `Tableswitch` mentioned in Sec, 4.2 to deal with continuations. As an example, we show in Fig. 5 the bytecode resulting from the translation of POPCONT. The code of all these functions can be found at http://dalila.sip.ucm.es/safe/certifsvm2jvm.

5   Certification of the Implementation

The main idea of the proof is defining a simulation relation between SVM and JVM states and showing that both machines evolve through states made equivalent by the relation when executing a SVM program and its translation.

To define the simulation relation we must consider that part of the JVM state is implemented by the static data structures kept in the RTS classes Heap and Stack, and that the rest is kept in the cell objects and arrays of the dynamic heap. The relation admits a SVM state to be simulated by several JVM states, since there is an abstraction when going from lists of cells in the JVM to set of cells in the SVM. The critical part of the relation is the existence of a bijection between the SVM heap locations and the JVM dynamic heap locations corresponding to active cells, i.e. cells linked in some list of the region stack. The bijection must preserve the heap structure in the sense that equivalent cells must point to equivalent cells. In the following, we will assume that P is a SVM program and $(P', cdm, ctm, com) = trSVM2JVM\ P$ its translation.

Definition 1. Given an injection $g :: dom\ H \Rightarrow loc$, and a constructor mapping com, the JVM dynamic heap h and the region stack $regS$ with k' regions *simulate* the SVM heap (H, k), denoted $equivH\ (H, k)\ h\ k'com\ regS\ g$, if:

$$range\ g = activeCells\ regS\ k' \wedge k = k' \wedge \forall l \in dom\ H . equivC\ (H\ l)\ (h\ (g\ l))\ com\ g$$

The first condition guarantees that g is in fact a bijection. Predicate $equivC$ (not shown) defines that two cells are equivalent under g and com when both live in the same region j and contain pointers made equivalent by g in equivalent argument positions. Equivalent constructor names are the string C in the SVM and the unique number $com\ C$ in the JVM.

Definition 2. The JVM state $s'=(None, h_s, h_d, h_i, ([], vs, \text{``PSafe''}, (\text{``PSafeMain''}, ts),$ $pc, tag)\#[])$ simulates the SVM state $s = (H, k_0, PC, S)$, denoted $cdm, ctm, com \vdash s \triangleq s'$, if there exists an injection $g :: dom\ H \Rightarrow loc$ such that:

1. $equivH\ H\ h_d\ k'com\ regS\ g$, where the region stack $(regS, k')$ is obtained from h_s and h_d by using the RTS class Heap.
2. $equivS\ S\ S'\ top\ ctm\ g$, where the stack (S', top) is obtained from h_s and h_d by using the RTS class Stack.
3. $k_0 = k'_0$, where k'_o is the static field k_0 of the class Heap.
4. $pc = cdm\ PC$.

Predicate $equivS$ (not shown) defines that the JVM stack (S', top) simulates the SVM stack S when, position by position, both contain either the same two basic values, or two heap locations made equivalent by g, or two continuations made equivalent by ctm^2.

Notice that the simulation relation guarantees that the heap structure is exactly the same in both machines. So, properties such as the number of active cells and the absence of dangling pointers are preserved.

The main correctness theorem states that, if the SVM and its implementation are started in equivalent states, then after the SVM executes its next instruction, and after the number of steps required by the JVM to execute its translation, both machines arrive to equivalent states. The Isabelle/HOL formalisation is:

theorem *correctSVM2JVM* :
  $[\![$ *(P',cdm,ctm,com)* = *trSVM2JVM P;*
  cdm, ctm, com $\vdash$ *S1* $\stackrel{\triangle}{=}$ *S1';*
  execSVM P S1 = *Right S2* $]\!] \Longrightarrow$
  $\exists$ *S2' . P'* $\vdash$ *S1' -jvm*$\rightarrow$ *S2'* $\wedge$ *cdm, ctm, com* $\vdash$ *S2* $\stackrel{\triangle}{=}$ *S2'*

A first set of lemmas deal with the static properties of the translation and prove that, if (p, i) and pc are two program counters made equivalent by cdm, then the JVM bytecode starting at pc is exactly the translation of the SVM instruction found at (p, i). The topmost one is the following:

lemma *fun_SVM2JVM [rule_format]:*
  (P', cdm, ctm, com) = *trSVM2JVM ((svms, ctmap), ini, ct, st)* $\longrightarrow$
  l < length svms $\longrightarrow$
  svms ! l = *(p,seq,fn)* $\longrightarrow$
  i < length seq $\longrightarrow$
  svm = *fst (the (map_of svms p)) ! i* $\longrightarrow$
  pc = *the (cdm (p,i))* $\longrightarrow$
  bytecode = *extractBytecode P'* $\longrightarrow$
  $(\exists$ *cdm' ctm' pcc inss bytecode' . inss* = *trInstr pc cdm' ctm' com pcc svm* $\wedge$
                      drop pc bytecode = *inss @ bytecode')*

After some initial massaging, the kernel of the main proof is done by cases on the instruction executed in the SVM. We have proved one auxiliary lemma for each SVM instruction. We show below the one corresponding to POPCONT:

lemma *execSVMInstr_POPCONT :*
  $[\![$ *(P', cdm, ctm, com)* = *trSVM2JVM ((svms, ctmap), ini, ct, ah, ai, bc);*
  cdm , ctm, com $\vdash$ *((hm, k), k0, (l, i), S)* $\stackrel{\triangle}{=}$ *S1';*
  (fst (the (map_of svms l)) ! i) = *POPCONT;*
  execSVMInst POPCONT (map_of ct) (hm, k) k0 (l, i) S = *Right S2;*
  drop (the (cdm (l, i))) (extractBytecode P') =
  trInstr (the (cdm (l, i))) cdm' ctm' com pcc POPCONT @ bytecode'
  $]\!] \Longrightarrow$ $\exists$ *v' sh' dh' ih' fms' . P'* $\vdash$ *S1' -jvm*$\rightarrow$ *(v',sh',dh',ih', fms')* $\wedge$
                      cdm , ctm, com $\vdash$ *S2* $\stackrel{\triangle}{=}$ *(v',sh',dh',ih', fms')*

The conclusion of the lemma is the same as that of the main theorem, but the premises inform us that the instructions about to be executed in the JVM are

---

^{2} More details can be found at `http://dalila.sip.ucm.es/safe/certifsvm2jvm`.

exactly those produced by the translation of POPCONT. The proof of this kind of lemmas is rather long and consists of passing through all the intermediate JVM states determined by the JVM bytecode and showing that the final state is equivalent to the arrival state in the SVM. If the bytecode contains loops, the proof become harder as we must introduce invariants and prove loop termination.

6   Conclusions and Related Work

We have presented a summary of the formalisations in Isabelle/HOL of two abstract machines, one functional (the SVM) and one imperative (the JVM). The latter is an extension of a previous one done by G. Klein [7]. We have also formalised the implementation of the first on top of the second, and defined a simulation relation between the abstract and the concrete states. As part of the relation, we have proved the existence of a bijection across the execution, guaranteeing that the number of cells and the heap structure is the same in both machines. In a previous work, we proved that a similar equivalence held between the *Core-Safe* and the SVM levels of the translation. Considering both proofs as a whole, this certifies that the memory consumption and the absence of dangling pointers properties certified at the *Core-Safe* level are preserved in the JVM code actually executed.

The complete specification in Isabelle/HOL of the syntax and semantics of both languages, of the translation functions, the theorems and the proofs, represent about one person-year of effort. Including comments, about 21 000 lines of Isabelle/HOL scripts have been written, and about 120 lemmas, some of them very long, have been proved. Isabelle/HOL features a Higher-Order Logic and gives enough facilities for defining recursive and higher-order functions. These are written in much the same way as a programmer would do in a modern functional language such as ML or Haskell. Isabelle/HOL provides also inductive predicates, inductive n-relations, transitive closures as well as ordinary first-order logic. This has made it easy to express the desired properties with almost the same concepts one would use in hand-written proofs. Partial functions have also been very useful in modelling programming language structures such as environments, heaps, and the like. Being able to quantify these objects in HOL has been essential for stating and proving the theorems.

Using some form of formal verification to ensure the correctness of compilers has been a hot topic for many years. An annotated bibliography covering up to 2003 can be found at [4]. Most of the papers reflected there propose techniques whose validity is established by formal proofs made and read by humans.

Using machine-assisted proofs for compilers starts around the seventies, with an intensification at the end of the nineties. For instance, [18] uses a constraint solver to asses the validity of the GNU C compiler translations. They do not try to prove the compiler correctness but to *validate its output*, by comparing it with the corresponding input. This technique was originally proposed in [21]. A more recent experiment in compiler validation is [12], where the source is the term language of HOL and the target is assembly language of the ARM processor.

More closely related to our work is [23] where the author uses Isabelle/HOL to formalise the translation from a small subset of Java (called μ-Java) to a stripped version of the Java Virtual Machine. He defines a big-step semantics for μ-Java and a sate-transition semantics for the small JVM (17 bytecode instructions). Then, the translation functions are defined and a correctness theorem similar to ours is proved. This work can be considered as a first attempt, and it was considerably extended by Klein, Nipkow, Berghofer, and Strecker himself in [7,8,1]. Only the latter claims that the extraction facilities of Isabelle/HOL have been used to produce an actually running Java compiler. The main emphasis is on formalisation of Java and JVM features and on creating an infrastructure on which other authors could verify properties of Java or Java bytecode programs.

A realistic C compiler for programming embedded systems has been built and verified in [3,10,11]. The source is a small C subset called *Cminor* to which C is informally translated, and the target is Power PC assembly language. The compiler runs through six intermediate languages for which the semantics are defined and the translation pass verified. The authors use the Coq proof-assistant and its extraction facilities to produce Caml code. They provide figures witnessing that the compile times obtained are competitive with those of *gcc* running with level-2 optimisations activated. This is perhaps the biggest project on machine-assisted compiler verification done up to now.

As we have said in Sec. 1, the motivation for verifying the *Safe* back-end arises in a different context. We have approached this development because we found it more rapid than translating the *Core-Safe* properties to certificates at the level of the JVM. Also, we expected the size of our certificates to be considerably smaller than the ones obtained with the other approach. Additionally to previous efforts, we have complemented functional correctness with a proof of resource consumption and memory structure preservation.

Acknowledgement. We are grateful to Delfín Rupérez for providing preliminary Isabelle/HOL code for the RTS, the JVM extensions, and the translation.

References

1. Berghofer, S., Strecker, M.: Extracting a formally verified, fully executable compiler from a proof assistant. In: Proc. Compiler Optimization Meets Compiler Verification, COCV 2003. ENTCS, pp. 33–50 (2003)
2. Bertot, Y., Casteran, P.: Interactive Theorem Proving and Program Development Coq'Art: The Calculus of Inductive Constructions. In: Texts in Theoretical Computer Science. EATCS. Springer, Heidelberg (2004)
3. Blazy, S., Dargaye, Z., Leroy, X.: Formal verification of a C compiler front-end. In: Misra, J., Nipkow, T., Sekerinski, E. (eds.) FM 2006. LNCS, vol. 4085, pp. 460–475. Springer, Heidelberg (2006)
4. Dave, M.A.: Compiler verification: a bibliography. SIGSOFT Software Engineering Notes 28(6), 2 (2003)

5. de Dios, J., Peña, R.: Formal Certification of a Resource-Aware Language Implementation. In: Berghofer, S., et al. (eds.) TPHOL 2009. LNCS, vol. 5674, pp. 196–212. Springer, Heidelberg (2009)
6. Klein, G.: Verified Java Bytecode Verification, PhD thesis, Institut für Informatik, Technische Universität München (2003)
7. Klein, G., Nipkow, T.: Verified Bytecode Verifiers. Theoretical Computer Science 298, 583–626 (2003)
8. Klein, G., Nipkow, T.: A Machine-Checked Model for a Java-Like Language, Virtual Machine and Compiler. ACM Transactions on Programming Languages and Systems 28(4), 619–695 (2006)
9. Klein, G., Nipkow, T., Schirmer, N., Strecker, M., Wildmoser, M.: Project VerifiCard (2001–2003), http://isabelle.in.tum.de/VerifiCard/
10. Leroy, X.: Formal certification of a compiler back-end, or: programming a compiler with a proof assistant. In: Principles of Programming Languages, POPL 2006, pp. 42–54. ACM Press, New York (2006)
11. Leroy, X.: A formally verified compiler back-end, 79 pages (July 2008) (submitted)
12. Li, G., Owens, S., Slind, K.: Structure of a Proof-Producing Compiler for a Subset of Higher Order Logic. In: De Nicola, R. (ed.) ESOP 2007. LNCS, vol. 4421, pp. 205–219. Springer, Heidelberg (2007)
13. Lindholm, T., Yellin, F.: The Java Virtual Machine Sepecification, 2nd edn. The Java Series. Addison-Wesley, Reading (1999)
14. Montenegro, M., Peña, R., Segura, C.: A Simple Region Inference Algorithm for a First-Order Functional Language. In: Trends in Functional Programming, TFP 2008, Nijmegen (The Netherlands), May 2008, pp. 194–208 (2008)
15. Montenegro, M., Peña, R., Segura, C.: A Type System for Safe Memory Management and its Proof of Correctness. In: ACM Principles and Practice of Declarative Programming, PPDP 2008, Valencia, Spain, July 2008, pp. 152–162 (2008)
16. Montenegro, M., Peña, R., Segura, C.: An Inference Algorithm for Guaranteeing Safe Destruction. In: Selected papers of Logic-Based Program Synthesis and Transformation, LOPSTR 2008. LNCS, vol. 5438, pp. 135–151. Springer, Heidelberg (2009)
17. Necula, G.C.: Proof-Carrying Code. In: ACM SIGPLAN-SIGACT Principles of Programming Languages, POPL 1997, pp. 106–119. ACM Press, New York (1997)
18. Necula, G.C.: Translation validation for an optimizing compiler. SIGPLAN Notices 35(5), 83–94 (2000)
19. Nipkow, T., Paulson, L., Wenzel, M.: Isabelle/HOL. LNCS, vol. 2283. Springer, Heidelberg (2002)
20. Peña, R., Segura, C., Montenegro, M.: A Sharing Analysis for SAFE. In: Selected Papers of the 7th Symp. on Trends in Functional Programming, TFP 2006, pp. 109–128. Intellect, Bristol (2007)
21. Pnueli, A., Siegel, M., Singerman, E.: Translation Validation. In: Steffen, B. (ed.) TACAS 1998. LNCS, vol. 1384, pp. 151–166. Springer, Heidelberg (1998)
22. Pusch, C.: Proving the Soundness of a Java Bytecode Verifier Specification in Isabelle/HOL. In: Cleaveland, W.R. (ed.) TACAS 1999. LNCS, vol. 1579, pp. 89–103. Springer, Heidelberg (1999)
23. Strecker, M.: Formal Verification of a Java Compiler in Isabelle. In: Voronkov, A. (ed.) CADE 2002. LNCS (LNAI), vol. 2392, pp. 63–77. Springer, Heidelberg (2002)

Formal Development for Railway Signaling Using Commercial Tools

Alessio Ferrari[1], Alessandro Fantechi[2],
Stefano Bacherini[1], and Niccoló Zingoni[1]

[1] General Electric Transportation Systems (GETS), Firenze, Italy
[2] Universitá di Firenze, DSI, Firenze, Italy

Abstract. This report presents the approach experimented by a railway signaling manufacturer for the development of applications through Simulink/Stateflow in a standard–regulated industrial framework.

The General Electric Transportation Systems (GETS) railway signaling division of Florence, inside a long-term effort of introducing formal methods to enforce product safety, decided to adopt the Simulink/Stateflow tool-suite to exploit model based development and code generation within its own development process [1]. Products traditionally provided by GETS, like any railway signaling application developed for Europe, shall comply with the CENELEC norms [2].

Introducing the Simulink/Stateflow tool-suite within a CENELEC based process is not a straightforward step, and GETS faced two crucial obstacles: the lack of a formal semantics for the Simulink/Stateflow languages, and the absence of a CENELEC compliant code generator.

The languages used by Simulink and Stateflow are not formally specified and their semantics is essentially given by the simulation engine itself. This increases the difficulty of defining an effective formal verification strategy, a highly recommended practice according to the CENELEC norms.

Code generators provided for the tool-suite (in particular Stateflow Coder) are not certified for railway software development, this complicating their adoption in this domain. In order to overcome these problems, GETS first introduced a set of modeling guidelines to restrain the semantics of the tools [3]. The idea is based on the intuition that reducing the Simulink/Stateflow languages to a semantically unambiguous subset enables proper code synthesis and formal verification. Once developed this set of modeling rules, a proper strategy including formal development, model based unit testing and formal verification of modules has been defined. Given a set of system-level functional requirements, these can be partitioned into separate sets of unit requirements and then formalized into Stateflow models according to the GETS guidelines. Each model represents an independently verifiable system component. Unit testing based on requirement coverage is then performed on the models through the Simulink environment, and during test execution a test observer is used to register the test-suite input data and the test results. The registered test-suite is executed on the auto-coded unit and results are automatically compared. Finally, the unit is analyzed through

M. Alpuente, B. Cook, and C. Joubert (Eds.): FMICS 2009, LNCS 5825, pp. 197–198, 2009.

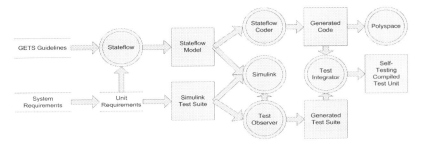

Fig. 1. Overview of our strategy for model based testing

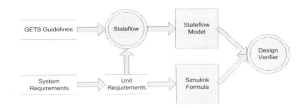

Fig. 2. Overview of our strategy for formal verification

the Polyspace tool, based on abstract interpretation, in order to increase the confidence on the correctness (in particular, absence of runtime errors) of the generated code (Fig. 1). This strategy basically settles the problem of having a qualified code generator, since certification of conformity is ensured each time code is synthesized from a model. Verification of functional requirements is provided at Stateflow chart level: unit requirements are translated into formulas made of Simulink blocks and validated against the Stateflow model through the property proving engine called Simulink Design Verifier (fig. 2). The presented approach is focused on the level of system modules, since the strategy has been fully put into practice only at this level during the development of the logic of an Automatic Train Protection system called SSC/SCMT BaseLine 3 (150K LOC of auto-generated code). Extension of the approach at the overall system level is theoretically feasible, but we are still working on strategies for putting it into practice in the most effective manner.

References

1. Bacherini, S., Fantechi, A., Tempestini, M., Zingoni, N.: A Story about Formal Methods Adoption by a Railway Signaling Manufacturer. In: Misra, J., Nipkow, T., Sekerinski, E. (eds.) FM 2006. LNCS, vol. 4085, pp. 179–189. Springer, Heidelberg (2006)
2. European Committee for Electrotechnical Standardization: CENELEC EN 50128, Railway Applications - Software for Railway Control and Protection Systems (1997)
3. Ferrari, A., Fantechi, A., Bacherini, S., Zingoni, N.: Modeling Guidelines for Code Generation in the Railway Signaling Context. In: Proceedings of 1st NASA Formal Methods Symposium (NFM), Moffet Field, California, U.S.A. (2009)

Integrated Formal Approach for Qualified Critical Embedded Code Generator

Nassima Izerrouken[1,2], Marc Pantel[1], Xavier Thirioux[1], and Olivier Ssi Yan Kai[2]

[1] University of Toulouse, IRIT-ENSEEIHT Laboratory
Toulouse, France
[2] Continental Automotive, Toulouse, France
{Nizerrou,Pantel,Thirioux}@enseeiht.fr,
{Olivier.Ssi-Yan-Kai}@continental-corporation.com

Abstract. This paper sums up the integration of a correct-by-construction components for the qualifiable GENEAUTO[1] automatic code generator (ACG). It transforms SIMULINK models to C code for safety critical systems. Our approach which combines classical development process and formal specification and verification using proof-assistants, led to preliminary fruitful exchanges with French certification authorities. The most rigorous objectives from qualification level and user standards conforms with DO-178B/ED-12B recommendations for a level A development tool. The resulting tool has been applied successfully to real-size industrial use cases from various transportation domain partners and led to detection of requirement errors.

Keywords: automatic code generator, formal verification, qualification, Coq proof assistant.

1 Problem Statement

Both the complexity of software in safety critical systems and the level of requirements from the certification authorities are rising regularly. There exists a huge background of work related both to ACG for model-based languages and to the verification of compilers such as [1,2,3,4,5]. Large part of these works is dedicated to synchronous language-based models such as SCADE-KCG [1]. Semantics of models supported by GENEAUTO [6], however, mix data-flow and control-flow. These can be expressed using synchronous languages [7,8], but they do not allow to respect easily the model/code structural traceability constraints expressed in GENEAUTO by several industrial partners. Also, to our knowledge, there is no formal verification applied to these code generators. The code generator of [2] focuses on the verification on source code. Important related works rely on compiler verification and validation [3,4], but the verification is focused on instances of compilation. A promising approach consists in the formal development of a correct-by-construction compiler, e.g. [5]. Our work is based on this later approach. However, there is a significant difference with our proposal. In order to avoid departing from the usual industrial approach to qualification and ease its acceptance by certification authorities, we do not work at the semantic level directly. In

---

[1] www.geneauto.org

M. Alpuente, B. Cook, and C. Joubert (Eds.): FMICS 2009, LNCS 5825, pp. 199–201, 2009.
© Springer-Verlag Berlin Heidelberg 2009

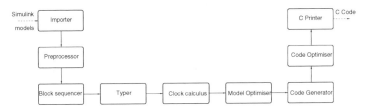

Fig. 1. GENEAUTO ACG architecture

fact, we developed a two-step approach: in a first step, translate natural specification of requirements into a formal specification using the COQ proof assistant; then in a second step, these requirements are proved correct w.r.t. the semantics of the languages.

2   Qualification of Critical Code Generators

The architecture of the GENEAUTO toolset (cf. figure 1) is composed of several elementary tools which exchange XML files representing either system or code models. The main purpose of splitting the ACG in several steps is to ease the verification of each one independently. Some parts (elementary tools) in GeneAuto are written with classical technologies using the JAVA programming language (Importer, Preprocessor, ...), and other parts are written with COQ (Block Sequencer, Typer, ...) and extracted to OCAML programming language. In order to interface the extracted code from COQ with the other parts of the GENEAUTO toolset, each elementary tool developed using formal technologies is composed of two software artifacts as illustrated in the figure 2. The JAVA front-end model (reader and writer) which, on the one hand relies on the common Model Factory to read and write the full XML model files representing the system and code models, and on the other hand executes the OCAML wrapper for the extracted implementation of the elementary tool from the COQ development. In order to exchange information with the concerned module, it writes simple text files which contain the minimal description of the model required for the current module. This choice relies on simple verification of text files printers and parsers by cross-reading instead of XML more complicated ones. Then, after executing OCAML wrapper, reads a simple text file which contains minimal required information for building the outputs of the elementary tool. This artifact will also read the text log file produced by the OCAML model wrapper and output the messages through the standard GeneAuto logging facility. The OCAML wrapper which reads the simple text model file and computes the necessary information for the wrapper. For instance, the OCAML model sequencer computes the input and output dependencies, sorts the blocks according to the rules in the tool requirements, assigns an execution order to all blocks of the model and writes these to the execution order simple file. This artifact will also produce a log file. As a result, the specification, implementation and proofs associated to the Block Sequencer have been done in COQ with more than 4500 lines of code and more than 130 proved theorems. The resulting software has many properties that have not been anticipated before using formal methods such as detecting lack of specification properties. Thus, mixing classical development process and formal specification and verification using

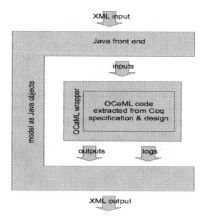

Fig. 2. Component architecture in GeneAuto

proof assistant was applied successfully and led to preliminary fruitful exchanges with some certification bodies.

References

1. Colaço, J.L., Pouzet, M.: Type-based initialization analysis of a synchronous data-flow language. International Journal on Software Tools for Technology Transfer (STTT) 6(3), 245–255 (2004)
2. Berry, G., Bouali, A., Fornari, X., Ledinot, E., Nassor, E., de Simone, R.: Esterel: A formal method applied to avionic software development. Science of Computer Programming 36(1), 5–25 (2000)
3. Pnueli, A., Siegel, M., Singerman, E.: Translation validation. In: Steffen, B. (ed.) TACAS 1998. LNCS, vol. 1384, pp. 151–166. Springer, Heidelberg (1998)
4. Necula, G.C.: Translation validator for an optimizing compiler. ACM SIGPLAN Notices 35(5), 83–94 (2000)
5. Leroy, X.: Formal certification of a compiler back-end or: Programming a compiler with a proof assistant. In: Proceedings of the 33rd Symposium on Principles Of Programming Languages (POPL 2006), vol. 41(1), pp. 42–54 (2006)
6. Tooms, A., Naks, T., Pantel, M., Gandriau, M., Wati, I.: Geneauto: An automatic code generator for a safe subset of simulink/stateflow. In: Proceedings of the 4th European symposium on Real Time Systems, ERTS 2008 (2008)
7. Caspi, P., Curic, A., Maignan, A., Sofronis, C., Tripakis, S.: Translating discrete-time simulink to lustre. In: Alur, R., Lee, I. (eds.) EMSOFT 2003. LNCS, vol. 2855, pp. 84–99. Springer, Heidelberg (2003)
8. Halbwachs, N., Raymond, P., Ratel, C.: Generating efficient code from data-flow programs. In: Małuszyński, J., Wirsing, M. (eds.) PLILP 1991. LNCS, vol. 528. Springer, Heidelberg (1991)

Visualising Event-B Models with B-Motion Studio⋆

Lukas Ladenberger, Jens Bendisposto, and Michael Leuschel

Institut für Informatik, Heinrich-Heine Universität Düsseldorf
Universitätsstr. 1, D-40225 Düsseldorf
{bendisposto,leuschel}@cs.uni-duesseldorf.de

1 Motivation

The communication between a developer and a domain expert (or manager) is very important for successful deployment of formal methods. On the one hand it is crucial for the developer to get feedback from the domain expert for further development. On the other hand the domain expert needs to check whether his expectations are met. An animation tool allows to check the presence of desired functionality and to inspect the behaviour of a specification, but requires knowledge about the mathematical notation. To avoid this problem, it is useful to create domain specific visualisations. One tool which performs this task is Brama. This tool is very important for ClearSy, and is being used for several industrial projects and has helped to obtain several contracts. However, the tool cannot be applied in conjunction with ProB. Also, creating the code that defines the mapping between a state and its graphical representation is a rather time consuming task. It can take several weeks to develop a custom visualisation.

In [1], we introduced a tool that like Brama allowed to create sophisticated visualisations using Macromedia Flash. The tool, however, still required the user to write some gluing code in Java to link the model and the visualisation. The visualisation built into ProB as described in [2] did not require to write code, as it uses a function written in B to link the model and its visualisation. These visualisations are rather simple and restricted. Also writing the required animation function can still be a considerable challenge.

We now introduce B-Motion Studio, a tool that allows to create visualisations as easy as using animation functions in ProB while being almost as sophisticated as our previous Flash based tool (e.g., see Figure 1). B-Motion Studio comes with a graphical editor that allows to create a visualisation within the modeling environment. Also, it does not require to use a different notation for gluing the state and its visualisation.

B-Motion Studio uses two important concepts: Controls and Observers. A control is a graphical representation of some aspects of the model. Typically we use labels, images or buttons to represent informations. For instance, if we model

---

⋆ This research is being carried out as part of the DFG funded research project GEPAVAS and the EU funded FP7 research project 214158: DEPLOY (Industrial deployment of advanced system engineering methods for high productivity and dependability).

M. Alpuente, B. Cook, and C. Joubert (Eds.): FMICS 2009, LNCS 5825, pp. 202–204, 2009.
© Springer-Verlag Berlin Heidelberg 2009

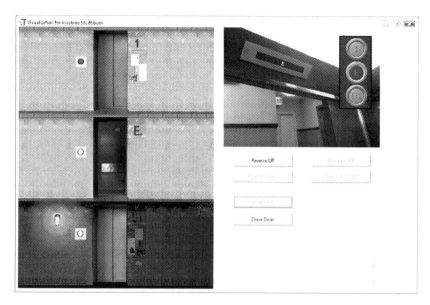

Fig. 1. The Visualisation in Action

a system that has a temperature and a threshold temperature that triggers a cool down, we might simply use two labels displaying both values, or maybe we can incorporate both information into a gauge display. It is also possible to define new controls for domain specific visualisations. Observers are used to link controls to the model's state, i.e., they do the same as the animation function in PROB. The main difference is, that we allow to decompose the animation function into different aspects, i.e., if our model contains information about the speed of a motor, we can separate all information regarding the speed from the information regarding the temprature. This allows us to write small functions and combine them rather than writing a single funtion covering all aspects of the model.

2   Conclusion

The main advantages of B-Motion Studio are:

- The modeler stays within a single notation. B-Motion Studio uses Event-B predicates and expressions as gluing code.
- An easy to use graphical editor, that allows to create visualisations with a few mouse clicks (see Figure 2).
- B-Motion Studio comes with a number of default observers and controls that are sufficient for most visualisations.
- It can be extended for specific domains.

Tool bar   WYSIWYG editor   Outline View

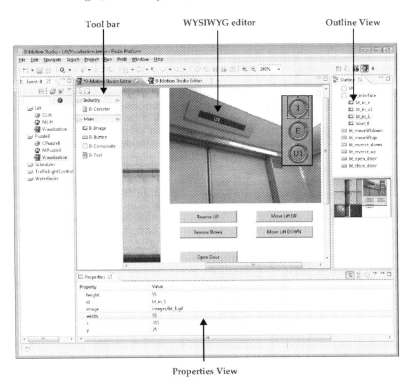

Properties View

Fig. 2. The B-Motion Studio Perspective

In summary, we hope that B-Motion Studio provides a way to quickly generate domain specific visualisations for a formal model, enabling domain experts and managers to understand and validate the model. We also believe that our tool will be of use when teaching formal methods, both during lectures as a way to motivate students to write their own formal models.

3   Further Information

More technical details, a tutorial and installation instructions can be found at the project's website http://www.stups.uni-duesseldorf.de/BMotionStudio.

References

1. Bendisposto, J., Leuschel, M.: A generic flash-based animation engine for ProB. In: Julliand, J., Kouchnarenko, O. (eds.) B 2007. LNCS, vol. 4355, pp. 266–269. Springer, Heidelberg (2006)
2. Leuschel, M., Samia, M., Bendisposto, J., Luo, L.: Easy Graphical Animation and Formula Viewing for Teaching B. The B Method: from Research to Teaching, 17–32 (2008)

Behavioural Analysis of an I²C Linux Driver

Dragan Bošnački[1], Aad Mathijssen[1], and Yaroslav S. Usenko[2]

[1] Technische Universiteit Eindhoven, The Netherlands
[2] Centrum Wiskunde en Informatica, Amsterdam, The Netherlands

Introduction. Formal methods for the analysis of system behaviour offer solutions to problems with concurrency, such as race conditions and deadlocks. We employ two such methods that are presently most applied in industry: model checking and static analysis on a common case study to analyse the behaviour of a Linux driver for I²C (Inter-Integrated Circuit).

An industrial client provided us with the source code of the driver for which it was known that it contained defects. Based on the code, some documentation, and feedback by the developers we extracted a model of the device driver. The model was checked using the mCRL2 toolset [3] and some potential defects were revealed which were later confirmed by the developers. The errors were caused by inconsistent use of routines for interrupt enabling and disabling, resulting in unprotected references to shared memory and calls to lower-level functions. In addition, we performed checks with UNO [4], a static analysis tool that works directly with the source code. We employed UNO to statically detect the errors that were found by the dynamic analysis in the model checking phase. Based on our findings, we modified the source code to avoid the discovered potential defects. Although some errors remained unsolved, an improvement was observed in the standard tests that were carried out with our fixed version.

The I²C Linux driver. In general, the Linux 2.6 kernel contains an I²C driver stack that is split up into three layers [5]: chip driver, core module and bus driver. The core module is part of the Linux kernel, as are a number of chip drivers and bus drivers. In our case, an I²C bus driver was supplied by the client. The code mainly performs two tasks: handle ioctl calls from user space, offered via the core module, and handle interrupts from the hardware.

To find race conditions we focused on the interaction between the two parallel components of the driver: the ioctl handler and the interrupt service routine.

mCRL2 analysis. The mCRL2 language and toolset [3] allows users to model and automatically verify the behaviour of distributed systems. Systems can be modelled using a process algebra enriched with data types. Automated verification is supported by checking temporal properties on all states of the model.

Based on the source code of the I²C bus driver we have created an mCRL2 model consisting of a translation of the ioctl handler and the interrupt service routine and the environment in which these functions occur. For the verification of our model we focused on violation of mutual exclusion of shared memory accesses. Exploration of all states and transitions revealed two types of violations: more than 100 concurrent shared memory accesses and one concurrent access of low-level functions.

M. Alpuente, B. Cook, and C. Joubert (Eds.): FMICS 2009, LNCS 5825, pp. 205–206, 2009.
© Springer-Verlag Berlin Heidelberg 2009

These violations were caused by misplaced or absent calls to functions that disable and enable interrupts. We fixed this by making a number of small changes to the source code, by moving or adding these functions to protect the usage of shared memory and low-level functions. We have also made these changes to our mCRL2 model. Verification of this model showed us that these violations have been resolved.

State space exploration for instances involving multiple ioctl threads became prohibitively large. To resolve this, we have employed symbolic techniques as implemented in the LTSmin toolset [1].

Static Analysis Results. We applied UNO to find the same violations as reported by the mCRL2 analysis. The mutual exclusion properties needed to be encoded as property automata. A property automaton monitors the traversal of the control flow graphs of the C functions. UNO produces an error trace, in case a violation of the property is found.

After formulating the property automata, UNO was able to reproduce all possible defects that were discovered with mCRL2: the errors of accessing shared memory without previously disabling interrupts and unsafe function calls.

Conclusions. By means of both model checking using mCRL2 and static analysis using UNO, we were able to find possible non-trivial defects, which have been confirmed by the developers. Furthermore, we have provided a verified fix for the found defects.

Although in general model checking is a more powerful technique than static analysis, in this case study it seems that they are evenly matched. We think that this is due to the low number of parallel components involved in the properties we wanted to check. Instead of choosing between model checking and static analysis, we can also use them in tandem, e.g. by employing static analysis as a light-weight analysis to locate possible problems. Once the possible defects are located, one can apply the more expensive fully-fledged model checking only to the critical modules in the code base.

A more detailed account of this summary can be found in [2].

References

1. Blom, S., van de Pol, J.: Symbolic Reachability for Process Algebras with Recursive Data Types. In: Fitzgerald, J.S., Haxthausen, A.E., Yenigun, H. (eds.) ICTAC 2008. LNCS, vol. 5160, pp. 81–95. Springer, Heidelberg (2008)
2. Bošnački, D., Mathijssen, A., Usenko, Y.S.: Behavioural analysis of an I²C Linux Driver, CS-Report 09/09, Technische Universiteit Eindhoven (2009)
3. Groote, J.F., Mathijssen, A.H.J., Reniers, M.A., Usenko, Y.S., van Weerdenburg, M.J.: Analysis of distributed systems with mCRL2. In: Alexander, M., Gardner, W. (eds.) Process Algebra for Parallel and Distributed Processing, pp. 99–128. Chapman and Hall, Boca Raton (2008)
4. Holzmann, G.J.: Static Source Code Checking for User-Defined Properties. In: Proc. World Conference on Integrated Design & Process Technology, IDPT (2002)
5. Kroah-Hartman, G.: I2C Drivers, Part I. Linux Journal (December 2003)

Model-Based Testing of Electronic Passports

Wojciech Mostowski[1], Erik Poll[1], Julien Schmaltz[2], Jan Tretmans[1,2],
and Ronny Wichers Schreur[1]

[1] Radboud University, Nijmegen, The Netherlands
[2] Embedded Systems Institute (ESI), Eindhoven, The Netherlands

Introduction

Electronic passports, or e-passports for short, contain a contactless smartcard which stores digitally-signed data. To rigorously test e-passports, we developed formal models of the e-passport protocols that enable model-based testing using the TorXakis framework.

E-Passport Protocols

Access to e-passports involves several protocols. All e-passports should conform to the standards of the International Civil Aviation Organization (ICAO) [3]. To prevent surreptitious access to the e-passport chip, ICAO specifies the Basic Access Control (BAC) protocol, which establishes a secure channel based on a symmetric session key. To prevent cloning of e-passports, ICAO specifies an optional Active Authentication protocol. The second generation of e-passports being introduced in the EU in the summer of 2009 contains more sensitive biometric data, namely fingerprints. To protect this information, the EU mandates the use of a stronger security mechanism called Extended Access Control (EAC) [1]. EAC requires the passport terminal to authenticate itself (with a chain of PKI certificates) to the passport before any sensitive biometric data can be read.

Formal Models and Model-Based Testing

The official standards give long and detailed descriptions of the individual protocols. Understanding the combination and possible interaction of the various protocols is difficult. To better understand the protocols, we developed formal models in the form of finite state diagrams. Initially we just drew these on a whiteboard to understand the specifications, but then we realised that they could be used to test e-passports using *model-based testing*.

In model-based testing a formal model is used to automate the testing process: a formal model of the desired behaviour is used to generate tests and analyse the test results. One theory for model-based testing uses labelled-transition systems as models, and an implementation relation called **ioco** that formally defines when an implementation is correct with respect to its specification model [5].

M. Alpuente, B. Cook, and C. Joubert (Eds.): FMICS 2009, LNCS 5825, pp. 207–209, 2009.
© Springer-Verlag Berlin Heidelberg 2009

We expressed our state diagrams as labelled-transition systems and then used the TorXakis model-based testing tool to test actual e-passports. TorXakis is based on the model-based testing tool TorX [6] extended with symbolic test generation capabilities [2]. TorXakis performs random walks through the model, sends commands to the passport chip and verifies that the responses conform to the model. TorXakis is implemented in Haskell.[1] For lower-level communication with the passport chip using a card reader, we used the open source passport-terminal software that we helped develop in the JMRTD project.[2]

Results and Conclusions

The most difficult part of the testing process was understanding the official specifications and constructing a formal model for them. Finite state diagrams turn out to be a very effective and perspicuous way to specify the combination of passport protocols. Indeed, it amazes us that the official specifications do not use finite state diagrams anywhere.

Once we had the model, the actual testing only took about a week, including developing the extra software. Here we did take advantage of the existing e-passport terminal software. But note that this software, like any passport terminal software, only executes one particular sequence of protocol steps, whereas to rigorously test the security of a passport all different possible sequences of these steps have to be exercised. This is what we let TorXakis do for us.

The tests were run fully automatically: an overnight test was able to perform over 100 000 protocol steps on a passport. Once the test infrastructure has been set up, model-based testing simply amounts to playing with models. By slightly changing the model, new tests are derived automatically with a simple key stroke. By refining and tweaking the model we could quickly find out how any underspecification or unclarities in the specifications had been resolved in the implementation that we tested.

We will publish our formal models of the e-passport protocols as an aid to anyone implementing or testing e-passport software, or indeed anyone just trying to understand the specifications. We plan to do the same for the 'twin brother' of the e-passport: the new electronic driving license [4].[3]

References

1. Advanced security mechanisms for machine readable travel documents – Extended Access Control (EAC) – Version 1.11. Technical Report TR-03110, German Federal Office for Information Security (BSI), Bonn, Germany (2008)
2. Frantzen, L., Tretmans, J., Willemse, T.: Test generation based on symbolic specifications. In: Grabowski, J., Nielsen, B. (eds.) FATES 2004. LNCS, vol. 3395, pp. 1–15. Springer, Heidelberg (2005)

---

[1] http://www.haskell.org

[2] http://jmrtd.org

[3] For which we developed the first (open source) reference implementation, http://isodl.sourceforge.net.

3. Doc 9303 – Machine readable travel documents – Part 1–2. Technical report, ICAO, 6th edn. (2006)
4. ISO/ICE. ISO-compliant driving license – Part 1, 2, 3. Technical report (2009), ISO 18013
5. Tretmans, J.: Model based testing with labelled transition systems. In: Hierons, R.M., Bowen, J.P., Harman, M. (eds.) FORTEST. LNCS, vol. 4949, pp. 1–38. Springer, Heidelberg (2008)
6. Tretmans, J., Brinksma, E.: TorX: Automated model based testing. In: Hartman, A., Dussa-Zieger, K. (eds.) First European Conference on Model-Driven Software Engineering, Imbuss, Möhrendorf, Germany, December 2003, 13 pages (2003)

Developing a Decision Support Tool for Dam Management with SPIN*

María-del-Mar Gallardo[1], Pedro Merino[1], Laura Panizo[1], and Antonio Linares[2]

[1] Dep. Lenguajes y Ciencias de la Computación, University of Málaga
{gallardo,pedro,laurapanizo}@lcc.uma.es
[2] BEFESA AGUA, SAU
Antonio.linares@befesa.abengoa.com

1 Motivation

Analysis of many critical systems is usually based on the simulation of numerical models. This solution is suitable for analyzing systems with continuous and deterministic behaviors that evolve over time. However, real critical systems are more complex and can exhibit non-deterministic behavior due to unexpected events. Furthermore, critical systems present both discrete and continuous behaviors, which interact regularly. Both features can be modeled with hybrid formal methods, taking advantage of exploration techniques like model checking.

We have selected dam management as a case study. A dam is a critical system that has a hybrid behavior, there are continuous variables such as the water level, and discrete states such as the opening degrees of the spillways. At present, Decision Support Systems, based on numerical models, are used to manage complete river basins. Dams are modelled as black boxes which store and release water. A Decision Support Tool (DST) for dam management provides information about the possible consequences of dam operator actions, which can help to ensure the safety of the dam, as well as the efficient use of the water. In this work we have used formal methods to model a dam as a hybrid system, and we have obtained decision support information from the analysis performed with model checking.

2 Modeling Hybrid Systems with PROMELA

In our previous work [4], we evaluated the same case study with the SCADE suite. Now we have used SPIN [2] to obtain a realistic model of a dam, by integrating numerical models into PROMELA, the formal specification language used in SPIN. In Figure 1, it can be seen how the hybrid model is built, taking into account the different outflow elements of the dam and other components necessary to carry out the analysis, such as the models of the environmental inflows and the user operations. In addition, the hybrid model includes properties that reflect the initial condition (weather forecast) and the desired evolution of the dam and its variables.

* Partially supported by Befesa Agua and by grants P07-TIC3131 (Andalusia) and TIN2008-05932 (Spain).

M. Alpuente, B. Cook, and C. Joubert (Eds.): FMICS 2009, LNCS 5825, pp. 210–212, 2009.

Discrete and continuous behaviors have to be reflected in the hybrid model of the dam. The discrete part can be easily defined in PROMELA. However, the continuous behavior presents some difficulties, mainly because PROMELA is an asynchronous language without a time model. Defining hybrid systems in PROMELA has two main goals: the first is to implement a model of time that allows us (a) to carry out time-bounded analysis, (b) to discretize the numerical models, and (c) to include timed processes. The second goal is to deal with continuous behaviors by integrating numerical models in PROMELA. A mechanism to emulate a timed operation has been developed based on [1], in which a discrete time model is proposed that uses a synchronization process to control the execution of the other processes. A timer variable is associated to each process, and a global timer is included to allow both the time-bounded analysis and the definition of timed properties. To manage continuous behaviors, we use the embedded C code extension for PROMELA [3]. Using this extension has some benefits: (1) functions implemented in C code can use more powerful libraries; (2) c_code statements are executed as atomic steps, which considerably reduces the number of states produced in the analysis;(3) C variables can be excluded from the state space when they do not hold relevant information for the analysis. The PROMELA model of the dam is composed of 3 processes that represent the 3 spillways that comprise the real dam. It has also a process that represents the water inflows and another one to model the dam operator that sends commands to the different elements of the dam to vary their discrete position.

3   DST with SPIN

To obtain support information, model checking is applied to the hybrid model. In Figure 1 the architecture of the DST developed is shown. The objective has to be expressed as a non desired behavior, and the result is a counter example with information about

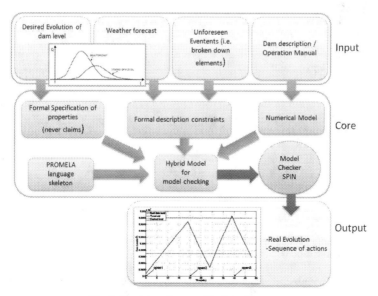

Fig. 1. Decision Support Tool Architecture

Table 1. Results of SPIN analysis

	Property A		Property B	
	1 Core	2 Core Cpu0	1 Core	2 Core Cpu0
State Vector	148	148	156	156
Depth reached	2837	2299	2839	1139
States(stored)	1117623	524113	8968761	112986
States(matched)	1025582	592117	9686355	136935
Transitions	2143205	1116230	18655116	249921
Atomic Steps	1231807	678326	11435409	186293
Total memory (MB)	132,583	192,558	1174,497	145,512
Elapsed Time (sec)	4,89	3,75	53,4	1,060

the operations performed to satisfy the user requirements. Two types of timed properties have been defined: a) properties that check if a condition is true in a period of time, and b) properties that check if the elapsed time between two conditions is within a given time range. Properties in SPIN can be expressed with LTL formulas or can be introduced with a special automaton called *never claim*. To express timed properties it is more suitable to modify the never claim automaton. We have carried out some tests to evaluate both the basic capabilities of SPIN and its multi-core extension. The system configuration is as follows: the period of time analyzed is 60 minutes, in our discrete time model one minute is equal to one time step. The user model can only act at time points 0, 20 and 40. The analysis has been performed on an Intel Core2 Quad PC with 2.40GHz and 3GB of RAM. The operating system is Ubuntu. Table 1 shows the results of analyzing two different timed properties with 1 and 2 cores, respectively. Property A checks that the dam level is in the range [53.07, 53.06] from minute 40 to 60. Property B checks that the time needed to decrease the dam level from more than $53.018Hm^3$ to $53.007Hm^3$ is less than 10 time steps. Both properties return a counter example with a possible execution path that satisfies the condition.

4 Conclusions

The analysis shows that the SPIN multi-core extension reduces the analysis time notably. Furthermore, the use of memory in each cpu can be reduced even more if a correct load balance is applied. The DST is still a prototype, but the results of the implementation are very promising and show the suitability of the methodology for this type of systems. Future work will focus on enhancing DST and the dam model, adding new elements with more complex behaviors. To improve the capabilities of DST, new property templates should be developed.

References

1. Bosnacki, D., Dams, D.: Discrete-time promela and spin. In: FTRTFT 1998: Proc. of the 5th Int. Symp. on Formal Techniques in Real-Time and Fault-Tolerant Systems. Springer, Heidelberg (1998)
2. Holzmann, G.J.: SPIN Model Checker: Primer and Reference Manual. Addison-Wesley Professional, Reading (2003)
3. Holzmann, G.J., Joshi, R.: Model-driven software verification. In: SPIN, pp. 76–91 (2004)
4. Gallardo, M.M., Merino, P., Panizo, L., Linares, A.: Using SCADE for decision support in Dam management. In: MSVVEIS 2009, pp. 125–131 (2009)

Author Index